Eric Rabjohns

Barrie S May

The Book of
Carharrack

Born of the Mines

Carharrack Old Cornwall Society

HALSGROVE

First published in Great Britain in 2003

British Library Cataloguing-in-Publication Data
A CIP record for this title is available from the British Library

ISBN 1 84114 244 1

HALSGROVE

Halsgrove House
Lower Moor Way
Tiverton, Devon EX16 6SS
Tel: 01884 243242
Fax: 01884 243325
email: sales@halsgrove.com
website: http://www.halsgrove.com

Frontispiece photograph: *A tranquil scene captured on this postcard view of Carnmarth Cove Shute, early-1900s. Little has altered since then, the water still emerges unflaggingly from the pipe. It is believed this flow has its source in underground springs within the granite of Carnmarth, the notion of it emanating from a mine adit is doubtful owing to the impurities prevalent in the latter. Water sources such as the shute have seen considerable usage over the years and despite the presence of 'tap water' in homes, there are still those who partake of the occasional bucket of 'shute water', indeed it was interesting to see the 'bus people of United Downs', during their stay in the early-1990s, filling a variety of containers from such a source, reminiscent of the convoys of villagers in the past engaged in the same routine.*

Printed and bound in Great Britain

FOREWORD

CARHARRACK – A MOMENT IN TIME

Morning breaks, the sun's rays try to force themselves through the smog which reluctantly refuses to relinquish its grip over the village. Movement begins; the early shift turn the latches and venture out from their squat terraced cottages along White Stocking, Croft and Foxes Rows on to the well-trodden tracks leading to the workplaces surrounding the village. As the tracks merge the workers' caravan expands: talk ranges from recent gossip as to the cause of William Henry's fall, to expectation of the day's labours ahead – will the lode hold good for a few more fathoms? Is Cap'n Odgers in a good mood? He should be; the returns for last month looked promising. 'I've heard tell there's rich pickings in the 15 level on North Lode.' Snatches of hymns, well loved and worn, pervade the air adding a touch of humanity and comfort to an otherwise often harsh industrial landscape.

Ahead at the surface the area reverberates to the sounds and actions of the mechanised giants; powerhouses creating pressurised steam, utilised to its full in the war against water that threatens to swamp the very survival of the district, if allowed. Nurtured like a child by their operators, who know their every idiosyncrasy and soothe them through their times of stress, these engines provide the mines' security and lifeblood of effort; they supply the forces for a vast array of equipment needed to treat the ore once it arrives on the surface.

Ever-present plumes of smoke – some innocuous, others of a more acrid nature – fill the atmosphere. Baskets of coal lay piled up close to their furnaces; water troughs, overhead launders and gutters dissect the workplace making sure every last drop of this priceless commodity reaches its destination in readiness for its desired purposes, feeding the hungry boilers, or mixing with the crushed ore to aid mineral separation. The sun is beginning to win its battle. Another day has begun.

Eric Rabjohns, 2002

Left: *This superb photo was forthcoming during our 1992 exhibition and shows the present fish shop as it looked in the 1930s when it was Peters' Second Hand Shop. Mrs Peters is holding baby Rosemary with Freda Peters by her side.*

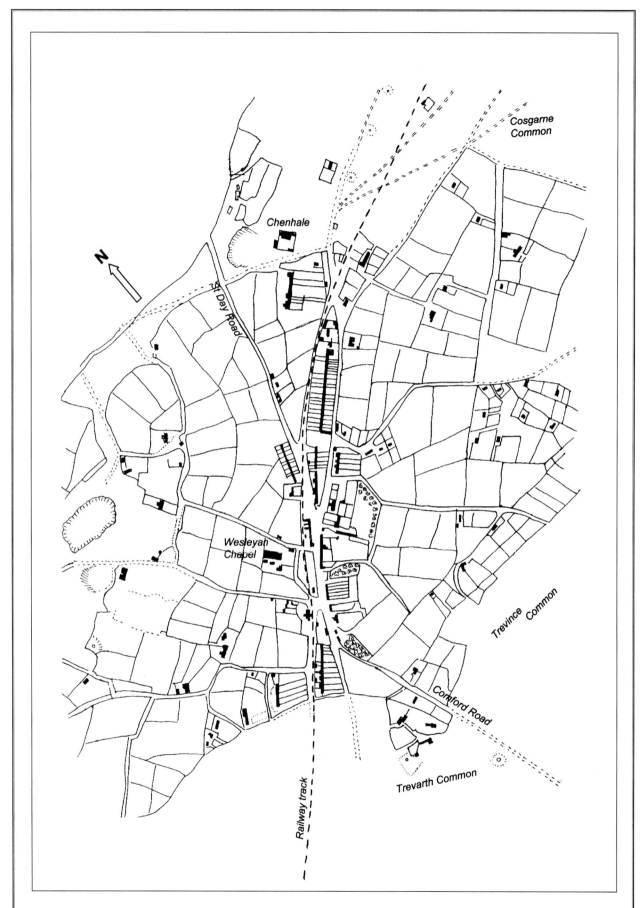

Section of the Tithe Map of Gwennap Parish, 1839. The surveyor was Robert Symons.
Reproduced by kind permission of the County Records Office. Ref. No. DDX 560/25.

CONTENTS

The earliest view of St Piran's Church, c.1910, probably taken by Mr Govier of Chacewater.

Foxes Row, c.1910. Apostrophe or not, we don't know! There has been little change since this photograph was taken, although the cold nightly winter visits to the bottom of the garden closets have been superseded by internal luxuries. The gabled structure on the far right covered the storage bays of the coal yard which were served by a short branch line from the main route of the railway.
(Courtesy of Paddy Bradley, Redruth)

ACKNOWLEDGEMENTS

Our special thanks go to the following village people, some sadly no longer with us, who have kindly agreed to be interviewed about their lives and experiences in and around Carharrack. Without their knowledge, patience and understanding, and a wealth of photographs and memories, this project would have proved a very difficult task.

Billy and Rose Penrose, Phyllis Nicholls, Ruby Wilton, Richard Kinsman, Pearl Lewis, Ted Woodley, Bertha Keats, Nancy Woodley, William Barrett, Wilfred Bawden, Billy and Rita Wright, Christine Odgers, Gerald Brown and family, Gerald and Joan Pellow, Trevor Pellow, Margaret Sedgeley, Brian Saundry, John and Terry Simmons, Courtney Butler, Cyril Hitchens, Alec Young, Barbara Nurhonen, Naomi Joslin, Douglas Honey, Harry Tredre, Elsie Hughes, Mrs Conduit, Teresa and Winnie Allen, Alec and Pat Williams, Billy Chown, George and Valerie Pellow, Roy and Rennie Leah, Nigel Jolly, Pat Smerdon, Peter Benbow, William Matthews, John Kellow, Nancy Evans, Sidney Albrook, Bernard and Jill Pearce, Malcolm Drew, Johnny Orchard, Tommy Ware, Janet Sandow, Kevin Rundle, Jean Homer, Stephen Speller, Florence Combellack, Jocelyn Brew, Thelma Odgers, Enid Fewins, Linda Williams, Margaret Dawes, Vanessa Stone, Claire Page, Alan Harris, Sylvia May, Gladys Tredre, Colin King, Alwyn Williams, Diane Andrew, Johnny, Joyce and Terry Chynoweth, Win Jewell, Dougie Thorncroft. If there are others who we have unfortunately omitted from this list we apologise.

Thanks also go to: Paddy Bradley for permission to use views from his postcard collection; Paul Annear and Lt Cdr Joe Mills for items of village interest which they have 'passed on' to us; Clive Benney for permission

to use views from his postcard collection; Joff Bullen for permission to use views from the Trounson/Bullen Collection of photographs; Derek White for his time and assistance in researching newspaper items; the Royal Institution of Cornwall (RIC) for their assistance and permission to use some photographs from their vast collection; to Terry Knight and his staff at the Cornwall Centre, Redruth, for their help and assistance.

We have, wherever possible, acknowledged the photographer or source of the photographs used in this publication and sought their permission to use their material. However, in many cases we have not been able to trace the photographer; we apologise for any unintentional omissions.

Left: *A watercolour of the Poldory pumping engine built in the early 1900s.*

INTRODUCTION
CARHARRACK - BORN OF THE MINES

This book was researched, compiled and written by Eric Rabjohns and Barrie May on behalf of the Carharrack Old Cornwall Society. The main aim of the society is to gather, collate and store information about the community which, until the formation of the society in 1987, had been overlooked in written publications relating to Cornwall's heritage. Carharrack possesses a fascinating and varied history which appeals to residents of the village and local family members as well as to those interested in mining, religion, railways and bottle collecting. It was felt by the Carharrack Old Cornwall Society that the information and knowledge it had collected needed to be captured for prosperity.

Over the years the society has held several village exhibitions displaying the accumulated information and artefacts. These successful events have proved very popular, with each occasion bringing forth more

priceless anecdotes and photographs. The society has also recorded the reminiscences of many long-serving local residents which, together with the other material, have enabled a definitive history of the village and parish to be compiled in words and pictures. *The Book of Carharrack – Born of the Mines* represents the culmination of that research for the benefit of the inhabitants of Carharrack.

Above: *This shows the huts and headgear relating to White Works Mine, which worked part of the old Carharrack Mine. The exact siting of these structures is at the back of the scrapyards. Several local lads remember playing around here and descending some of the shallower shafts after the war.*
(Photo courtesy of the Trounson/Bullen Collection)

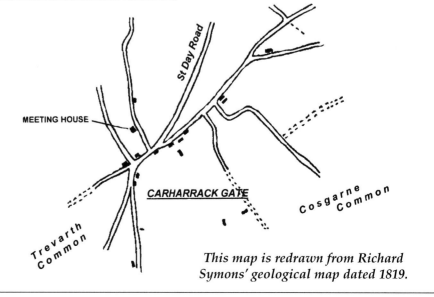

This map is redrawn from Richard Symons' geological map dated 1819.

ONE

⌘

A VILLAGE DEVELOPS

WHY CARHARRACK?

Placenames and their derivation can often tell us something of a settlement's early history, and may provide an insight into the nature of the locale and features that existed there in the past. There are three possible explanations for how Carharrack got its name.

One line of thought (based upon *Car* referring to 'a building of a friendly nature') put forward by local schoolmaster and historian Mr Blewett in his writings about the village maintains that it refers to a dwelling of a religious purpose, a meeting-place for travellers. This possibly relates to a property in Little Carharrack where the inscription *Roman 117* appears above a window. There was once a pilgrimage trail connecting the religious centres of Canterbury and St Michael's Mount which took in St Day, so it seems likely that the route could have passed through the Little Carharrack hamlet on course for Lanner, another calling point.

Another meaning emanates from *Caer* or *Car*, which is a Cornish-language term meaning a camp, enclosure or fort, and *harrack*, a corruption of the personal name Hartoc – hence Harthoc's fort/camp. In 1989 a member of the Redruth Old Cornwall Society stated that he had recently located the site of a hillside fort within the grounds of Carn Villa, Carn Marth. Undoubtedly there is an unusually wide hedge system in one area of the farm which could be remnants of a peripheral wall embankment. The final derivative comes from the two Cornish words *Car* or *Caer* and *Harrack*, the former meaning a camp or enclosure and the latter a rock – thus a settlement near the rock or carn which presumably refers to the Carn Marth granite mass. Which one of these is more likely? Suffice to say that each derivative has a degree of evidence to substantiate it.

A granite marker stone, with the letter E and a numeral, which is thought to relate to the boundary of the Edgcumbe estate.

IN THE BEGINNING

Carharrack only materialised as a thriving community well into the 1800s, as a result of the development of the Gwennap mining area. Earliest references to the name Carharrack date back to 1290 when it was written as Cararthek. Since then various other spellings of the name have appeared. Morton Nance in his writings on place names quoted in *The History of Gwennap* by C.C. James dates them as follows:

Cargarek	*1308*
Carharthek	*1422*
Carartek	*1542*
Carharrack Veor	*1589*
Carharrock Mill	*1591*

C.C. James sheds some light on the early history of the area now known as Carharrack. The Domesday survey (1086) mentions the manors of Chenmerch (Carn Marth) and Talgolle (Tolgullow) which would appear to have one of their boundaries within our present village site. The lands of Chenmarch occupied the western sections and the manor of Tolgullow the northern and eastern areas. During the period 1083–1199, the aforementioned manors were sub-divided into the manors of Tolcarne, Trevethan, Carharrack, Trevarth, Cusgarne, St Day, Treskirby and Cossawes. Interestingly the Trevince estate, which occupies a large area bordering the village and has ownership of several local properties and farms, never received manorial status.

In the hedgerows surrounding the present Ting Tang and woods south of the Howard Beauchamp Recreation Field are several granite stones incised with the initial E followed by a single numeral. To date, the numbers one, four, five, six and seven have been found. These presumably designate the boundaries of the estate of Lord Edgcumbe who owned

Above and left: *Detailed drawings of the White Cross of Penhalvyngam Moor which stands 4ft 11ins tall and depicts a standing figure of Christ on the front section and a Latin cross on the reverse. The cross now stands on private land belonging to the Williams family of Scorrier House, whom we thank for their kind permission to produce these sketches. (Sketches by Eric Rabjohns)*

Top left: *One of the several boundary stones still to be found between the manors of St Day and Carharrack in the vicinity of the area between the pound and School Hill Road. This one is inscribed with the number 51.*

Left: *A close-up of one of the three unmarked boundary stones between the manors of Cusgarne (Coisgarne) and Carharrack, which are visible in the village centre.*

several stretches of land in the region dating back to the sixteenth century. Prior to this point these areas were in the hands of the Bodrugan family.

During the early 1900s the Earl of Mount Edgcumbe sold off Trevarth House and a tract of mining wasteland and rough moor. The latter was sold to the Beauchamps of Trevince House who set about developing a new coniferous plantation there. This is the wooded area between Ting Tang and the road that joins White Stile Hill to the Trevarth Road. A narrow strip of land wedged between the larger manors of St Day to the east, Tolcarne to the north, Cusgarne to the south and Trevarth Common to the west, made up the manor of Carharrack. According to C.C. James' research, it comprised the land which lay between the roads from Carharrack to Comford and Trevarth which is now called Ting Tang.

Around 1300 the area was called Penhalvyngam Moor and a boundary stone in the form of a cross, now in the grounds of Scorrier House, once stood there, erected for the soul of the Lord of Talgollow (Tolgullow). The cross, which stands at 4ft 11ins, has a representation of Christ on the face and a Latin cross in relief on the reverse. It was more commonly known as the White Cross and a description of it can be found on pages 48-49 of C.C. James' book. Recent research by the author has revealed that the series of granite stones along the pound to Tolcarne Road constitute some of the boundary markers between the manors of St Day and Carharrack.

The Royal Institution of Cornwall holds maps dating from the 1820s which clearly indicate a set of 79 numbered stones stretching from Crofthandy, inscribed number 1, to Tolcarne, number 79. Close to the hedges just north of the lane which passes from the pound to School Hill Road are several granite posts with numbers 46, 48, 50, 51, 63 and 65 inscribed on them, which correspond exactly to the numbering system on the manor map. Another map, this time referring to the Cusgarne/Carharrack manor boundary, shows a series of stones starting just to the west of the Trevarth and Comford Road junction, skirting the southern edge of the road through the village and ending on United Downs. Within the area of pavement from Sparry Lane to St Piran's Church there are three small unmarked granite posts which could have formed part of the Cusgarne boundary (spelt Coisgarne on the maps). An early picture postcard of Carharrack depicts a stone opposite Albion Row.

The earliest references to dwellings or tenements in Carharrack date from the 1700s when the names Carharrack Veor and Vean appear on deeds and leases relating to transactions involving the land and properties of the Hearle estate. The family homes of the Hearles included Trebartha Hall and Helligan. By the late 1770s it is recorded that 12 cottages existed and the name Carharrack Gate prevailed. One can only presume that the term gate arose due to the fact that the area was a boundary between two estates.

The first-known detailed map of Carharrack is Symons' geological map from 1819 (see page 8). This shows road structures which resemble exactly, apart from interconnecting tracks, the system found today and also enables one to plot the existence of the building sites listed below. At this juncture it needs to be emphasised that these sites may or may not be existing homesteads. It is relatively certain that a building of some form was to be found close to the site in 1819.

Fir Tree Farm   Manor House   Alma Cottage
Alma Stores   Elm Farm   Part of Church Row
Mini Market   Trelawney   Primrose Cottage
Thorn Cottage   Rosewood Farm
A site opposite the present Carharrack club
Two sites at the entrance to Sparry Lane
The beginning of United Road
Sites in the Carn Marth Cove region
Some sites in Little Carharrack

The only named building is the Meeting House which refers to the present chapel. By 1815 the original Octagon Chapel had been demolished and the present Methodist Chapel built.

RAPID GROWTH

By 1840, when the Tithe Map (see page 4) was published, most of the village terraces had been built, the only exception being Chapel Terrace. Through the research of house deeds, which were kindly loaned to the author, it appears most of the terraced properties built in the village at this time were in the hands of descendants, or relatives, of the Hearle family. Nearly all of the documents include references to the Rodds of Trebartha Hall, situated on the north-eastern side of Bodmin Moor near North Hill village, and/or the Tremaynes of Helligan near Mevagissey. These families seem to have held the freehold to most village developments until relinquishing them in the early 1900s. Prior to this many properties were leased to local families for renting, and in some instances this is still the case. The date at which the building of Church Street took place is problematic. One map seems to indicate that the railway, which was built in the mid-1820s, came first, followed by the dwellings which were squeezed into the space between the road and the track.

It is certain that the rapid growth of Carharrack was a result of the expansion of the local mines, notably the Consolidated Mine (Consols) which employed 3,000 people. Housing such numbers became imperative and Carharrack was not only the closest settlement but also provided good access to local towns and plenty of space for building. The village was in need of expansion.

1843 TO 1870

The year 1870 saw the publication of the next map to feature Carharrack. This was the first Ordnance Survey map and it proved much more accurate in its observations and recordings. The following structures had appeared in the Carharrack area between 1843 and 1870:

Giew House   Chapel Terrace
Rock House   Ashfield House
Lansbury   Pelmear Villa
Manor House (Little Carharrack)
The brickworks along Trevarth Road
Carn Marth Castle (Hillside Terrace)
Croft Row extended westward, numbers one to six (?)
Railway Terrace extended, numbers 12 onwards

1870 TO 1907

The next Ordnance Survey map appeared in 1907/8 and, with the benefit of the strong memories of surviving relatives, it is possible to link buildings with their constructors. New buildings appeared at:

Carndene and Carnside nos 1, 2 built by the Kinmans; Grove View development began, built by the Allens, numbers one to four started in 1891; Pine View, Grove View and Sunnydene began in 1907; St Piran's Church, 1884; Milk/pop yard, Railway Terrace; Billy Bray Memorial Chapel in 1883.

1907 TO 2002

The beginning of the 1900s saw little major development in Carharrack with the exception of the construction of bungalows along United Road in the 1930s. The later bungalows were built by Billy Wright in the 1960s, apart from one which was built by Ernie Andrew. The 1960s saw the beginning of the boom years of building in the village:

Mid/late 1960s Consols Road, builder Burns and Bray.
Late 1960s to early 1970s Tremayne Road, builder Billy Wright; Polkerris Road, builder Derek Bell.
1968 to 1975 Trevince Park, builder Sowden.
Early 1970s Bungalows further along Chapel Terrace, builders E.J. Allen & Sons, Shortlanesend; Treyew Place, builder Tony Williams, Blackwater.
Mid-1970s Menakarne Estate, builders Camborne & Redruth UDC; Manor Road, builders Simmons.
Late 1970s Tresithey Estate, builders Ladds.
1980s Parc Stenak, builders Ladds.
Late 1980s to early 1990s Manor Road extension, builder John Simmons; Billy Bray's Mews, builders Ladds.

Since the completion of the latter, apart from a few solitary dwellings being erected as infills, there have not been any large-scale developments, although a proposal for 12 dwellings, listed as an 'affordable housing scheme' off Sparry Lane, was being discussed by Kerrier Council in August 2002.

NAMES WITHIN THE VILLAGE

The recording of place names depended upon the diligence of the census officer. In 1871 the officer was very thorough, but in 1891 only nine areas/roads were noted. Usually the same route was taken by the census official who would begin at the Carn Marth end of the village and continue along the north side to United Downs, before taking the southern path to record properties west to Ting Tang. House names were not usually noted:

1841 Ting Tang, Wheal Squire, Trevethan, Carharrack Cove, The Village.
1851 Little Carharrack, Wheal Damsel, Sparry Bottom, Lower Trevethan, Ting Tang, Carharrack.
1861 Chapel Terrace, Little Carharrack, Carharrack Village, Ting Tang, Trevethan (Higher and Lower), Carn Marth Cove (Carharrack Cove), Old House Road – probably Church Street.
1871 Albion Row, Carn Marth Cove and Row, Wheal Damsel plus Wheal Damsel Row, Foxes Row, Croft Row, Chapel Terrace, Church Street and Road, East Wheal Damsel, Ting Tang, Higher and Lower Trevethan, Little and North Carharrack, Sparry Bottom, Mount Pleasant, Thorn Cottage, Bunt's Row (four homes included – probably Higher Railway Terrace), Timber Yard Row (possibly Higher Albion Row), White Stocking Row (Albion Row).
1881 Stephen's Row – possibly part of Croft Row, Carharrack Road mentioned – United Road, Trevethan, Sparry Bottom, Church Row and Street, Foxes Row, Carn Marth Cove and Row, Chapel Terrace, Croft Row, Chenall, Albion Row, Carharrack Village, Little Carharrack.
1891 Squire Lane, Croft Row, Albion Row, Shoot Row (Carn Marth Cove and Hillside Terrace), Foxes Row, Church Street, Sparry Bottom, Little Carharrack, Higher and Lower Trevethan, Carharrack Road (United Road southern side), New Road (Squire Lane), Sparry Bottom, Fore Street, Church Row, Albion Row, Croft Row, United Road, Railway Terrace, Church Street, Chapel Terrace, Foxes Row, Shute Row, South Carn Marth, Little Carharrack, Ting Tang, Trevarth Road, Trevethan, Cusgarne Common (beyond United Road).

BIBLIOGRAPHY
The History of Gwennap, C.C. James
Mr Blewett's notes and recordings on the Gwennap area
Manorial Maps of St Day and Cusgarne, housed at the County Records Office and the Royal Institution of Cornwall Library
Richard Symons' geological map, dated 1819

Two

Born of the Mines

Mining in the Gwennap Parish

'Born of the mines' is the subheading for *The Book of Carharrack*. It is fitting in that it acknowledges that without the development of Gwennap, especially the United Downs area, as a centre of mining, Carharrack would probably have remained a small hamlet signposting road traffic to Lanner, St Day, Redruth, Truro and beyond. However, the sudden upsurge of mining activity in the early- to mid-nineteenth century laid down the foundations for a society which has changed little up until the present day, 180 years on. The development of mining in Gwennap Parish, the immediate area around Carharrack, enables one to see how such a population explosion occured.

The Hunt for Minerals

The earliest working of minerals in the parish was by streaming methods, a technique which was used throughout Cornwall. Streaming occurred in low-lying moorland areas or river beds and estuaries where the erosion of tin deposits further up the valley led to a deposition of tin particles as sediment. The Restronguet Creek basin was one such deposit.

Around 1600, when lode or shaft mining began, waste material from mining still contained a small amount of tin which could not be extracted. This waste was discharged into streams close to the mines and a new breed of tin streamer emerged who could glean a living by retrieving these tin residues. The method of streaming involved digging the sediment in stream beds, thus stirring the material up. Gravity would then deposit the heavier material, which contained the metal particles, in the launders or settling tanks provided. The waste was 'creamed off', leaving the tin concentrate to be dug out. Practically all local streams had tinners working in their lower reaches. Lower Carharrack stamps utilised the waters of the Tolcarne/Vogue area and stream works were evident in the Poldory,

Trehaddle and Hale Mills valleys, tapping the mineralised waters issuing from the Carn Marth granite mass.

Copper was recovered from the streams by a process of cementation and several of these works existed in the Bissoe Valley beyond the outfall of the Great County Adit at Twelveheads, which carried cupreous waste from the whole region. The stream was directed into a pit which held a superb collection of rusting ironmongery – kettles, pans, etc. The copper in the waste water changed places with the iron in the rust as the iron was dissolved in the water and the copper was deposited on the kitchen utensils. This copper was then periodically scraped off and sold. Even the iron further downstream settled out in the form of ochre and was sold.

Alongside these ongoing streaming activities, mining methods proper (underground lode extraction) were beginning. By the early 1700s the following mines were active: Ting Tang, Tolcarne, Wheal Lovelace and Poldice, working from relatively shallow depths, about 80 fathoms (480 feet). Indeed, some of these concerns had been recovering minerals for several years. Deeper working proved very difficult at this time as the principal pumping engines were designed by Newcomen and could only successfully pump from depths of 50 fathoms.

During the mid-eighteenth century there was a turning point as the ability to mine deeper was mastered. This was due to improved steam power and the inauguration of the Great County Adit, which meant that the copper lodes hidden beneath the surface tin were now attainable. The copper era had arrived. Those mines mentioned above began to prosper, as did Wheal Maid, West Wheal Virgin and Carharrack Mine.

The Wheal Virgin story itself warrants further mention. On an initial outlay of £100 in 1757 the first fortnight saw the raising of copper ore to the value of £5,700. By 1779 copper was ousting tin as the chief mineral extracted from the area. A year later saw the amalgamation of several mines working in the Maid

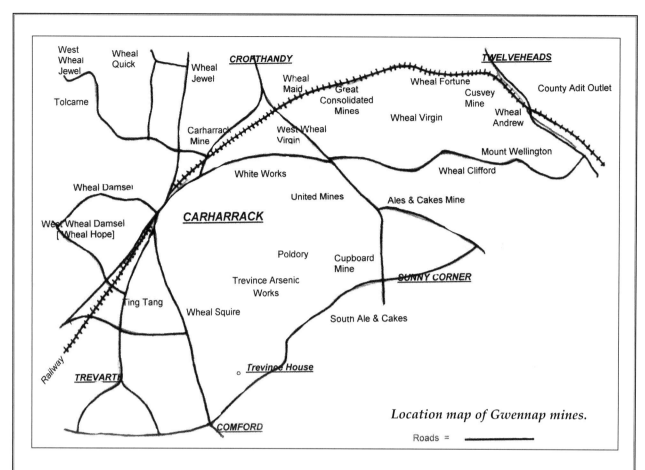

Location map of Gwennap mines.

Roads = ————

Consolidated Mines, 1980s. Very little remains intact of this once world-famous site. Left of centre are the surviving walls of Davey's whim, or winder; in front of this to the right is the site of the pumping engine-house on Davey's shaft, which was built for an 80-inch engine in 1834. In the distance the stacks and engine-houses around Taylor's shaft can be seen. The engine-house existed prior to 1835 when a new 85-inch engine replaced a 70-inch one bought from Wheal Alfred in 1826. Behind Taylor's house and stack – dead centre of the horizon – is the stack and part wall of the winding engine-house. The stack furthest to the left is known as the clock tower – it once housed the mine clock.

Close-up of Hockings engine-house, built for the 85-inch engine.

A watercolour of Garland's engine-house. When it was restarted in 1905/6 it was quite an occasion. It was 'put to work' by Joe Odgers of Carharrack.

Viewed in the late 1990s, the 1900–05 stamps engine is on the left and Garland's house is next with Eldon's far right. Some renovation aimed at preventing further decay has occurred to the structures over the last ten years.

Valley as Consolidated Mines (Consols); these included West Wheal Virgin, Fortune, Carharrack, Andrew and Cusvey. During the same period a number of mines south of Consols (Poldory, Wheal Cupboard, Ales and Cakes and Squire) were all active individually, although little is recorded of their histories. No doubt their development followed the same pattern with early tin production and greater depths resulting in copper returns.

By 1815 Poldory was down to the 110 fathom level and Ales and Cakes to 150 fathoms. It was at this time that they joined under the title Gwennap United Mines. Several other mines besides the conglomerates were active surrounding the 'big two'. Wheal Damsel began its run c.1795 and by the turn of the century, when most local mines were failing, it was the richest in the area. Prior to 1800 Wheal Jewel worked under the banners of Wheal Quick and North Damsel, giving profits of £200,000 and employing 300 people at its height.

The demise of most of the local concerns during the early 1800s – Consols and United both closed in 1805 – was principally due to the inability to mine at depth. The miners were awaiting the advent of better drainage, which would enable them to mine deeper in search of more profitable lodes. The ability to pump water from greater depths arrived with the introduction of a new breed of steam engine exhibiting increased efficiency and power. The cessation in 1800 of the restrictive patent placed on James Watt's engines by his organisation led to the engine being redesigned and built. This may have been lucrative for Boulton and Watt and associates but proved frustrating for those who wanted to expand mining activities. Many local engineers were now using their talents to bring the steam engine 'up to date' so that it could meet modern mining requirements. These engineers included Richard Trevithick, Arthur Woolf, Michael Hocking and Matthew Loam, who were among many using their skills to further the expansion of the mining industry in the area. Another asset was the continuing development of the County Adit, its relieving fingers ever reaching and connecting more mines to the 'adit web'.

Coupled with the above improvements and the involvement of two families – the Williamses of Scorrier and the Taylors – the coming of the 1820s saw a turn in fortunes for the local mines. John and Michael Williams had taken charge of United Mines in 1814, a company which had been restarted three years previously. John Taylor and Sons, who had several mining interests within the county, purchased Consols in 1819. This new breed of managers poured money into renovating machinery, improving mining techniques and utilising and encouraging talented engineers. The ground was being prepared for the next chapter in Gwennap's mining history, 'The Boom Years'.

THE BOOM YEARS: C.1820–40

The years 1820–40 saw copper mining reach its peak in Gwennap Parish. The boom had begun and the area soon became the greatest and the richest in the mining world, with Carharrack emerging from a cluster of dwellings to form a village. The local scene must have been one of great activity linked to the Devoran–Chasewater Railway, which was begun in 1824. Workers came flooding to the area, eager to partake in the emerging bonanza. From 1819–40 Consols yielded close on 300,000 tons of copper ore which sold for £2 million, with an initial outlay of a 'mere' £65,000 realising £480,000 in dividends.

This mining boom spearheaded the usual ancillary spin-offs, as Jack Trounson continually pointed out – 'It took several people up top to keep one miner under it.' The local railway meant that Devoran became the nearest port, thus ousting Penryn in prominence. Precipitation plants were spread along the Carnon Valley, extracting any remaining copper from the adit water, and arsenic works billowed forth their foul clouds. There were also the more usual trades and occupations surrounding a mining region – the blacksmiths, carters, wheelwrights, engineers, candle makers, rope makers, carpenters, coal merchants, horse traders and brick makers.

The genius of the shrewd John Taylor, manager of Consols, meant that many technological advances were witnessed. Taylor surrounded himself with some of the Cornish engineering giants such as Arthur Woolf, William Sims, John Hocking and Michael Loam and he was eager to promote new machinery. Experiments were under way within Consols to discover the most efficient type of steam engine. In around 1830 these experiments found that the less powerful but more economical single-acting engine was to be favoured. Hawke's shaft, close to the present racetrack at United Mines, was the site of one of the first man engines used in the county. This was a moving ladderway, originating in Germany, for the raising and lowering of the workforce to the different levels of the mine.

By this time industrialisation had reached Gwennap. Facts and figures relating to Consols were, to say the least, impressive. No less than eight large pumping engines were required to deal with the ever-insurgent water (despite all mines being connected to the County Adit) and 11 other engines were employed for winding, crushing or stamping duties. These were supplemented by water-wheels of 48ft and 40ft diameters, plus five smaller ones. The majority of the shaft depths were in excess of 200 fathoms with Woolf's reaching 300 fms (1,800 feet). It was estimated that the overall development underground (levels and tunnels) was 63 miles in length.

In 1841 Gwennap Parish was the most populous in the county, reaching figures of 10,796. However, do not imagine that Consols was alone in its fortunes.

Ales and Cakes, 1939.

Left to right, engine-houses: *Eldons (built in 1829 to provide a water supply for mine machinery when United was at its most productive), Stamps (built c.1900, when Messrs Cohen and Moss were attempting to rework nearby waste dumps for tin, plus some dewatering of Garland's shaft), Hockings (built in 1835 for an 85-inch pumping engine, it was used for target practice and was demolished by US troops during the Second World War), Garlands (built in 1857 for an 85-inch pumping and reused 1900–05 when an 80-inch was installed. After closure it was moved to Condurrow Mine, Beacon.).* (Photo by H.G. Ordish)

During the 1820–40 period the following mines were also at their zeniths:

Wheal Jewel   Wheal Damsel   Carharrack Mine
Poldice   Cathedral   Cusvey
Ting Tang   Wheal Maid   Wheal Unity Wood
Wheal Unity   Wheal Quick   West Wheal Damsel

As the mid-1800s approached, Gwennap and district were enjoying the successes of the copper boom. Consols and United Mines employed 3,196 people and Jewel Mine a further 1,354.

The Decline: 1860–2002

By the 1860s the copper industry in Cornwall was on its last legs. A drop in the demand for copper, the exhaustion of many local ore bodies and the emergence of more cost-effective mining in other countries were all contributing factors. The mines in the immediate area were either closed or floundering amid adverse conditions.

A healthier situation existed in the Camborne and Redruth area where substantial quantities of tin had been found beneath the copper lodes. During this time profitable amounts of tin were never discovered at depth and once the copper had been exhausted little could be done by the mines other than to close. Combining several mine setts, and thus avoiding the costly duplication of working practices, appeared to be the only saving grace.

In 1861 Wheal Clifford alone was working steadily in its search for tin. Fear of flooding from the interconnecting levels when United Mines and Consols announced their closure forced Clifford to acquire both redundant concerns, thus becoming Clifford Amalgamated Mines. However, falling tin prices plus crippling pumping costs led to the closure of this enterprise in the 1870s.

During the 1850s Wheal Maid and Carharrack Mine had been swallowed up by the St Day United and Poldice Mine which worked until 1873, centring on the Poldice sett. Tresavean also soldiered on as a copper mine with some tin returns in its latter workings until the mid-1880s.

So by the end of the 1880s Gwennap's position as a centre of mining had ceased. Practically overnight thousands of job opportunities were lost and very few openings were available to the local workforce. The great Cousin Jack exodus had begun as many local men boarded trains at Redruth to later find themselves aboard ships bound for the mining fields of Australia, South Africa and the Americas. Others sought work in the coalfields of Britain. The effect on the district must have been catastrophic, especially in a close-knit village community such as Carharrack. It is no wonder that little expansion in housing took place until the 1930s.

The Redruth–Chasewater Railway almost closed but for the continued success of the Basset and Pedn-an-drea Mines further west. Even then, at times only one train a day was needed. However, in typical resilient Cornish manner, several dozen men continued to scratch a living from the burrows by re-treating the dumps and extracting any remaining metals that they could. Indeed, so successful, or should it be hardworking, were they that over the 25 years up until 1890 120,000 tons of waste had been treated producing 5,100 tons of tinstone. The total amount of ore raised in the parish was 1,593,000 tons, resulting in 134,700 tons of copper – the largest quantity raised in any parish with only Illogan Parish being comparable.

Despite the adversities, mining continued in some form or another right through the twentieth century. Between 1900 and 1905 an ambitious attempt was made to reclaim ores from the still-extensive burrows in the area. Messrs Cohen and Moss set up a considerable mill and treatment plant on United Downs. Added to this was the building of a new steam stamps and the re-equipping of an old pumping engine-house with an 80-inch cylinder steam engine. Owing to the inadequacies of the mineral processing plant, the company were unable to extract sufficient quantities of metal.

Tresavean was reopened in 1907 in the hope of discovering tin beneath the copper, and towards this end remained working until 1928, although some small deposits of tin were encountered.

Up until the 1930s several small crushing mills and treatment plants were to be heard in the vicinity of the Poldory Valley where a Mr Moor had previously owned an arsenic treatment works, during the years running up to the early 1900s. The stack that

Left: *A watercolour by the author of the site of the 1905/6 attempted reworking by Messrs Cohen and Moss. The engine-house on the left worked 120 head of Cornish stamps purchased from Killifreth – it was the last big stamps erected in the county. The long building housed the dressing plant which included belt-driven vanners. To the right is Garland's engine-house.*

Above: *A view, c.1940, looking east of the valley bottom along Poldory. The nearest stack formed part of the Trevince Arsenic Works which was active in the later part of the 1800s and was at one time worked by the same management team as a similar set-up in the Bissoe Valley. The stack to its right is still just managing to hang on to its existence – the rubbish is gradually burying it. On the left of the nearest stack the treatment plants of Ernie Teague and John Pelmear can just be made out.*

Left: *View of a dressing plant further down the Poldory Valley taken by Govier, Chacewater. Wilfred Bawden remembers two such plants working in the area; one run by Ernie Teague and the other, further east, by John Pelmear. Presumably this is the latter concern. Both were active around 1910 but had ceased prior to 1939. The adventurers would have reworked the vast waste dumps, carting the orestuff to their set-up. There are two water-wheels in this view; the right-hand one is hidden by the wooden structure overhead. This one drove a small set of three to four Cornish stamps which would have reduced the orestuff to a small enough size to be treated on the accompanying buddles, which in turn separated the tin from the waste by gravitational methods. These buddles would have been inside the shed and run by the other wheel via a series of cogs, gear wheels and drive belts. Once the tin ore had been treated it would be bagged and transported to one of several local tin-dressing plants for further refining. Such plants were at Trehaddle and Tolgus. Launders supplying the water to these floors can be seen behind the structures. A system of feeder troughs and launders brought water across the valley floor. (Photo courtesy of the Royal Institution of Cornwall)*

remains, now almost engulfed by the United Downs rubbish tip, marks the site of a small ore-treatment plant. This could possibly be the site of a concern run by Alf Burrows and John Pelmear. They had water power running four head of stamps which could be heard in Carharrack, thumping away all night. The machinery was tended or fed with orestuff in the evening which it would grind into smaller fragments. This caused much annoyance for villagers wishing for a quiet night's rest.

Further down the valley, near the sewage-treatment plant, was another small mill run by Ernie Teague, again using water power.

During the 1930s the area at the back of the scrapyard was worked by a Mr Kellow under the name of Whiteworks, due to the colour of the ore obtained. It is said that the ores were carted to Redruth Smelting Works in Andrew's Yard to be treated.

In the mid-1930s the Non Ferrous Mining Co. Ltd acquired Whiteworks, as well as working the eastern sett of Wheal Clifford and Mount Wellington Mine, locally called Magpie. Wellington's mill plant was utilised during the war years in the search for wolfram and tin due to the loss of the Malayan sources through enemy capture. Since then little work had taken place until the late-1960s to mid-1970s, when Wheal Jane began exploratory drilling on

United Downs in preparation for the contemplated dewatering of Consols and United Mines and the creation of the Wheal Maid decline. This decline was started but was later abandoned as a result of the tin price collapse of the mid-1980s, the intention being to recover tin beneath the copper lodes. With the demise of the latter attempt it seems as if Gwennap's mining days were over and alas 16 years on in 2001 there seemed no future possibility of mining in Cornwall at all, let alone within earshot of Carharrack, which owes so much to the search for and discovery of minerals within the locality.

MINES SURROUNDING CARHARRACK

With all mining activities the fortunes and development are dependent upon market forces and the quality and availability of orestuff. It should be noted that local mines were at the forefront of technological advances of the period, and several new inventions were first tried out in the following concerns:

Ting Tang

The generic name Ting Tang applies to three, at one time separate, mining setts. Ting Tang made up the

Above: A closer view, taken in the 1970s, of Alfie Burrows' treatment plant. In the foreground are the circular depressions holding two convex buddles, which were used to recover tin from the waste material. The stack presumably was linked to a calciner, which roasted the tin ore to extract some of the impurities.

Inset: This photograph was taken in the 1940s. Poldory engine-house stands in the centre with the remains of a small treatment plant in the valley floor. The engine-house is probably the one mentioned in 1907 as being built by Fred Long of St Day.

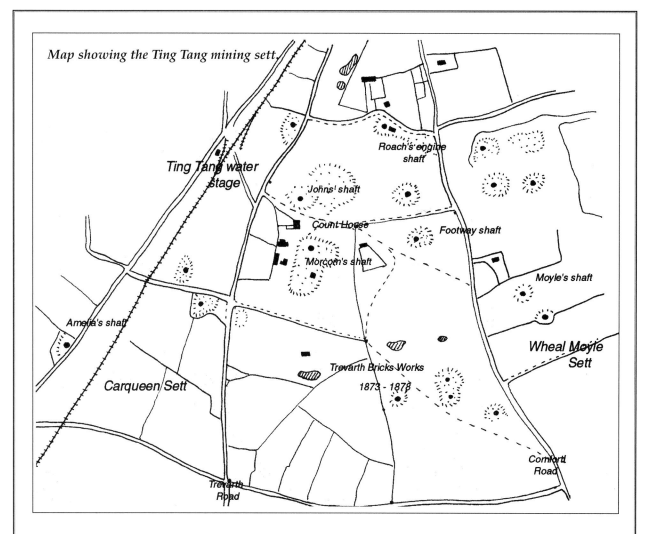

Map showing the Ting Tang mining sett.

Left: *Ting Tang count-house, photographed by H.G. Ordish, prior to further demolition in recent years, a shadow of its former glory status. The count-house proved to be the nerve centre of most mines. Besides being the administrative hub of the mine, it was the place where the workforce assembled on a regular basis when the sections of the underground pitches were bid for by the pares (a term used for a group of miners). During the most productive period of working there was a monthly, quarterly or biannual examination of the books. It was often an excuse by the adventurers for indulging in excess eating, drinking and generally enjoying themselves. However, these count-house dinners were part and parcel of Cornish mining folklore, albeit a pastime of the wealthier merchants and entrepreneurs. Several mines, notably the larger ones, possessed their own dinner services, suitably labelled with the mine's monogram. Since its use as a count-house this particular one has had a variety of inmates. In the 1870s, prior to the building of St Piran's Church, hymns and sermons of worship would have been heard inside. Other sounds to emanate from its walls from 1910 onwards were children's voices during its temporary classroom status, the musical tones of the Carharrack band whilst practising, and the workshop noises associated with Fred Williams' wheelwrighting business.*

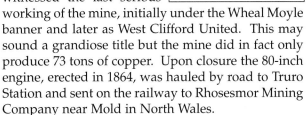

Right: Many of the larger mines had their own 'mine bell' like the Ting Tang one pictured. Unfortunately very few, if any, still exist, apart from this one now on show as part of the Museum Exhibition at Poldark Mine tourist attraction, Wendron. The bell was used to signal changes of shift, or core, periods of the mine. Its solemn peal would have rung out if tragedy struck in the form of an underground accident. This particular bell, cast by Perran Foundry, Perranarworthal, in 1844, weighed two hundredweight. It would have been hung on tall, wooden shear legs which straddled the mineshaft top.
(Photograph courtesy of the management of Poldark Mine)

northern section while the south and eastern part was Wheal Moyle and the western end Carqueen.

The earliest mention of mining here dates from 1700–10 when work was concentrated in the northern sett retrieving tin ore at shallow depths. Working continued during several phases until the late 1860s when it was known as West Clifford United. The years 1816–35 were the most profitable with the predominant metal 'won' being copper – 40,000 tons of copper ore were extracted. At this time Michael Williams, one of the Williamses of Scorrier House, was the manager and worked the mine in conjunction with the nearby United Mines which obviously reduced costs in certain areas of production and management. Some 180 people made up the workforce and the deepest point underground then was 74 fathoms (444 feet). A 63-inch pumping engine was erected in 1818 to extract the inflowing water and thus make further development in depth possible. Transportation was aided from the mid-1820s when the Devoran–Chasewater Railway was formed with the track passing close by the mine to the north. No doubt the ores were ferried to the port of Devoran while the imported coal and other materials were carried on the upward journey, thus superseding or at least supplementing horse-related transport.

The 1870 Ordnance Survey map shows a watering stage for the railway steam engines approached by a spur of track and a passing loop nearby, so it may be assumed that these track sections would have been used for loading and unloading mine materials.

After abandonment in 1834 the mine was opened with renewed vigour for a couple of years from 1845–47. Work centred on the western end of the sett where some good mineral-producing ground was found. A Sims compound 60-inch and 100-inch pumping engine was erected which was then the largest of its type in the county. It was built by Harveys of Hayle and required three boilers 33ft in length with a diameter of 5ft 9in. The pistons were packed with hemp and tallow and required attention every six to eight weeks. A *West Briton* reporter commented upon the oppressive nature of this maintenance early this century by stating that the men, who entered the bottom cylinder through special manholes, found conditions so hot that a blacksmith's bellows was directed into the cylinder to cool the worker. This situation soon came to an end when, in 1846, the engine was stopped and later sold to Treloweth Mine in St Erth Parish as a 60-inch. By now the depth below surface had reached 173 fathoms (1,038 feet).

The years from 1861–67 witnessed the last serious working of the mine, initially under the Wheal Moyle banner and later as West Clifford United. This may sound a grandiose title but the mine did in fact only produce 73 tons of copper. Upon closure the 80-inch engine, erected in 1864, was hauled by road to Truro Station and sent on the railway to Rhosesmor Mining Company near Mold in North Wales.

From the point of view of industrial archaeology the seventeenth-century working proved the most intriguing. Despite being connected to the County Adit in 1750, work was halted due to a lack of powerful pumping capacity. Newcomen's atmospheric engine only permitted the raising of water from up to 80 fathoms. By 1770 a Newcomen engine installed in 1745 could not cope with the inflow of water. As a result a Cornish delegation visited the Soho Works in Birmingham of Boulton and Watt. The outcome was that an offer was made to the Ting Tang adventurers to erect a trial engine on their sett free of charge, an offer not to be declined. Dutifully a 52 inch was ordered in November 1776, thus being the first B&W engine erected and used in Cornwall. Because the ship's hold hatches were too small for their load, the engine did not reach Falmouth until 1778.

Meanwhile, Thomas Wilson, manager of Wheal Busy Mine, ordered and received a 30-inch engine, which was set to work in September 1777. The Ting Tang 52-inch finally worked in July 1778. Both engines proved very successful and spearheaded B&W's superiority over Newcomen's engine design.

Few traces of the mine now exist, apart from a few shaft sites, the main feature being the truncated walls of the count-house.

Carharrack Mine

At one time this mine appears to have worked in conjunction with or under the label of East Wheal Damsel, which lay nearby. Started in the 1750s for copper, the mine worked the western extension of the rich lodes of Wheal Virgin and Wheal Maid mines to the east. As East Wheal Damsel it was worked by the Williamses of Scorrier from around the 1820s up until 1835. Along with Wheal Maid it raised 24,000 tons of copper between several periods of activity from 1821

Wheal Jewel site looking east along the line of south lode to the Consols valley. Michael's shaft lies to the right, with Foxes in the centre of the view. This area now makes up the Wheal Jewel caravan park.

Left: In the early years of the nineteenth century the Tolcarne Valley resounded to the thumping of a small set of water stamps which dutifully crushed the orestuff fed into it from the local mine waste dumps. One Mr Rundle ran the concern, utilising the water by means of a wooden launder, which traversed the valley. Alas the launder has departed the scene, but beneath a few generations of gorse and bracken lay the foundations of the water-wheel that drove the stamps. This H.G. Ordish view dates back to the 1950s. On the skyline are the waste dumps of West Wheal Damsel.

∞ Poldory ∞

Above left: During the early 1900s an asserted attempt was made to rework the Poldory waste piles. The buildings in this Govier photograph seem to be completed; quite a substantial complex, which probably housed crushing and gravitational separation machinery. (Photo courtesy of RIC, Truro)

Above right: All that survived of the site by the 1980s. Sadly even these small remnants have now been buried beneath the household rubbish.

northern section while the south and eastern part was Wheal Moyle and the western end Carqueen.

The earliest mention of mining here dates from 1700–10 when work was concentrated in the northern sett retrieving tin ore at shallow depths. Working continued during several phases until the late 1860s when it was known as West Clifford United. The years 1816–35 were the most profitable with the predominant metal 'won' being copper – 40,000 tons of copper ore were extracted. At this time Michael Williams, one of the Williamses of Scorrier House, was the manager and worked the mine in conjunction with the nearby United Mines which obviously reduced costs in certain areas of production and management. Some 180 people made up the workforce and the deepest point underground then was 74 fathoms (444 feet). A 63-inch pumping engine was erected in 1818 to extract the inflowing water and thus make further development in depth possible. Transportation was aided from the mid-1820s when the Devoran–Chasewater Railway was formed with the track passing close by the mine to the north. No doubt the ores were ferried to the port of Devoran while the imported coal and other materials were carried on the upward journey, thus superseding or at least supplementing horse-related transport.

The 1870 Ordnance Survey map shows a watering stage for the railway steam engines approached by a spur of track and a passing loop nearby, so it may be assumed that these track sections would have been used for loading and unloading mine materials.

After abandonment in 1834 the mine was opened with renewed vigour for a couple of years from 1845–47. Work centred on the western end of the sett where some good mineral-producing ground was found. A Sims compound 60-inch and 100-inch pumping engine was erected which was then the largest of its type in the county. It was built by Harveys of Hayle and required three boilers 33ft in length with a diameter of 5ft 9in. The pistons were packed with hemp and tallow and required attention every six to eight weeks. A *West Briton* reporter commented upon the oppressive nature of this maintenance early this century by stating that the men, who entered the bottom cylinder through special manholes, found conditions so hot that a blacksmith's bellows was directed into the cylinder to cool the worker. This situation soon came to an end when, in 1846, the engine was stopped and later sold to Treloweth Mine in St Erth Parish as a 60-inch. By

now the depth below surface had reached 173 fathoms (1,038 feet).

The years from 1861–67 witnessed the last serious working of the mine, initially under the Wheal Moyle banner and later as West Clifford United. This may sound a grandiose title but the mine did in fact only produce 73 tons of copper. Upon closure the 80-inch engine, erected in 1864, was hauled by road to Truro Station and sent on the railway to Rhosesmor Mining Company near Mold in North Wales.

From the point of view of industrial archaeology the seventeenth-century working proved the most intriguing. Despite being connected to the County Adit in 1750, work was halted due to a lack of powerful pumping capacity. Newcomen's atmospheric engine only permitted the raising of water from up to 80 fathoms. By 1770 a Newcomen engine installed in 1745 could not cope with the inflow of water. As a result a Cornish delegation visited the Soho Works in Birmingham of Boulton and Watt. The outcome was that an offer was made to the Ting Tang adventurers to erect a trial engine on their sett free of charge, an offer not to be declined. Dutifully a 52-inch was ordered in November 1776, thus being the first B&W engine erected and used in Cornwall. Because the ship's hold hatches were too small for their load, the engine did not reach Falmouth until 1778.

Meanwhile, Thomas Wilson, manager of Wheal Busy Mine, ordered and received a 30-inch engine, which was set to work in September 1777. The Ting Tang 52-inch finally worked in July 1778. Both engines proved very successful and spearheaded B&W's superiority over Newcomen's engine design.

Few traces of the mine now exist, apart from a few shaft sites, the main feature being the truncated walls of the count-house.

Carharrack Mine

At one time this mine appears to have worked in conjunction with or under the label of East Wheal Damsel, which lay nearby. Started in the 1750s for copper, the mine worked the western extension of the rich lodes of Wheal Virgin and Wheal Maid mines to the east. As East Wheal Damsel it was worked by the Williamses of Scorrier from around the 1820s up until 1835. Along with Wheal Maid it raised 24,000 tons of copper between several periods of activity from 1821

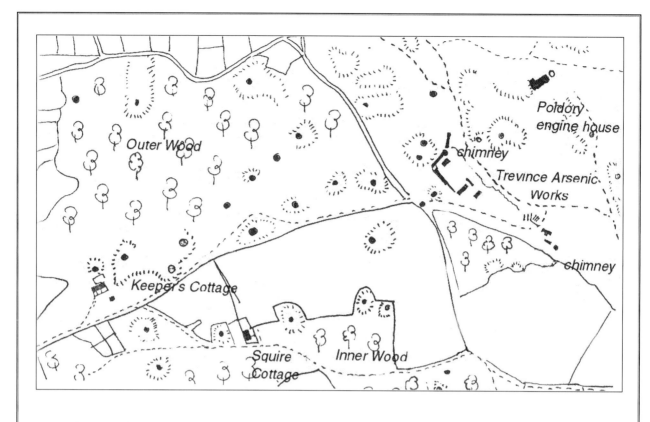

Above: *Wheal Squire sett including Trevince Arsenic Works.*

Right: *Whilst cleaning up some of the dumps of Carharrack Mine this wooden pump rod, dating from the early workings of the mine, was exposed. In mines with very acidic water, leather was used to line these rods.*

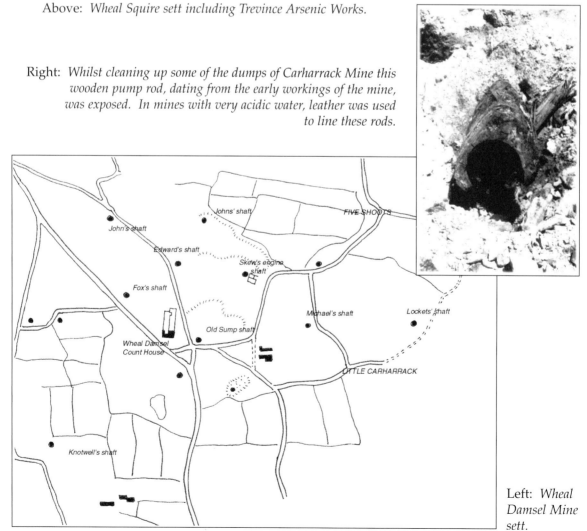

Left: *Wheal Damsel Mine sett.*

West Wheal Damsel's dumps dominate the skyline when viewed from the road to Lower Trevethan.

An H.G. Ordish photo of West Wheal Damsel, 1930s. The bob wall of the pumping engine is at the centre with the shaft directly in front. The winding engine stands to the right. Today only a small section of the pumping-house remains.

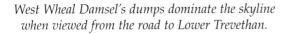

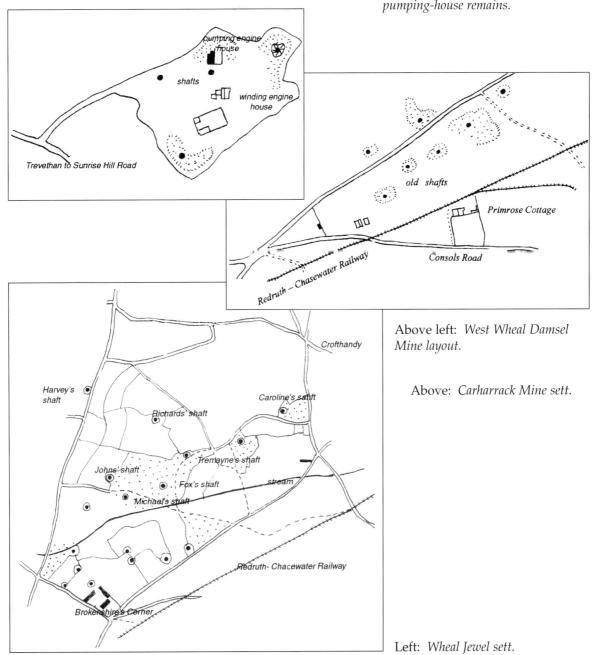

Above left: *West Wheal Damsel Mine layout.*

Above: *Carharrack Mine sett.*

Left: *Wheal Jewel sett.*

Wheal Jewel site looking east along the line of south lode to the Consols valley. Michael's shaft lies to the right, with Foxes in the centre of the view. This area now makes up the Wheal Jewel caravan park.

Left: In the early years of the nineteenth century the Tolcarne Valley resounded to the thumping of a small set of water stamps which dutifully crushed the orestuff fed into it from the local mine waste dumps. One Mr Rundle ran the concern, utilising the water by means of a wooden launder, which traversed the valley. Alas the launder has departed the scene, but beneath a few generations of gorse and bracken lay the foundations of the water-wheel that drove the stamps. This H.G. Ordish view dates back to the 1950s. On the skyline are the waste dumps of West Wheal Damsel.

⌘ Poldory ⌘

Above left: During the early 1900s an asserted attempt was made to rework the Poldory waste piles. The buildings in this Govier photograph seem to be completed; quite a substantial complex, which probably housed crushing and gravitational separation machinery. (Photo courtesy of RIC, Truro)

Above right: All that survived of the site by the 1980s. Sadly even these small remnants have now been buried beneath the household rubbish.

to 1852. One of the early fire engines, the forerunner of the much more powerful and efficient steam engines of Watt's time, was erected in 1779.

During the mid-1970s, after the removal of waste dumps in the area, a wooden pump rod was uncovered on the sett. It was a section of wood about 12 feet in length and 12 inches in diameter, hollowed out by manual boring. The section was removed by members of the Carn Brea Mining Society and is now in the Tolgus Tin Stream Museum along the Portreath Road. In 1935–39 a trial called Whiteworks was carried out on part of this sett to the south-east. Some work was carried out here on the shallower levels, around 60 to 70 fathoms, and about two tons of tin were raised. Mr Kellow was the manager at the time.

Wheal Squire

Over the years this sett has been engulfed by woodland and many of the dumps and shafts have been smothered by undergrowth. In its prime, c.1810–1820s when over 400 people were employed, Wheal Squire must have been a hive of activity. Little is recorded of the concern save that it had a 36-inch pumping engine and was draining down to the 98-fathom level in 1818 when the Williamses of Scorrier were its managers. Some 20,000 tons of copper ore realising £148,000 were obtained, and the greatest depth reached was 143 fathoms.

West Wheal Damsel

This mine was also entitled Wheal Hope and was included in the Wheal Damsel mine sett. It began as a separate concern in about 1850–56 when it had a 36-inch pumping engine and a 22-inch crusher. From 1857–74 150 people were employed and 30,000 tons of copper ore raised. In 1864 the management purchased the adjoining Wheal Damsel sett, intending to call the amalgamation Wheal Damsel United, but little work was done.

Wheal Damsel

The sett comprises the Wheal Spinster section in the north and Wheal Hope, also called West Wheal Damsel, in the west. Damsel began in about 1795, at first having little success because of poor values, but by 1806 fortunes had changed. At a time when most of the surrounding mines were having problems Damsel was at its most productive. The mine worked the same lodes as Wheal Maid and these lodes were almost two miles in length. One special feature of the Damsel sett is the existence of some goffins, or open-cast workings, to be found on the slope of the hill adjoining the Shute to Trevethan road. Periods of activity encompassed the 1790s to the 1870s and two engines are recorded on the mine, a 42-inch and 50-inch. It was one of the first mines to

make use of tramroads, which made the movement of ore underground easier. These were introduced in 1824. Some 37,000 tons of copper ore were produced.

One dominating feature long since demolished was the Damsel count-house which, during the 1820s, was known as the Copper Office and was used by 'Old' John Williams as the family's main admin centre. Just prior to this, in 1805, it was used as the place for handing out the poor relief in the parish, quite a trek for some parishioners of the day. The count-house stood at the junction of the tracks and road, just opposite the farm buildings belonging to the Penroses. Billy Penrose remembers his father mentioning that there was once a row of cottages there and he thinks they were owned by the Teague family, but they were ruinous when he was a lad.

Wheal Jewel

Most readers will recall the scare involving St Day and Carharrack Community School in the early-1990s when a shaft was 'discovered' in close proximity to one of the classrooms. This shaft, plus others which have been capped in the nearby town playing area and the plot now frequented by residential caravans opposite Tresaddern Farm, were all part of the extensive Wheal Jewel mine sett. The section in and around the southern end of St Day town constitutes the Wheal Quick, or North Jewel part, the caravan settlement being the site of the mine workings on Wheal Jewel.

Wheal Quick sett saw its first activity in around 1750. It was very profitable up until the beginning of the nineteenth century, at which point water inflow problems, coupled with impoverished lodes, caused closure. From 1815 to 1822 the Williams family of Scorrier took control and made profits. Other periods of working followed until the 1850s, by which time 58,000 tons of copper ore had been extracted realising £407,000. The depth then was 150 fathoms and there were 300 employees. In reports about the mine, mention was made of the poor ventilation experienced underground. The air was said to be 'scalding to the miners throats' and igniting a candle was nigh impossible, often taking hours.

Tolcarne Mine

This mine proved to be one of the biggest disappointments for its adventurers. Immediately to the east was Wheal Jewel, which was productive and extremely rich. It was assumed by the Tolcarne management that the profitable lodes in Jewel would prevail in their sett, but this was not so. Despite sinking several shafts, the lodes, which to the east had proved rich, proved very hard and poor in quality in Tolcarne. It so happened that the Great Cross Course, a vein of material that intersects the true lode sometimes causing upheavals and displacement of that lode, had moved the Jewel lodes 60 to 80 fathoms northwards. The owners persisted for about 20 years, finally succumbing to the fact that their sett was not profitable and not worth continuing with.

Gluttons for punishment, other intrepid mining buffs made attempts to earn a crust from Tolcarne between 1832 and the mid-1870s. Various titles were used for their efforts; West Wheal Jewel was one, North Wheal Damsel another and in its last reworking, when a 54-inch pumping engine was coupled with a 26-inch winder, it was North Wheal Jewel.

EMIGRATION

Mining has always been a very uncertain business, fluctuation in the price of minerals can be sudden and lasting or just a short-term 'blip'. Ore values and reserves likewise vary considerably and lack stability, making it difficult to plan for the future. A mining county such as Cornwall has suffered highs and lows over its entire mineral history. The Carharrack mineralised area has shared in the 'boom and bust' culture. However, certain consistencies remain, such as the knowledge and skills that the mining fraternity acquire and practise. These are invaluable and always in demand wherever mining exists.

The migration of miners has always been a feature of Cornwall's mining centres and therefore plays an important role in Carharrack's social history. Practically every village family prior to the Second World War can claim at least one 'cousin Jack or Jenny' in their fold, and in many cases several more such migrants. With the vast majority of the Carharrack mining workforce involved in copper, migration was firmly linked to the presence and market value of that commodity. Even in the early 1800s there was an exodus of mining talent when most copper mines surrounding Carharrack were either closed or having financial difficulties. At that time the principal destinations were the Americas, with Peru, Chile, Brazil, Cuba and Mexico luring workers with incentives of a financial nature or promises of an improved lifestyle. Such regions needed the skills and experience of men from proven mineral areas.

During the 1840s the copper fields in South Australia were developing quickly on a vast scale. The British Government enticed miners with the offer of assisted passages, at first just for selected tradesman and their families but later the offer was extended to the unskilled workers. Ten years on it was the copper and iron deposits around Quebec and the Keweenan Peninsula in Michigan that proved the attraction, along with the Californian Gold Rush that was taking place simultaneously.

Literature began to appear in the Mechanics Institute in the village offering placements abroad and sailing package deals. Monthly remittances sent home to support remaining family members were mounting in frequency and quantity. In the census

The family of James Enstice, born in 1838, who emigrated with his family to the United States in search of better times. Left to right, back row: *Sam, John, William, Edwin, Frank;* seated: *Anne, Anne (mother), Mary.* (Photo courtesy of the Nurhonen family)

returns the term *annuitant* usually referred to such situations, with the breadwinner living abroad. Concurrent with these attractions was the distress and suffering caused by unsatisfactory working conditions in the local industry. A miners' strike at Consols, when 200 people marched to Carn Brea Mine to gain support, was not even mentioned in any of the local newspapers. We wonder why not!

Emigration agents soon moved to the Carharrack area offering loans and incentives to 'seek a new life and experience' in these developing 'utopias'. By the mid-1840s the departure of emigrant ships was commonplace from Restronguet, Malpas, Hayle and Penzance and from larger ports 'up country'. Their destinations: Port Philip, Port Adelaide, Quebec, Natal, Hobart, New Brunswick and New York.

The real crunch came in the 1860s with the first signs of a decline in the area as a major copper-mining centre. Vast deposits of an alluvial nature could be won with much less effort and expense. The price of copper fell from a high of £115 per ton in 1880 to £18 by 1890. This price collapse, plus the absence of tin deposits beneath the copper ores, forced the workforce to migrate. Initially they would go to nearby areas which were developing tin ore, such as the great Dolcoath Mine and the Redruth region in general, but soon these work prospects were oversubscribed and foreign fields were sought. 'Local News' sections of the *West Briton* were regularly listing local inhabitants, usually male, who were emigrating from the district.

Data stored at the Royal Institution of Cornwall shows instances of migrant deaths recorded in the obituaries of the *Royal Cornwall Gazette*. From these details it is possible to trace the movements of village ancestors in their quests for work. It makes interesting reading, proving how adventurous, or perhaps desperate, they were in their efforts. Today we may travel in the luxurious comfort of a modern jet to some exotic island paradise, but to imagine these 'journeys of hope' endured by Carharrack villagers, aboard creaking, lurching sailing ships of dubious seaworthiness amid cramped and insanitary conditions, defies belief. The following mines and mining areas were home to ex-Carharrack folk:

Africa: Roodepoort, Transvaal, the Gold Coast.
USA: Hanker Mine, Park City, Utah. Gardner Mine, Bisbee, Arizona. Warren Davies and Co., Illinios. Jackson City, Richmond, Bessemer Mine, Humboldt and Marquetti Co., Michigan.
California: Grass Valley, Amadori City, Guadalope Mine, Smartville, Yuba County, Plumes Eureka Mine.
Brazil: Morrow Velho Mine, Morr de Santa Anna.
Bolivia: Dwendes Mine, Huanchaca.
Mexico: Real del Monte, Pachuca.
Chile: Caldera, Copiaco, Carrizal Alto, Coquimbo, Capitana; Mines de las Arienas.
Australia: Redfern, Sydney. Pleasant Creek, Victoria. Clunes, Scaradale, Ballerat, Wallarroo.

As expected the fortunes of the migrants were varied. Monetary rewards were undoubtedly to be had, albeit involving some sacrifice. Some of the people who made the sacrifice were listed in the *Royal Cornwall Gazette*:

Edwin Brown, aged 28, died 16 June 1871 as a result of an underground explosion in Real del Monte Mine. He was the son of John Brown, a local grocer and draper.

John Mitchell died aged 35 in 1895 at Bessemer, Michigan. He was the only son of John and Ann Mitchell of Ting Tang.

Ada Chynoweth Pelmear, aged 4 months, daughter of George and Jane Pelmear died in Buena Vista, Tocopilla in 1882.

The birthplace of LeRoy Gumma (senr), born 1896, in Colorado, USA. He came home to Carharrack at the age of 11. (Photo courtesy of Pearl Lewis.)

Joseph Roberts and his wife suffered tragedy upon tragedy between the years 1876 to 1880 with the loss of five young infants during their time in Chile. Further tragedy occurred to the family when the death of Joseph, aged 40, was reported. His wife was the daughter of James Sampson, a village bookseller.

Samuel Simmons, aged 27, died in an accident at Hanker Mine, Park City, Utah in 1895. His parents were William and Louise Simmons, who lived at Shute Row and Foxes Row in the 1880s and '90s.

Peter Benbow of Redruth has kindly allowed the author to use some sections of his extensive research into his family's history in Carharrack, which makes fascinating reading and superbly illustrates the events of a typical family living in a mining village:

Joseph Benbow, born in Carharrack in 1807, was christened in Gwennap on 12 April 1808; died at Sparry Bottom 20 April 1848; married Ann Phillips, who died in 1840; remarried one Elizabeth Phillips in 1841. After Joseph's death his second wife sailed to Australia with five children in 1848. She had an assisted passage of £8.12s. from Gwennap Parish. First Elizabeth and children would have gone to Penzance and boarded the steamer Lady de Saumarez *for Plymouth, where they embarked on the ship* Santipore *heading for Australia. (West Briton, 16:06:1848)*
William Benbow, born at Trevethan in 1825, christened in Gwennap Parish in 1823. Immigrated to Chile with brother Robert.
Francis Benbow, born at Tolcarne in 1826; died 1859; married Margaret Trebilcock and they had six children, one of whom was Caroline (born 1858; died in New Zealand 1935). Caroline then aged 20 sailed from Plymouth on the Piako *for Lyttleton, New Zealand on 11 October 1878; the voyage turned out to be quite eventful.*
The Piako's third passage and Capt. Boyd's second, almost ended in disaster. She sailed on 11 October with a crew of 40 and 317 passengers. Just a month out, about 180 miles from Pernambuco, smoke was reported to be rising from the fore hatch in between decks. In order to get to the seat of the fire, the fore hatch was removed upon which a 20 foot flame lept out of the hold. The foremost tier of cargo was ablaze! They tried to put the fire out with the fire hose to little effect. They decided to batten down the hatch again and try to get at the fire from another direction; from below decks through the married quarters, but the dense smoke prevented them from advancing very far. The situation looked grim.
The Captain then gave the helmsman a new course to steer, towards Pernambuco. The boats were then provisioned and lowered. It required every effort by Capt. Boyd to avoid panic amongst the people. There were 160 men among the passengers as well as families that were going to New Zealand. The Captain stood at the break of the poop, pistol in hand. He was calming

the women on board at one moment and the next ensuring his orders were being obeyed. Once the boats were lowered into the water, there was a rush upon the Captain by some of the rougher characters, but the Captain met the rush with 'Stand back everybody! Women and children first!' Just then a cry of 'Sail Ho!' filled the air. Captain Boyd took one look to make sure a ship was in sight, then happily said, 'Well done! You'll all be saved if you don't get excited. Keep yourselves calm and don't make a noise.' From this time the situation settled down and things were calmer on board. The vessel on hand, the Loch Doon, still took three hours to come

IN LOVING MEMORY

OF

WILLIAM JAMES ALBERT,

Eldest and dearly beloved Son of W. J. A. and M. J. HUNT,

OF CARHARRACK.

Who was accidentally killed at the Chapin Mine, Iron Mountain, Michigan, U.S.A., April 8th, 1910,

AGED 19 YEARS AND 8 MONTHS.

An in memorium card says it all.
(Loaned courtesy of Keith Manley)

alongside so that the passengers could be transferred. A few ex-sailors volunteered to stay on board the Piako and help fight the fire.

Having reached Pernambuco the Captain found more problems; smallpox was raging at the place and 400 were dying each day. It was decided to make for a small island seven miles up river called Coconut Island which was uninhabited and had a grove of coconut trees surrounded by a lot of sand. The passengers were landed here and had to endure this island for nine weeks.

Food was sent from the ship, which Captain Boyd and his crew managed to save. The fire was smothered by the expedient of scuttling it into the level of her poop deck. This most effectively put out the fire, and when she was raised again very little damage was done to the ship herself. However, the fire destroyed most of the cargo in the forward hold, the greater part of the emigrant's baggage and effects. The Piako finally arrived at Lyttleton on March 5th after necessary repairs had been made, being 145 days out of Plymouth.

Richard Benbow, born Carharrack 1886, known to have gone to Atlantic Mine, Michigan. John Benbow, born in the village 1868 and died here in 1923, having mined in Africa and India. William Benbow, John's brother, born Carharrack 1874 married Rosina Cann (daughter to William and Jane Cann). They had one son, Reggie, born 1909 who was born 6 months after his father's death. He attended a school for the blind and in the 1930s had a basket making business in a loft adjacent to the Mills' Hall.

The following reports are taken from the local news sections of the newspapers:

Royal Cornwall Gazette, *April 1909*
On Friday the following young men left St Day and District for the USA: Stephen Harry, T. Johns,

J. Barrett, H. Knuckey, J. Trevithick, Richard Williams.

West Briton, *July 1932*
Death of Frederick Chynoweth at Iron Mountain, Michigan, USA. Left Carharrack in 1907. Relatives J. Chynoweth, St Day, and Miss B. Chynoweth, Railway Terrace.

West Briton, *March 1935*
Death in Butte City, Montana, of William Arthur Mills, aged 44, who emigrated in 1921; son of Mr T. Mills. Wife and son still live in village.

West Briton, *January 1936*
WJ Weatherhead, Railway Terrace, sailed from Liverpool bound for South Africa to take up a mining appointment at Grootfontein, South West Africa Co. Ltd.

West Briton, *May 1936*
Returned from India on furlough from Kolar Gold Fields is Mr and Mrs Robert H. Teague and daughter Margaret. Mr L. Pelmear arrived from Nundydroog Gold Mines.

Interviewing villagers in Carharrack brought the following information about emigrants to light:

Harry Tredre's father and Ernie Teague sailed to South Africa together circa the late 1800s early 1900s. Harry's Uncle Tom, a teacher, went to Johannesburg. Harry also remembers that at Christmas time some of the village parties were funded with money sent home by absent parents mining abroad.
Phyllis Nicholls' grandfather died in Brazil.
Bennett Dower, a relative of Ruby, died as a result of a mining accident in Chile in 1888.

BIBLIOGRAPHY
Mines and Miners of Cornwall VI Around Gwennap, A.K. Hamilton Jenkin
The Cornish Miner, A.K. Hamilton Jenkin
Copper Mining in Cornwall, D.B. Barton
History of Gwennap, C.C. James
The Cornish in America, A.C. Todd
Observations on the West of England Mining Region, J.H. Collins
The Metalliferous Mining Region of South West England – Vol. I, H.G. Dines
The Cornish Beam Engine, D.B. Barton
Mining in Cornwall Vol. I and II, J. Trounson
The History of Tin Mining & Smelting in Cornwall, D.B. Barton

THREE

༒

RELIGION: CHURCH OF ENGLAND & METHODISM

One imagines the area around Carharrack as having been fairly desolate with mine dumps, buildings, engine-houses and smoking mine stacks. Where the village now stands there would only have been a handful of houses, a few around the area occupied by the Square, known as Carharrack Gate, and a few more at the eastern end, known as Chynhale. This would have been Carharrack in 1830, the year of the copper-mining boom and a time before the village began to develop as a sizeable mining community.

During this period the Church of England found that it was necessary to address the problem of rapidly expanding villages. The people of Carharrack had to travel to Gwennap Parish Church in order to worship until, in 1828, a new church was built at St Day (see *The Book of St Day*). This then became a separate parish, as did Lanner in 1845. Despite this there was still no church in Carharrack.

At some point in the nineteenth century the first change came for Carharrack Anglicans. Charles James was the lay reader and he was also a local historian writing many notes about the parish. These notes were edited by his son C.C. James and were published as *The History of Gwennap* in 1947. Mr James was in charge of worship which took place in Ting Tang count-house.

ST PIRAN'S CHURCH

It was not until the 1880s that Carharrack had its own church and even then it did not become a separate parish within the Church. Under a scheme to provide mission churches in industrial areas, St Piran's Church was built. Canon Mason was the principal organiser of these churches and he preached in the open air when the foundations were laid. He took the opportunity to praise the district's lay readers.

St Piran's Church was opened in February 1884 and was immediately active as a mission church to Gwennap. Early in 1885 it was reported that an Improvement Class in connection with the Church Temperance Society had been formed, Thomas Tredre and Joseph Blamey were secretaries. Shortly after this a quarterly meeting of the church Sunday school was held, at which a training lesson was given by Mr C.C. James' class of boys.

The well-known architect Sylvanus Trevail who designed the church was also the architect of St Day School. The dual-purpose concept was introduced into both buildings. A folding screen in the church was used to separate part of the space for use as a schoolroom. The single bell which came from one of the closed-down mines nearby was cast by W. Taylor of Oxford in 1848.

A small second-hand pipe-organ was installed. It had first been in place at St Day as a barrel-organ. Such organs worked on the same principal as fairground organs and were provided with a set number of tunes. Later a pedal board was added to the one manual. An electric blower was installed much later.

The church contains a memorial to Mr J.C. Edwards who ran the Commercial School for many years. There are also memorials to Mr Charles James, lay reader for 40 years, and Mr Edwin J. Enstice, whose service exceeded Mr James' by two years.

The schoolroom has been used for many purposes over the years. During the period 1910–25 Miss Johns held her school there and in the 1950s Madame Norman had a dancing class there. In 1986 the schoolroom became the meeting venue for the first session of the Old Cornwall Society.

The church closed for some years during the 1930s and was reopened in the 1940s, still in association with Gwennap. The last two vicars of Gwennap lived in Carharrack in Wingfield House. Recent years have seen a reduction in the number of Anglican clergymen and as a result incumbents are responsible for more than one parish. Gwennap Parish became associated with Perran-ar-Worthal and Stithians (see *The Book of Stithians*). Carharrack, which was transferred to St Day, is now part of a United Benefice with St Day and Chacewater.

Above and right: *The hymn written by Charles Wesley after a visit to Carharrack.*

Above: *The old bell thought to have been used to call miners to shifts at a local mine. Photographed on display in October 1991.*

The Lord Jesus Christ

All thanks be to God,
Who scatters abroad,
Throughout every place,
By the least of His servants, His saviour of grace!
Who the victory gave,
The praise let Him have,
For the work He hath done
All honour and glory to Jesus alone!

Our conquering Lord
Hath prospered His word,
Hath made it prevail,
And mightily shaken the kingdom of hell.
His arm He hath bared,
And a people prepared
His glory to show,
And witness the power of His passion below.

He hath opened a door
To the penitent poor,
And rescued from sin,
And admitted the harlots and publicans in;
They have heard the glad sound,
They have liberty found
Through the blood of the Lamb,
And plentiful pardon in Jesus's name.

And shall we not sing
Our Saviour and King?
Thy witnesses, we
With rapture ascribe our salvation to Thee.
Thou, Jesus, hast blessed,
And believers increased,
Who thankfully own
We are freely forgiven through mercy alone.

His Spirit revives
His work in our lives,
His wonders of grace,
So mightily wrought in the primitive days
O that all men might know
His tokens below,
Our Saviour confess,
And embrace the glad tidings of pardon and peace!

Thou Saviour of all,
Effectually call
The sinners that stray;
And O let a nation be born in a day!
Then, then let it spread,
Thy knowledge and dread,
Till the earth is o'erflowed,
And the universe filled with the glory of God.

Left: *During May–June 1992 the wooden spire was overhauled ready for the rehanging of the bell which was being repaired. As far as is known this is the only wooden spire in the county.*

THE COMING OF METHODISM: THE WESLEYS

Although Methodism dates from as early as 1738 it was not until 1743 that it came to Cornwall. Charles Wesley arrived first and made St Ives his base. On Saturday 23 July he travelled to the Carharrack area and recorded in his journal:

I preached at Gwennap to near 2,000 hungry souls, who devoured the word of conciliation. Half of my audience were tinners from Redruth.

By Gwennap he meant the whole parish. A tradition which certainly dates back to the early-nineteenth century records that Charles Wesley preached somewhere in front of the present chapel. His brother John came to Cornwall shortly afterwards and on Saturday 3 September preached at Gwennap. He estimated his congregation as numbering 400–500. The place became for him a 'usual place' where he preached on 17 occasions. In 1762 he was supposed to preach there but a gale prevented him. He was taken to Gwennap Pit instead and on succeeding occasions, a total of 18, he preached there.

Charles Wesley came to the county again in 1744 and 1746. In July 1744 he wrote that 'a little one has become a thousand'. In total he visited Gwennap 15 times and on his last visit he estimated that 9,000 or 10,000 people heard him preach for nearly two hours. When he left he was so pleased with the success that he wrote the hymn 'The Lord Jesus Christ' which can be seen opposite.

John Wesley described the preaching place as 'the plain'. He often stood on a wall but once said he preached from a little hill. It was here that he said he saw a strange sight, 'a man who was old and rich but not covetous.'

When the Wesleys first arrived a Methodist Society was formed. In 1744 it had about 50 members, three of whom had begun to preach. They met in a room, the whereabouts of which is unknown although we have an idea of what it looked like. A letter to John Wesley tells how a mob broke in during a preaching service and beat out the candles and broke down the desk. The people most likely stood or sat on backless forms and the desk was probably a cupboard. Charles Wesley went to meet the society members after preaching but found almost the whole congregation following. He stood at the window so that those both inside and outside could hear.

By 1767 there were 63 members of the society. In the following year they built a preaching house to succeed the room – this was the Gwennap Octagon. The octagonal shape was a favourite of John Wesley and there were a number throughout the country. Charles Rule of Wheal Rose attended the opening. Thomas Rankin preached that on 'This day has Salvation come to this house.' The first trustees were

seven in number, described in the deed as tinners and yeomen. Such places of worship as the Octagon had to be licensed by the diocese of the Church of England, but rather strangely the licence for this preaching house was not granted until 1797.

The Methodist Society kept growing and in 1799 there were two significant developments. The society petitioned conference to hold its own Communion services and the chapel was enlarged. It requires little imagination to realise that the only way to enlarge an octagon is to demolish one wall and build a piece on. It is likely that the extension provided both additional accommodation and a Communion area.

THE WESLEYAN CHAPEL

In 1814 membership had grown to 833 and the Gwennap Octagon could no longer cope. The trustees made a bold decision and demolished the octagon in order to build the present chapel. It is dated 1815 but was opened on 1 June in the following year. The chapel was built by J. Williams & Sons after the style of Wesley's chapel in London. The gallery was a horseshoe shape instead of oval and the apse built into the chapel would have been used for Holy Communion. Little is known of the early days of the chapel because there are no records prior to the 1850s.

The mining boom saw an increase in the population of Carharrack. The village began to take on the shape which is familiar to us today and chapels were built in different parts of the parish. The membership of the society, which had reached its highest number of 1,118 in 1823, was then distributed between the newly-built chapels. In 1841 the number of members remaining at Carharrack was 500.

There was a religious census on 31 March 1851 and the minister returned congregation numbers of 240 in the morning and 900 in the evening. The sittings available totalled 871. He gave the average congregation as 1,000. He added this note 'Chapel in the evening generally very crowded, numbers being unable to sit down.'

In 1857 a new trust decided to spend £350 on the chapel. They wanted to lay a wooden floor, raise the seats three inches, wainscot the ground floor and gallery stairs and also build a vestry (this is the large vestry which now links the chapel and the schoolroom). Mrs Blamey was appointed chapel cleaner at 25s.0d. per quarter. The property was leasehold then and in 1861 application was made to the Lords for a new lease. It cost £200 and was settled in three lives:

Hugh, son of Hugh and Jane Phillips, Tresavern, Stithians, aged eleven.
Elizabeth, daughter of Richard and Elizabeth Goldsworthy, Carharrack, aged eight.
Joseph, son of James and Sarah Holman, Menerdue, Stithians, aged fourteen.

The Wesley Chapel schoolroom team in the charge of Mr Moyle, the contractor of Chacewater. Left to right, back row: ?, Mr Brown, ?, Charles Pelmear, John Charles Treweek. No one else has been named.

Left: *Interior of the chapel prior to the 1906 alterations, showing the leaders' seats at the front and only a curtain for the organ blower – to hide his exertions!*

Right: *A 1900 view of the first schoolroom with Victorian rounded windows. The building on the right housed four classrooms.*

Right: *A busy scene at the ceremony for the laying of the foundation stone.*

Below: *Dated 21 November 1905, work seems to be progressing well.*

Right: *An 1899 photo of the Manse and Chapel. This postcard view was sold in aid of the Organ Fund.*

The grand opening, 5 February 1906.

At one meeting it was agreed that members of miners' and philanthropic clubs be admitted to the vestry to hold meetings by contributing 3d. per member annually.

Other developments which took place included the small pulpit being replaced by the present rostrum. Following this a house was built containing four classrooms. Permission for Carharrack to have an organ had to be sought from the Circuit Quarterly Meeting, and it was agreed that they could have 'the best they can afford'. In 1890 a pipe-organ was installed. In the event they could afford £250.

In 1906 ambitious plans were put into effect with the classrooms being demolished and the present schoolroom built. In the chapel the ground-floor pews and leaders' seats were removed and replaced with the present pews. The ceiling was replaced with one made up of metal plates, the trade name for which was *Steelite*. A three-day bazaar was held in 1909 to pay off the debt incurred. It raised £428 which was a considerable sum in those days.

The chapel and Sunday schoolroom, 2002.

The centenary was celebrated in 1915 with a morning service followed by a luncheon. In the evening a meeting was presided over by Col George Smith, and Mr W.J. Trebilcock gave a talk on the history of the chapel. The chapel had been the head of the Gwennap Wesleyan Circuit from 1828. At Methodist Union (the joining of Wesleyans, Primitive Methodists and United Methodists to form the Methodist Church) in 1934 the circuit was split and Carharrack became part of the Redruth Circuit.

TREVARTH CHAPEL

In 1861 the Wesleyans at Trevarth asked for their own meeting-house. It was agreed that a building costing £50 be erected and settled on the present Carharrack Trust. The lease was granted on the lives of:

Harriet Mariah Williams, daughter of John and Caroline, aged eleven.
Elizabeth Odgers, daughter of William and Emily, aged six.
John Teague Letcher, son of James and Mary, St Day, aged eleven.

In 1865 it was agreed that the evening anniversary service of the Trevarth Sunday School would be allowed to be held in Carharrack Chapel in the event that the weather was inclement. In 1866 and 1867 special services were held to try to defray the cost of constructing the new meeting-house. It was later agreed that a porch could be added to the chapel.

In 1903 the building was renovated at a cost of £2.10s.0d. It was also lent to Lanner Primitive Society while their chapel was renovated. Later on in the century it was felt that the ground-rent paid for the building was exorbitant. Colonel Trefusis could not sell the freehold but agreed to a nominal rent of 1s.0d. By 1924 the chapel had ceased to function and the building was let to the Carharrack band at a rent of 10s.0d. per year.

BILLY BRAY & THE BIBLE CHRISTIANS

One of a number of different Methodist denominations appearing in the nineteenth century was a Bible Christian Church. It was strong in Cornwall and set up a Gwennap Circuit. It is not known where the Bible Christians first met locally but in 1840 Billy Bray built a chapel on the outskirts of Carharrack. He was a charismatic local preacher and evangelist who had previously built two other chapels. The Bible Christian Chapel was first known as The Fishing Net because Billy described it as 'a fishing net near Carharrack to catch the fine fish that might be found in such large shoals in the neighbourhood.' The thought possibly came from his receiving a donation of fish at St Ives when collecting money to build the chapel.

In *Bible Christian Magazine* in 1874 a note says that Great Deliverance Chapel (as it was by that time known) had been very little altered. The main change had been the substitution of a modern plat-form for the pulpit. The note goes on to say that a new chapel was to be built in the village of Carharrack. Billy Bray had died in 1868 but before then there had been talk of the possibility of moving into the village.

A footnote on Great Deliverance Chapel is that in 1884 the Salvation Army considered using it but instead decided to go to St Day. After standing in ruin for many years the remains of the chapel were built into a stable. This can still be seen at the junction of Consols and United Roads.

A lease was taken on a yard and store in the centre of Carharrack and the store was made into a chapel which was opened on 19 November 1874. There was an afternoon service followed by a tea and public meeting, the latter being held at the Wesleyan Chapel with addresses given by at least five minis-ters. This chapel was used until 1885 when a new chapel was completed and the old one then became the Sunday schoolroom. The rear section, which was separated by a screen, was once used by J.C. Edwards as part of his Commercial School.

Great Deliverance Chapel. This illustration comes from
The History of the Bible Christians *by F.W. Bourne.*

THE BILLY BRAY MEMORIAL CHAPEL

The new chapel had a plaster roundel in the frontage inscribed 'In Memory of Billy Bray 1883'. The chapel, which cost £758, was built by Messrs Gilbert and Moyle and was opened on 28 May 1885. The villagers made a full day of the celebrations with the morning service being followed by a luncheon. The press reported that there were no toasts made because an afternoon service quickly followed. There was a tea and an evening meeting later on.

In 1894 there was another full-day celebration for the centenary of Billy Bray's birth. Revd F.W. Bourne, author of *The King's Son: A Memoir of Billy Bray*, preached in the morning and public meetings were held in the afternoon and evening in the Wesleyan Chapel. Revd H. Stafford Smith who visited Carharrack in 1908 was obviously a devotee of Billy Bray and had his photograph taken at each local place connected with Billy.

The Jubilee celebrations were held on 8 June 1933. There were public meetings in the afternoon and evening accompanied by a tea. These meetings were addressed by former ministers. The chapel had been part of the Hicks Mill United Methodist Circuit which disappeared at Methodist Union. The Billy Bray Memorial Chapel, like the Wesleyan Chapel, became part of the Redruth Circuit.

For a time Carharrack band had used the schoolroom for practices. During the Second World War the ladies of the casualty centre met there. In the early days the yard at the back of the chapel was used for preachers to graze their ponies; there was also a shed provided for traps. This yard was later let.

There came a time when numbers attending Methodist services had decreased considerably and the first result of this was to abandon the evening service. It was then found that the premises needed considerable repair and redecoration and the estimated cost was far beyond anything the folk could afford. On 6 February 1975 it was decided at a meeting of the trust and society to close the chapel at the end of June.

SUNDAY SCHOOLS & OTHERS

During the nineteenth century and until comparatively recent times Sunday schools played a large part in church life. The one at Carharrack Wesley was established in 1808; it met in the afternoon and there was quite a large number of children who attended. The *Royal Cornwall Gazette* reported:

On Midsummer Day about 300 children belonging to the Methodist Sunday School assembled in the chapel, where an excellent and appropriate address was delivered by the Revd Mr Mowat, the superintendent. The children and their teachers afterwards paraded the neighbourhood, with a band of music, and in the evening were liberally regaled with tea and cake in a field adjoining the chapel, kindly lent for the occasion by Mr Powning. About 2000 were present and the teachers and singers, about 100 in number, took tea in the chapel. The business of the day concluded with singing and prayer; and the company separated highly gratified with the proceedings.

The tea treat was held on Midsummer Day until well into the 1900s. Looking at the numbers mentioned in the above report it is questionable whether the schoolroom built in 1857 was ever big enough.

There was variety in recorded tea treats. In 1864 there was a trip on the Redruth and Chasewater Railway to Devoran. Headed by the band of the 17th DCR Volunteers in 1872 they proceeded to Trevince, then they returned to the village and to 'the lawn in front of the noble house of Mrs T. Martyn.' There was the usual tea and it was noted that 80 elderly people were invited. There were 400 children in attendance and an estimated total of 2,000 people.

The Bible Christians had a Sunday school at Great Deliverance. At one of their tea treats there was a slight mishap when the day was spoiled because the band did not turn up! At the Billy Bray Memorial Chapel the Sunday school was quite strong.

In the twentieth century there were three main events during the year for both of the Sunday schools. First there was the distribution of prizes which involved awards for attendance being presented at a concert given by the children. There were songs, recitations and often a play and the schoolroom would be full of parents and friends enjoying the occasion. There was also the Sunday School Anniversary when special hymns were practised for some weeks for the three services. In the afternoon there was a flower and egg service, during which the children filed into the chapel and presented these items, which were later taken to sick and elderly people. The third event was the tea treat which has already been mentioned. The route of the processions at these events became standardised – leaving their respective premises the children would walk behind Foxes Row, down the lane to Trevarth Road

Above: *Postcard view from 1908 showing the Revd H. Stafford Smith standing in front of the main chapel with the then schoolroom on the right. The schoolroom was originally the first actual Bible Christian Chapel in the village.*

Above left: *A superb view of the Billy Bray Memorial Chapel showing the full beauty of the decorative brickwork and lettering.* (Photo by Ray Bishop, Mulberry Studios, Wadebridge)

Left: *Interior of Billy Bray's at the time when they still had a pipe-organ, c.1910.*

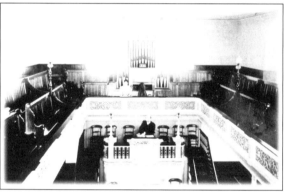

Right: *Poster advertising a visit from Revd Stafford Smith.*

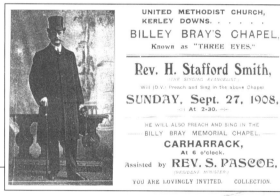

Wesleyan tea treat parade in 1952/53 venturing along Railway Terrace, photographed by Barrie May. Leading the procession from left to right are: T.J. Allen, Olga Richards, Matt Moyle, ?, Stevie Daniel (holding the flag) and Revd Alan Freeman.

Left: *A 'goodly' crowd for this Bible Christian tea treat, c.1900s.* (Postcard courtesy of the Paddy Bradley collection)

Right: *An attentive group of United Methodists at their 1919 tea treat eagerly awaiting sustenance. Several chapels had their own crested tea service for such occasions.* (Postcard view courtesy of the Paddy Bradley collection)

This Bible Christian tea treat is of interest, not because of the assembled gathering, but because of what is in the background. This view looking towards the end of Railway Terrace from the railway-track bed is now the site of Numbers 17 and 18 Polkerris Road. Behind the raised dais, on which are seated the band, can be seen a small cottage with an orchard adjacent on the right. This dwelling was the one prior to Rock House, which was constructed by Mr Joseph Odgers around 1907.

Wesleyan Choir in about 1915. Left to right, back row: ?, ?, ?, Rutter Stephens, LeRoy Gumma, ?, ?, ?, ?, Joe Allen. No ladies known; front: Harry Allen, second from the left.

Left: *United Methodist Choir, c.1920s. Left to right, back row: ?, W. Murton, Albert Wills, T.J. Sims, ?, Edward John Williams, Ernie Pascoe; middle: ?, ?, Miss Chinn, Mrs Mills, Albert Pengilly, Beattie Moore, Lilian Dyer, Katie Chinn; front: ?, Redvers Chinn, A. Furriner, Elsie Joules, Jack Mills, ?, ?, ?.*

Right: *The Billy Bray Memorial Choir at the time of the Jubilee Celebrations in 1933. Left to right, back row: Wilfred Kellow, John C. Murton, Richard Penberth, Harold Bosanko, Bill Bellow, George Evans, Ivor Collins, Percy Bawden (inset); middle: Edward J. Williams, Joyce Collins, Flo Smith, Elsie Pascoe, Gwen Mitchell, Elsie Mitchell, Winifred Bosanko, Josephine Thomas, Sylvia Thomas, Joe Ash; seated: Gwen Murton, Mrs L. Wills, Hilda Ash, Robert Stephens (conductor), A.M.*

Thomas (organist), A. Paull, Katie Chinn; front: Ivan Lawry, Artley Hitchens, Douglas Martin, Albert Wills.

and back to the Square where a serpentine walk took place. They would then go down the front of the village to Pound Crossroads before finally walking up North Hill to the Square and on to the playing-field. The children would be given saffron buns and mugs of tea while adults had a sit-down tea.

The band, which had led the procession, played at intervals and there were sports for the children. Young adults often indulged in 'pat on the back' and 'kiss in the rings' in the evenings. Often the day came to an end with another serpentine walk around the playing-field. Sometimes romances resulted from these events.

At the end of the nineteenth century both chapels had a Band of Hope, which continued into the 1920s. This was a temperance organisation whose meetings included a lot of entertainment as well as frequent visits to other groups to give concerts.

The class meetings, which had been a feature of early Methodism, ceased along with week-night services. The Wesleyan Chapel had a weekly Bible class which lasted into the 1960s with varying fortunes.

The Billy Bray Memorial Chapel began a guild in the 1940s which lasted for some 20 years. One was started at Wesley but only survived a few seasons. There was a Youth Club at the Wesley Chapel for some years in the late 1950s. A Good Templars Club functioned at the Billy Bray Memorial Chapel after the Second World War but this was short-lived. Members were given a blue sash and a medallion.

Two organisations, which had joint membership, were the Girls' League and the Sisterhood. The latter has only ceased recently having for some years also included ladies from the Church of England.

MUSIC & CHOIRS

During the period when the Octagon Chapel was in use and the Wesleyan Chapel was in its early years there were no musical instruments at either of the religious buildings. The singing would have been led by a precentor who would pitch the tunes; later there were instrumentalists. On Christmas Eve in 1868 the chapel choir, under Mr Martin Pope, gave a programme of anthems and carols. The *West Briton* gave special mention to the flute playing of Messrs Pope, the violin playing of Mr Dennis and that on the horn by Messrs Elijah Whitford and Trengove. By 1874 there was a harmonium and Miss Pope was paid £8 per annum for playing. Two years later the trustees were discussing a new organ which resulted in the pipe-organ being installed in 1890.

The choir had established a reputation and they sang anthems at evening services. It could be that it was as leading singers, or the only official ones, that William Perry and William Whitford were paid £1 each annually. Programmes of anthems and solos were given on the afternoons of special services and after the Second World War the choir gave a performance of 'Judas Maccabeus'.

More recently in 1993 a special service of Charles Wesley hymns was given to celebrate the 250th anniversary of Methodism coming to the area. A year later a service of singing and readings was held for the bicentenary of the birth of Billy Bray. Sadly numbers fell to such an extent that the choir had to be disbanded.

In its early days the Billy Bray Chapel had a harmonium which was later replaced by a pipe-organ. Unfortunately it appears that this organ had a persistent fault and so it was removed by the trustees. From then on there was a succession of harmoniums. The choir there was quite good and, like the Wesleyans, they rendered special services of anthems and other music. They also rendered services of song and cantatas. They were well known for their variety concerts. In times past the carol services at both chapels highlighted Thomas Merritt. At the time of writing there is no chapel choir. While the interest in Merritt's carols continues, the singing of them often takes place in combined choir concerts.

Left: *The Wesley Choir in 1988.* Left to right, back row: *Gerald Pellow;* middle: *Gary Pearce, Percy Odgers, Rut Stephens, Sylvia May (who began as a deputy organist back in the 1960s and is still playing regularly);* front: *Joan Pelow, Roma Pill, Thelma Odgers, Joyce Tucker, Olga Treloar, Jeanette Dunstan, Sharon Pascoe, Naomi Joslin, Helen Sedgwick.*

Above: *This superb postcard view of Crofthandy 'station' shows the main track bed in the left-hand bottom corner – Carharrack to the left, Devoran to the right. The gatekeeper's hut can easily be seen along with the loading bay siding (bottom right). Inside the walled yard were sidings raised on trestles for supplying the needs of the Crofthandy and surrounding areas. St Day school and church tower are silhouetted on the skyline.*

Right: *Ting Tang water stage in close-up, c.1899, looking towards Carnside. Note the see-sawing-type water filler being worked by the fireman standing on the tank to the left. The locomotive is actually resting on one of the little mainline spurs at the site. Tommy Lavin is the guard standing on the right with Mr Brewer, the driver, next to him. Prior to 1856 the section of line above here was horse-drawn.* (Photo courtesy of the Trounson/Bullen Collection)

Left: *Railway Terrace with one of the wide wooden gates in view. Just to the left of this scene is a property called Railway House which was occupied by the Williams sisters at the turn of the twentieth century. They were very punctual as gatekeepers and also ran a laundry service – 2d. a clothes basket. 'Bring 'em in one day, they mangled 'em ready for the next.'*

Four

The Redruth & Chasewater Railway

Mrs Tredre emerges unhurried from the doorway of her small wooden hut at the junction of Wheal Damsel Road and Alma Terrace, just as she has done repeatedly over several years as a railway gatekeeper. A small group of children aware of her moves call out, 'Please Miss can we help?' – knowing full well from experience that a polite request should result in their goal, lending a hand to haul the hefty wooden crossing gates into place temporarily blocking the carriageway to Pennance and beyond. A pony and trap manoeuvres itself slowly to a halt – inside, the Jory family: Henry at the helm, wife Annie with eldest children Mary and Edwin filling the sides, all bound for the weekly market trip to Redruth, it's Friday today. The animal, slightly restive as a result of the sudden gathering of people, fidgets on its hooves; the iron-rimmed wheels gently rocking in response.

The gatekeeper having been moved to action not by a pocket watch or the like, but by the up coal train's pre-arranged signal of five blasts on the whistle as it drags its burden along the inclined track from the Crofthandy gate crossing, a mile distant. Escaping steams, belching smoke and grinding metal become the prevalent features as the then modern beast of technology powers along, dissecting the village with its tail of laden trucks bound for the western coal yard just a few yards ahead.

Such an evocative scene can now only be a figment of

Left: *The gate crossing outside the upper coalyard which inspired the descriptive text in this chapter. Note the crossing gate itself, barring the entrance to the coalyard spur in the bottom left-hand corner. Beyond the pony and trap, the wooden gatekeeper's hut is plainly visible.*

the nostalgic imagination but, to a certain man and his fellow adventurers back in the early days of 1820, the need for a more efficient mode of transport to supersede the sight of laden packhorse trains carting orestuff and the like to and from mines and ports was paramount to the area's mining future.

Why this sudden urgency to discover another mode of conveyance? To smelt copper ore required a ratio of 16 to 1 of fuel coal to finished copper metal produced, unlike for tin whose coal to metal count was far lower. To maintain a suitable copper smelter in the county would have required so much coal being transported from the nearest producing coalfield, namely the South Wales area, that it was more financially viable to convey the ore directly to the smelters.

Four months after a proposal to build a mineral railway, which would serve the Gwennap mines along with Wheal Busy at Chacewater, appeared in the *West Briton*, a meeting of the adventurers was held at the Albion Tavern in London on 15 January 1824. Soon after this, in June, the Redruth and Chasewater Railway Act was passed by Parliament. Negotiations with landowners, dealt with by Richard Thomas, the line's surveyor, began right away and work commenced without delay on the line's construction. John Taylor was the main instigator of the project; he had recently acquired the Consolidated Mines complex. He was the man who required an alternative source of transport for the ores produced.

The total length of the mainline was to be nine

Left: Miner and Smelter were the first two locomotives used on the railway in December 1854. They were 0-4-0 saddle tanks built by Neilson and Co. of Glasgow. Due to the excessive track wear they were fitted with 2ft 6in trailing wheels in 1859. A decade later Miner was rebuilt and converted to a 0-6-0. Along with Spitfire she worked the upper section of track above Carharrack, nine wagons being the maximum load. Smelter, her sister engine, could only manage three to four wagons at her best. Miner had the privilege of hauling the last train down to Devoran on 25 September 1915.

and a half miles; the track gauge would be 4 feet. The opening ceremony took place on 30 January 1826 despite both ends of the line being incomplete. At the outset the proposal was to begin adjacent to the newly constructed Devoran wharves with the line then proceeding up the Carnon Valley to just below Nangiles Mine, Twelveheads, where a loop for passing and the transference of wagons could take place. From here the line would feed its way up the valley towards Hale Mills where it was envisaged there would be a branch line to connect with Wheal Busy. Due to difficulties with failing production figures of the mine in question, this section was never completed. In 2003 the embankment and tunnel which traverse the site at Hale Mills, plus a length of cutting heading for Poldice, can still be seen. Between the hillsides the line continued and later reached Crofthandy 'station', a small yard with a siding and loading facilities.

Half a mile further on, behind Primrose Cottage, lay the Great Yard built in 1850 which played an important role prior to the introduction of steam-powered locomotives in the mid-1850s. Here wagons were loaded, unloaded, stored, etc., with some being diverted along branches to the Consols and United Mine areas which were not adjacent to the main track. The former branch ran for a good mile 'backalong', parallel to the Twelveheads route, but at a greater height above the valley section. Granite sleeper blocks in the floor of the lane leading to Poldory mark the track bed of this United link.

The routeway through Carharrack has a few anomalies which cannot be fully answered. An existing plan of the route places the line to the south of the village, but for some reason this idea was dispensed with in favour of the present location. Another unanswered query is 'Which came first, Church Street dwellings or the railway track?' Evidence from comparing early village maps suggests that the houses were built after the laying of the track. Such issues are dealt with later in this book, so suffice to say that such a major engineering project undoubtedly had a great influence on the settlement's daily life. Apart from those directly involved as a member of the company's workforce, the movement of the villagers must have been restricted on many occasions during the day and the dangers resulting from

the passing trains would have caused concern to those whose families included young and elderly members. Surprisingly few serious accidents were recorded during the existence of the railway.

In 1852 the decision was made to purchase two locomotives from the Glasgow firm of E. Neilson and Co. and thus two years later 'Miner' and 'Smelter' appeared, proving very successful. The reasoning behind this move was that since the inception of the line, horses that were used on it belonged to subcontracted carriers who considered shorter journeys more feasible and lucrative. Indeed, the Redruth and Chasewater Railway company first acquired their own horses as late as 1852. With the new steam engines working the line from Devoran to Ting Tang, the upper section from here to Wheal Buller and Redruth would be horse hauled. New wagons holding four to six tons were bought to work with the locomotives and in all about 120 wagons were used.

At Ting Tang there was an interchange of materials between the horse-pulled and steam-hauled wagons, which proved inefficient and uneconomic, so by 1859 it was decided to upgrade the remainder of the track to Buller and Redruth and purchase a heavier and more modern locomotive with its added traction to work this steeper section. 'Spitfire', with a wheel arrangement of 0-6-0, was put into service.

Above: Spitfire, the last and most powerful of the locomotives, was purchased from Neilson and Co. of Glasgow in 1859. She took 14 weeks to build at a cost of £1,340, paid in two instalments. She was a 0-6-0 saddle tank with 3ft 6in diameter wheels and a boiler pressure of 100lbs per square inch. Because of the superior adhesion qualities she mainly worked the line above Nangiles.

Although the railway continued to be used until its closure in September 1915, the fortunes of the line were by no means consistent. Closure of the mainstay of the business – Consolidated, United and Clifford Mines – by the 1870s caused plummeting incomes. The line struggled on, finding increasing trade from the blossoming mines in the Buller Hill region and the Redruth trade. Other cargoes were sought during the following years and several local concerns emerged which benefited the line. China clay was carried from the Ting Tang and Carn Marth areas along with some granite, although the latter commodity proved inferior to other county sources. In 1874 a siding and loop was added to the line at the eastern end of the village along Consols Road to facilitate the St Day Brickworks merchandise.

Things looked bleak in 1877 when the company went into receivership, although this made little difference to the outward running of the line. Mineral trains continued to run on a daily basis until total closure on 25 September 1915, when 'Miner' took the last haul of wagons to Devoran.

FULL STEAM AHEAD

Speed regulations for descending trains were set out in the company rulebook:

Above Carharrack, not to exceed 8mph.
Carharrack to Nangiles, not to exceed 10 mph.
Through Carharrack, not to exceed 5mph.

Wilfred Bawden remembers the railway:

I'd come home from working in Basset Mine... I'd be walking that week and I'd try and catch it at Buller Yard. The train was in and the guard was Tommy Lavin, and 'ee wouldn't let 'ee ride if 'ee could help it! "You can't ride... no!"
When the train started it never went too fast, so we'd jump up on the back. Mind, we had some job to get off here in Carharrack. The train would be rolling through and the women would be cursing... they'd have blacks on the clothes hanging out on the lines.

William Barrett, who spent his early childhood from 1905 in the village, recalls being 'up Pennance' when the trucks were descending by gravity full of smelted 'white tin'. He could hear the movement of the fine-grained mineral inside the wagons. The brakesman was in control of the wagons and would let the boys have a free ride. Because there was no

A loaded coal train, nearing the Great Yard having just left the Crofthandy yard. Near this point any train wishing to use the Carharrack Yard would give fives hoots on the whistle to warn those ahead of its arrival. (Photo courtesy of Trounson/Bullen Collection)

engine, there were no warning whistles to alert the gatekeepers, so the boys would jump off and run ahead to warn the keepers. Mrs Herons looked after the Trevarth Shute gate crossing.

The above account and the *Cornish Post & Mining News* article about a fatal accident in January 1891 prove very interesting, as the later article contradicts the report of the same event in the *West Briton* dated 26 January 1891. It is generally thought that the Railway Company policy did not permit wagons to descend by gravity alone, but this seems not to be the case. In the *Cornish Post* the following statement was made at the inquest:

When the engine requires water feed at the Ting Tang reservoir, it is generally the custom of the engine driver to go down with the engine alone. The brakesman in charge of the wagons slowly allows the latter to go down by means of the brakes until it overtakes the engine, which by this time has been supplied with water.

There is little remaining of the railway that is of major significance. Most of the granite sleeper blocks have been removed and used to construct hedges around the village. The angular granite pieces with bolt holes and rusty residue from metal chairs are easily visible opposite the Mills' Hall, they can also be seen in walls along the Pennance Road near to the site of the water feeder, and are still in situ in the ground at the top of the track connecting the Pennance and Trevarth Roads.

Richard Kinsman, who farmed at Carndene, remembers his father removing the granite setts along Pennance and using them to construct a hedge. Whilst packing some of these hefty blocks onto a cart one slipped and crushed one of his father's fingers. The air was blue... it was the first time he had heard such expressions uttering forth from his Dad! Posts with the angle irons that supported the huge wooden gates still stand at the Railway Terrace and Mills' Hall crossing points, although the latter one is not at its original site. The iron bridge above the old coal yard at the start of Pennance Road is the most impressive structure remaining and includes some sections of rail from the time of horse-drawn hauling. Its condition is a credit to Carharrack's local Parish Council which, way back in 1986-7, made the bridge's renovation one of its first projects.

The Great Yard, which is sited on private land, can still be traced amid the decaying walls and foliage, despite no track bedstones or suchlike existing.

POINTS OF INTEREST RELATING TO THE RAILWAY
CLOSE TO THE VILLAGE

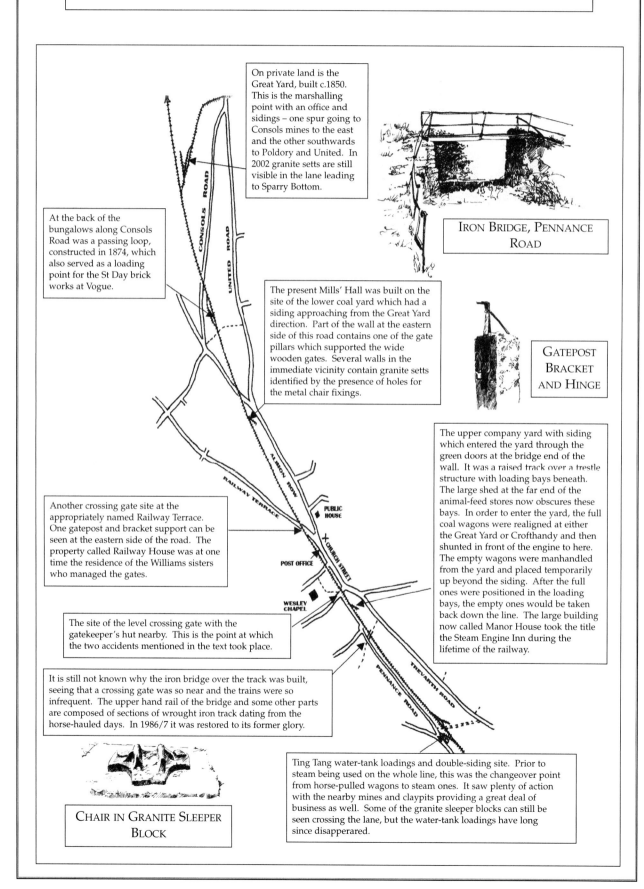

On private land is the Great Yard, built c.1850. This is the marshalling point with an office and sidings – one spur going to Consols mines to the east and the other southwards to Poldory and United. In 2002 granite setts are still visible in the lane leading to Sparry Bottom.

IRON BRIDGE, PENNANCE ROAD

At the back of the bungalows along Consols Road was a passing loop, constructed in 1874, which also served as a loading point for the St Day brick works at Vogue.

The present Mills' Hall was built on the site of the lower coal yard which had a siding approaching from the Great Yard direction. Part of the wall at the eastern side of this road contains one of the gate pillars which supported the wide wooden gates. Several walls in the immediate vicinity contain granite setts identified by the presence of holes for the metal chair fixings.

GATEPOST BRACKET AND HINGE

The upper company yard with siding which entered the yard through the green doors at the bridge end of the wall. It was a raised track over a trestle structure with loading bays beneath. The large shed at the far end of the animal-feed stores now obscures these bays. In order to enter the yard, the full coal wagons were realigned at either the Great Yard or Crofthandy and then shunted in front of the engine to here. The empty wagons were manhandled from the yard and placed temporarily up beyond the siding. After the full ones were positioned in the loading bays, the empty ones would be taken back down the line. The large building now called Manor House took the title the Steam Engine Inn during the lifetime of the railway.

Another crossing gate site at the appropriately named Railway Terrace. One gatepost and bracket support can be seen at the eastern side of the road. The property called Railway House was at one time the residence of the Williams sisters who managed the gates.

The site of the level crossing gate with the gatekeeper's hut nearby. This is the point at which the two accidents mentioned in the text took place.

It is still not known why the iron bridge over the track was built, seeing that a crossing gate was so near and the trains were so infrequent. The upper hand rail of the bridge and some other parts are composed of sections of wrought iron track dating from the horse-hauled days. In 1986/7 it was restored to its former glory.

CHAIR IN GRANITE SLEEPER BLOCK

Ting Tang water-tank loadings and double-siding site. Prior to steam being used on the whole line, this was the changeover point from horse-pulled wagons to steam ones. It saw plenty of action with the nearby mines and claypits providing a great deal of business as well. Some of the granite sleeper blocks can still be seen crossing the lane, but the water-tank loadings have long since disappeared.

Samples of the metal chairs which held the rails plus one of the holding nails. These items are resting on one of the angular granite sleeper blocks at Devoran.

CARHARRACK BOUND

A maximum of six loaded wagons with a gross weight of 38 tons, net 25 tons, could be hauled up from Devoran. The return journey time was 90 minutes. Although numbers varied with demand, during the busiest periods six trains a day were the norm. As the up-train, bound for Buller or Redruth, passed a manned crossing, the driver would shout to the gatekeeper informing them of the time of the return journey.

TYPES OF WAGONS

There were two types of wagon used on the lines. The first type were *flats* which had hinged sides allowing for unloading on level surfaces. The second type were *deeps* which had ends that sloped inwards to two bottom doors worked by a side lever which were designed for elevated sections of track.

IN THE FIRING LINE

At the peak of their tractive effort the locomotives powered their load up the steep gradient beyond Ting Tang belching out clouds of smoke and showering the immediate vicinity with red-hot cinders. Thus, it was not unusual for hedgerow fires to occur and as a result precautionary measures were taken in the early days of steam. West Trevarth House, a thatched dwelling close to the line, was in the 'firing line' and the railway company decided to rebuild the house away from the track with a slated roof. An interesting point of note was that the owner of the aforementioned property, W.H. Tregoning, just happened to be a shareholder in the company.

ACCIDENTS ON THE LINE

West Briton, Wednesday 22 August, 1827
Catherine Davis, returning from Devoran, where her husband worked, to Gwennap, was riding on a loaded

coal wagon. The driver advised her to change her seat from the back to the front of the wagon which she attempted to do but fell off and under the wheels before the horse had stopped. She suffered two crushed legs, one of which was later amputated.

West Briton, Wednesday 22 September, 1832
Mr Harvey of St Day, going to Devoran, got onto one of the wagons loaded with copper ore when he felt a giddy spell and fell onto the track. His head was crushed by the wheels of the second wagon and he died instantly. He left a wife and four children.

West Briton, 9 November, 1876
On Tuesday a fatal accident happened to Jane Coad, aged 76 years, while in the act of crossing the railway line near the Steam Engine Inn, Carharrack. The train was on the down journey and when within 20 yards of the place where she stood the brake whistle was blown, but before she got out of the way the train came upon her and so injured her that she died in about half an hour. An inquest was held before Mr Carlyon, county coroner, on Wednesday and the jury returned the following verdict:

That the death was purely accidental, but the jury are of the opinion that two gates should be immediately placed at the crossing where the accident occurred, and that in addition to the two gates the road be placed in a proper state of repair to ensure the protection of the public.

Mr Jolly of Falmouth was retained on behalf of the company. The jury spoke highly of the conduct of the officials of the company under the painful circumstances.

The following two articles covering the same fatality were published in the *West Briton* and *Cornish Post & Mining News* respectively:

West Briton, 26 January, 1891
On the Devoran railway at Pennance on Tuesday afternoon a little boy, son of Mr Thomas Faull, stonecutter of Carn Marth, had his leg severed below the knee by a railway goods truck. The little fellow was

This view of the Great Yard looking east shows the route of the mainline, passing from left to right, skirting the walls of the yard. In front of the large tree to the right is the route of the Poldory spur with the inclined track bed leading up to the entrance bay in the wall crossing the photo from the right to the middle.

taken to the Miner's Hospital at Redruth where he died on Wednesday morning. The accident was caused by a coupling of the truck breaking and as the little boy was attempting to cross the line he was knocked down and run over.

On Thursday afternoon Mr J. Carlyon, county coroner, held an inquiry into the death of the boy. Mr H. Grylls (of the firm Paige and Grylls) represented the father, and Mr J. Hollaway appeared on behalf of the railway company. Mr William Wales junr was the foreman of the jury. William Francis Faull, brother of the deceased, said he was with the deceased when he was hurt. 'The truck came down and cut off his leg.'

William Clear, guard of the train, said they were on their way down and stopped the train to allow some bullocks to pass. Then the engine driver eased the brake to start again and the coupling of one of the trucks broke. There were nine trucks – six empty and three laden. When the coupling broke the trucks separated from the rest of the train about the width of a truck and the three boys thinking the end carriages were the last part of the train, dashed past. Two got through and the other was run over. Replying to Mr Grylls, witness said the accident happened at a level crossing. There was no protection there, but there was a gate which was never closed. Replying to Mr Hollaway he said the train was perfectly coupled. Mr Grylls hoped the coupling would be preserved.

Mr Paull, the engine driver, said the train was going four or five miles an hour. When they eased the engine brake the coupling broke.
Mr Grylls: 'What moved the loaded trucks?'…
Witness: 'Well I suppose the engine and the weight of the other trucks.'
'Who coupled the trucks?'…
'A man named Jonathon Webber'…
'Did you see him?'…
'No, but he told me he did it.'
Mr Hollaway: 'The train must have been coupled, or the

trucks would not have started.'

Several jurymen were of the opinion that there should be protection at all crossings, and the coroner intimated that he should submit the facts to the Home Secretary. Mr Grylls: 'I submit that there is no distinction between that line and any other line of railway.' The jury returned a verdict of 'Accidental death'.

Cornish Post & Mining News, 24 January, 1891
On Tuesday 20 January 1891 at Carn Marth the six-year-old son of Thomas Faull, who lives near the coal yard level crossing, was playing when an engine stopped for water at Ting Tang reservoir. The engine had gone down alone followed by the coal wagons which were being controlled by the brakesman. The boy had gone onto the track after the engine and was struck by the following wagons, crushing his legs. One of the railway employees questioned stated:

'When the engine requires water feed at the Ting Tang reservoir, it is the generally the custom of the engine driver to go down with the engine alone. The brakesman in charge of the wagons slowly allows the latter to go down by means of the brakes until it overtakes the engine, which by this time has been supplied with water.'

The boy was taken to the Miner's Hospital at Redruth, where he died the following morning.

The company which formed the railway mistakenly spelt Chacewater with an 's'. This usage continued throughout the company's existence.

BIBLIOGRAPHY.
The Redruth and Chasewater Railway, D.B. Barton
Photographs of 'Ting Tang water stage' and 'Miner pulling away from Crofthandy' by kind permission of the Trounson/Bullen Collection

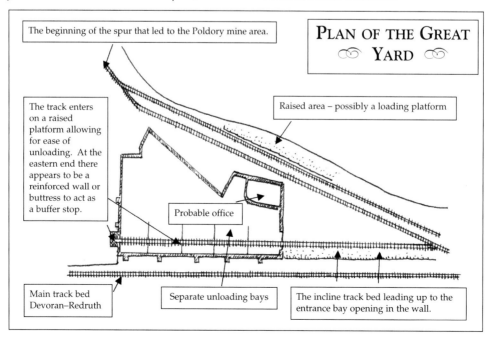

The beginning of the spur that led to the Poldory mine area.

PLAN OF THE GREAT YARD

Raised area – possibly a loading platform

The track enters on a raised platform allowing for ease of unloading. At the eastern end there appears to be a reinforced wall or buttress to act as a buffer stop.

Probable office

Main track bed Devoran–Redruth

Separate unloading bays

The incline track bed leading up to the entrance bay opening in the wall.

FIVE

❧❧❧

VILLAGE OCCUPATIONS & BUSINESSES

Church Street, No. 5, in 2002

In Carharrack, as with all settlements, occupations and businesses are closely linked with or emanate from the requirements and features of the community and its surrounding land usage. If one looks closely at the inaugural census of 1841 it presents a picture of a village totally engaged in supplying the surrounding mining industry with its labour force and skills. Over 75 per cent of the males worked as miners, principally involved with 'winning' copper, 30 per cent of the females as bal maidens, adorned with their 'gook' head coverings and tough cloth aprons, cobbing the ore with spalling hammers into smaller pieces to aid separation and improve the grade quality. Other ancillary trades linked to such an industrial base were prevalent in the figures with blacksmiths, cordwainers, carpenters, engineers, masons, carriers of materials, wheelwrights and mine agents accounting for 10 per cent of the workforce. One local family that became a feature of village life were the Wakems whose wheelwright business, begun prior to 1841, continued well into the 1900s. Initially it was run by John and subsequently by James his son.

It can be seen from the 1841 census that there was a lack of retail traders with Grace Barnett, Grace Annear and John Lean of Sparry Bottom Farm being listed as grocers, Tristram Powning as butcher and Richard Smith as fishmonger, whereas two public houses plied their wares, the Seven Stars and Steam Engine Inn. This era predated the storage of food in tin cans so therefore most foodstuffs were grown or reared by the people themselves (many a miner possessed a small garden area devoted to vegetable growth or animal rearing), or items were purchased at markets which were held regularly in local towns such as St Day. No doubt much trading of produce occurred between households.

The percentage of people, principally female, linked to the 'rag trade' either as seamstresses, dressmakers, tailors or milliners suggests that many households supplemented their meagre income by providing services which involved easily acquired skills and little outlay. It is unlikely that many of these individual ladies actually worked outside the village in larger manufacturing set-ups, although no doubt some did. Perhaps one or two provided their

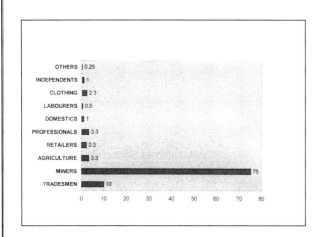

PERCENTAGE OF MALE
OCCUPATIONS, 1841

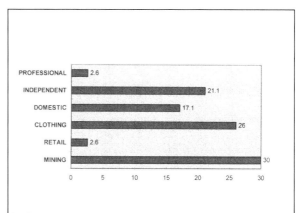

PERCENTAGE OF FEMALE
OCCUPATIONS, 1841

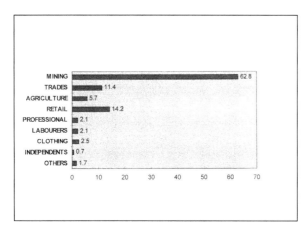

PERCENTAGE OF MALE
OCCUPATIONS, 1871

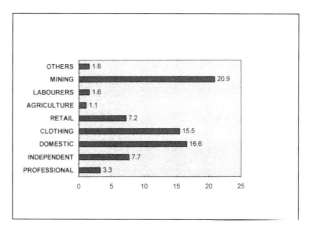

PERCENTAGE OF FEMALE
OCCUPATIONS, 1871

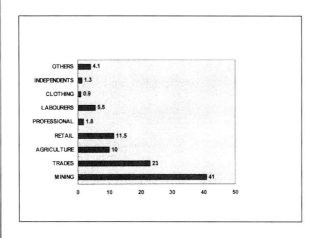

PERCENTAGE OF MALE
OCCUPATIONS, 1901

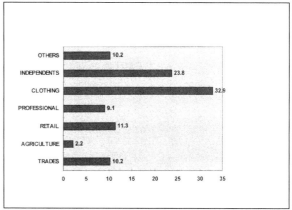

PERCENTAGE OF FEMALE
OCCUPATIONS, 1901

skills to Carharrack's drapery store, owned by the Rooke family, which was up and running by 1841 and continued in the family until the mid-1920s when the Poulters took over. Unfortunately a few years later this structure, which dominated the eastern end of the main street, was destroyed by fire.

Mining was sustained as a predominant source of employment throughout the 1870s but the majority of the workforce were now involved with the production and dressing of tin. United and Consolidated Mines – the copper boom giants – so dominant in shaping the fortunes of the village, now lay dormant and so it became necessary for the workers to take one of two options if they wanted to continue in mining. They could either emigrate to the recently-discovered rich mineral fields of South Africa, Australia or the Americas, or take advantage of the boom in tin production in several local districts such as Illogan, Camborne and Carnkie, where unexpected windfalls of tin were found beneath the copper lodes, something which did not occur in the Carharrack locale.

Indicative of the trend to emigrate was the rise in women classified in the census as being 'of independent means', which often refers to them receiving funds from husbands or relatives seeking their fortunes through mining ventures abroad. Census returns for 1841 indicate 21 per cent of women as being 'of independent means' as many miners had been lured by the newly-developing Australian mines. By 1871 this figure had fallen to 8 per cent, but with the great exodus of the 1880s and 1890s it rose again to 24 per cent. This time destinations covered the globe. Evidence of the involvement with mining areas a great distance from our shores can be noted in several house names within in the village: Guadaloupe at the beginning of Sparry Road, and Bendigo (later Pelmear Villa) at Brokenshire's Corner, taking its name from an Australian mining district.

By the turn of the twentieth century the retail trade was changing. The family business run from the front room was declining in favour of the purpose-built shop premises, although Gumma's Shop near Brokenshire's Corner and Minnie Darlington's along Albion Row continued to trade as such until the late 1920s and early 1930s.

During the twentieth century mining still provided a nucleus of jobs, albeit continually dwindling in numbers, because inherent skills and technical knowledge still prevailed. This soon ceased with the demise of South Crofty and Cornish mining in the mid-1990s. Likewise, although on a much smaller scale, the 'pop' industries kept several families and their helpers employed throughout the century and, despite Jolly's move in 1977, they still maintained a village workforce presence. Obviously other family trades, from haulage carriers and builders to grocers, have regularly provided vital part-time and full-time employment for villagers. Over the last 40

years the United Downs area has been an increasing source of jobs, initially with the influx of scrap-metal merchants such as the Drews, Wares and the Orchards in the early 1960s and, since the 1970s, with the blossoming industrial estate.

Village food stores maintained a strong presence right up until the late 1960s when about six establishments were still active. However, from this point on the demise of the local shop was gathering pace due to several factors including: the greater mobility of the public as private-car ownership increased; the widespread introduction of refrigeration units in homes thus negating the need to buy fresh food regularly at local sources; and multi-national stores beginning to move into local shopping centres, stocking a wider range of produce at reduced prices under one roof. Greater public mobility saw Carharrack begin to develop as a dormitory settlement. More people commuted from the village to work and purchased goods close to their workplaces where the larger, inviting sales outlets were sited.

Gradually the family grocery businesses declined in numbers until 2003 finds us with only one general store, the Convenience Store, stocked to the gunnels with commodities ranging from groceries to stationery and basic medicinal items, and a Post Office which supplements its sales with stationery, toys and literary material. Some assistance over the past 20 years has been offered to smaller village outlets with them being incorporated under the umbrella of a national purchasing supplier – such as Mace – but the struggle for survival seems ever present.

Farming in and around the village has taken the form of smallholdings covering a few dozen acres, combining a mixture of livestock, poultry, pigs and cattle, and arable crops. There does not appear to have been a large acreage supporting one crop or animal. Prior to the early 1900s most of the land to the west, south and east was rough common strewn with mine waste. It was the likes of families such as the Andrews at Ting Tang and the Kinsmans at Carndene, along Pennance, that first 'broke in' and fenced these areas. In the 1920s Little Carharrack Farm amounted to seven acres and was worked by the Combellacks. At the same time the Simmons family had a smallholding at Fir Tree Farm, Ting Tang. Other farms were worked at Elm Farm (behind the church), Tresithney, Rosewood, Sparry, Little Sparry, Chenhale, Primrose, Woodbine, Lower Trevethan, and the following in the Higher Trevethan area: Norway (also known as Bloomsbury), Carn Villa, Well Farm and Sunrise Hill. At the time of writing there is little chance of seeing cattle grazing or hearing piglets squabbling and squealing in the pastures. Much of the former pasture now provides forage for ponies and horses kept privately for riding. The farms run by Billy Penrose at Wheal Damsel, the Osbornes (with land along Pennance) and the owners of Lower Trevethan remain as smallholdings.

Left: *Church Street, No. 1. At the turn of the century the house was run by Ann Webster, widow of Joseph, as a tea dealers and grocery. The business had been in the village since the 1880s and by 1914 William Brown lived there followed by Ernie Teague's shop-cum-Post Office. Until the 1960s the interior still contained the original shelves and drawers, but then it was converted into 1 and 1A Church Street by Brian Scanlon.*

Above: *Church Street, No. 4. William Prater moved into the property from St Gluvius by 1860 and continued his cordwainer's (boot and shoe repair) business up until the First World War. Richard Chinn then had a wet-fish shop there until the mid- to late 1920s. It was then run by Alfred Teague, Ernie's brother, selling fish and chips. Bert and Elsie Woodley took over in the 1940s and continued the fish-and-chip trade until the mid-1950s. The counter was on the right as one entered the shop and there was a door into the seated area at the back. The store was in the small backyard.*

Top right: *Elsie Woodley outside the fish-and-chip shop in the 1940s.*

Left: *'Ted' Woodley lending a helping hand 'spud bashing' out the back of his parents' business.*

Left: *Church Street, No. 5. This is a little tarnished but is the only picture we have of the shop in 1909 with Bessie Jane Penrose and her children Tom, Hilda and Kathy. The postcard view appeared in the West Briton in 1977 when Tom Penrose, one of the children, was mentioned in one of their articles. From the 1870s to c.1905 Mrs Mary Brown ran it as a grocery and tea dealers. Her son George lived and worked there as a shoemaker. Bessie Penrose, and later her daughter Kathy, ran it up until the 1930s then Hilda Scholar (Kathy's sister) carried on into the 1940s. Later owners were the Newman and Shaw families. In 1971 it became the village Post Office after Thelma Odgers closed her shop. John and Joan Teather lived there until 1987, when Mike and Betty Nicholls, who came from Bath, took over until 1997. Richard and Hettie Tye, hailing from America, are the latest owners (2002).*

Church Street, No. 7. The shop was a grocer's from the 1890s through to the early 1930s and was in the hands of the Pelmear family. Richard and Louisa were followed by their daughter-in-law, Omira. It then became a private dwelling. Albert Pengilly used it as a rate office from the 1940s onwards, and this remained so until the 1970s. It has since had various uses, most of them of a professional nature, some of these being Paul Harris' accountant office, a factory outpost for South West Leisure Wear, an estate agent and builders (W.J. Ladds).

Left: *Church Street, No. 8. William Penrose had a butcher's here for almost 50 years from 1871 to the 1920s when his son Frederick was in charge. Prior to William it seems that John, his father, used the premises for a tailoring business. William Simmons took over and had a killing house along Chapel Terrace. From 1932 it was John Pascoe's grocery until the Thomases, Bill and Margaret (née Simmons), took over. He had a small butcher's shop in the back. Owners since have included the Hockings, Mrs Dalton, Dot and Dave Rice-Smith (1971), John and Barbara Parsley (late 1970s to the 1980s), Dan and Marie-Ann Gibbs (until 1987), Alan Blaby (for a short while), then Trisha Webb with Steve kept it as Today Stores until 1995 when it was redesigned by Dawn and Nigel Wearne and named the Carharrack Convenience Stores.*

Above: *Church Street, No. 9, in 2000. Elizabeth Ann Clymo and Katie her daughter had a general stores here from c.1910 for 20 years. It was then taken over by Mr Peters who lived at Chenhale Farm and dealt in furniture. He had it as a second-hand shop. In the mid- to late 1940s it took on the role of a fish-and-chip café and has remained so ever since. Various people have run the place. Jack Polkinghorne was first, followed by Mrs Richards, Amy and William Grant, John Gribble, Neil and Jacquemina Roberts (remember 'Aracini and Chips'), Harold Coates was next ('Yesteryears and Chips!') and Eileen and Sue took over until 1994. The Andrews sisters then arrived, Wendy, June and Marion, aided by Treve who painstakingly and lovingly restored the shop's frontage to resemble its past glory c.1900. In doing the work he uncovered the original coloured-glass panels above the doorway. In 2001 Ross and Dawn Morgan took over.*

Above: *Church Street, No. 10. John Mitchell and his wife ran this property for about 30 years from c.1910 until the late 1930s, selling fruit and vegetables. He had a mobile round using a cart which he housed in the old building which was in front of Alma Stores. He also looked after the orchard plot just along from the stores. Mrs Mitchell ran the shop with the help of Violet, her pet Pomeranian, who was at times rather 'snappy'.*

Above: *Glenwood, which was run as a general stores and Post Office by Charlotte Mildred 'Millie' Cock for ten or so years from the 1920s until the 1930s.*

Alma Stores (soon after closure as a shop).

ALMA STORES

This property was probably built around 1819 – a building definitely appears on this site on a map of that date. Beside the shop at the western end was a shed used at one time by Joe Allen of Trevarth Road for storing building materials. This shed has now been incorporated into the shop structure, which has been extensively redesigned and refurbished since its closure in 1990. From the late 1890s and for nearly 60 years this was run as a general store by the Kent family. Mrs Grace Kent, who is listed as a shopkeeper living at Trevethan in 1881, started and was followed by John and Annie Rowe (Annie being Grace's daughter). William Barrett recalls that Mrs Kent used to sell a lot of dried fish, stacks of it! His family would buy some on the Saturday and soak it overnight ready for cooking at Sunday lunchtime. She had a bell near the door which was rung to summon her from her garden patch. Since then there have been numerous incumbents: Henry Andrew, Mrs Banbury, Mrs Heal, Mrs Bellas, the Fletchers, Bill and Anne Neighbour ('Do you recall the recycled toilet rolls!'), Dennis and Margaret MacFarlane, and finally David Garston. In front of the shop there used to be a whitewashed building which was used as a meat store by Fred Penrose who had a place up at Trevethan. Mr Mitchell, the greengrocer from No. 10 Church Street, kept his delivery cart here. Until recent road improvements you could still see the metal base plates upon which the sliding doors ran.

Left: Recently remembered as the Mini-Market Cash and Carry, to older residents it remains Treweek's General Stores. John William and Phillipa Treweek ran it from c.1890, with their son, John Charles, taking over in the mid-1920s. Since the mid-1950s the proprietors have been Jane Andrew, Marion and Treve Combellack (her daughter and son-in-law), the Elliots and John and Adele Bentham in 1992. The shop closed in July 2000.

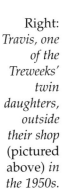

Right: *Travis, one of the Treweeks' twin daughters, outside their shop (pictured above) in the 1950s.*

Above: *Pictured in the late 1940s, Annie Rowe stands in her shop doorway. The window display looks very attractive and some of the produce for sale includes Colmans Extract and Tea, Hudson's Soap and Bluebell herbal products. 'Annie kept the place absolutely spotless,' says Christine Cann. 'She'd get up early and clean the floors before laying down sacking.' Note the changes in the shop frontage and window arrangement since then.*

Right: *Ashfield House Stores, viewed in the 1970s when the Dowsons had it. The front of the shop was cobbled and it is believed that the stones still exist beneath the present skin of tarmac. There is a possibility that it was a piano shop at the turn of the twentieth century, but this has not been proven. By the beginning of the First World War 'Long Joe' Odgers and family were in ownership and carried on a grocery*

business until the mid-1930s. It is believed the Mr Odgers owned the first motor car in the village. The shop sold cream, milk and during summers was noted by locals for its ice-cream, 'delicious' was the general opinion! It then passed into the hands of his niece and her husband, Clifton Teague. They kept a herd of cows at the back and had a local milk round. Next came the Dowsons who kept the shop until the late 1970s. In January 1980 a serious fire occurred, destroying the interior which consisted of small drawer containers along the sides. After renovation the Etherington's Freezer Centre emerged drawing many customers from the outlying districts. In 1996 the business moved premises and the property reverted back to a private dwelling.

Left: *This small shop was built by the Gummas. Originally the front room of the house served as the shop and then the extension was built. Pearl vividly recalls helping her father with the construction back in the 1930s. They kept the place until the 1960s. Then George Need ran it as the Magpies Nest. Stephanie Nankivell's antique shop and Mrs Orchard's wool shop followed, then Pots and Pans run by Jeremy Edwards. The late '80s saw Baby Bits courtesy of Judith Joslin.*

Right: *This United Methodist tea treat photograph, taken in 1911, shows John Mitchell with his handcart selling his wares, namely fruit and vegetables. The man standing beside him is John Hingston of Woodbine Farm. The lettering on the side of the two crates stacked in front of the cart reads 'John Jolly, Carharrack'. It is interesting to note that the bottles in the crates are upside down. Does this mean they are empties, or is that the way they carried Codd bottles in those days?* (Thanks to John Kellow for this postcard view.)

The cottage on the left was blacksmith Walter Lock's between the 1890s and 1920s. Local children on their way home from school would hang around waiting to be allowed to work the bellows. The blacksmith's shop stood in front and to the left of the cottage. The right-hand dwelling was a wheelwright's run by Frederick 'Fred' Williams, who moved into the village from Cusgarne c.1915. When the adjacent blacksmith's property became available he bought that as well. Besides basic carpentry items he also made complete farm carts. In his back garden there was a binding plate which was used for placing the metal binds or tyre rings onto the wooden-framed wheel. The binds were heated until 'white hot' in the blacksmith's forge then carried – using special grippers – to the garden, placed over the wheel on the binding plate, hammered onto the frame and doused with cold water to shrink them tight. After leaving this site he had his business in Ben Moyle's coal yard opposite Alma Terrace before moving to the Ting Tang count-house. Fred retired in the mid-1950s. It is possible that before Mr Williams, John Wakem used to have his wheelwright's premises here, because one villager mentions that Mr Wakem made the wheel and then the adjacent blacksmith heated up the metal-ringed rim ready to place on it. (Thanks to Mr Williams' daughter, Nancy, for the above information.)

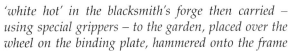

Above: One of two views the Society possesses of Walter Lock's blacksmith's shop. Walter is tending the horse with his two assistants, clad in protective leather aprons, on hand. The man holding the young child's hand is Ernest Andrew, the child is his son Ernest John Andrew.

Above: A close-up of the village's prestigious drapery store which dominated the scene at the eastern end of the Square. The premises may possibly have been a drapery shop since the 1840s when John Rooke was listed as a tailor in the village. His son, also called John, carried on the trade until retiring in the 1870s. Ten years later John Rooke and his wife, Caroline, began their involvement in the shop which lasted until 1925 when the Poulter family took over the business. The latter Mr Rooke came from St Day and may have been related to the previous Rookes, although probably not directly. The Poulters traded for two more years but this came to an abrupt end when a serious fire completely demolished the shop and house. Residents who frequented the store during its reign spoke of the quality garments available. One lady remembers them selling lovely 'smellies', a reference to 'Jockey Club' perfume which a female resident purchased from the store and wore with pride. In the early 1930s Henry Treloar bought the site and a large workshop-cum-store was erected. This was required for storage of machinery needed to run his motorcycle and bicycle maintenance business. Later on an extension was added which served as a Post Office and was run by his wife and daughter, Thelma, who later married Mr Percy Odgers. The Post Office closed in 1974.

The Post Office just prior to closure with Mr Treloar's motorcycle workshop behind.

HONEY'S GARAGE

Honey's Garage was situated at the site now occupied by the Pound residential area. Sydney and Emily Jane Honey, plus sons Bernard and Douglas, moved into the village from Plymouth in 1926 and Sydney built the garage set-up, which included a shallow-roofed main workshop with a pit inside, a small office and two petrol pumps. They also ran a taxi service using a Sunbeam, which had large headlamps that 'shone like new dollars'. Bernard helped out on the mechanical side and Douglas was by this stage pursuing a career in the Navy. Sydney died in 1934 and Bernard took up the reins but the business ceased trading soon after in 1935.

Above: *Edward Simmons' delivery van photographed in the 1940s, a common sight around the area.*

THE NORTH HILL GARAGE

The Simmons family have been involved in several business concerns over the years. Initially Edward Simmons, who lived with his family at Ting Tang, was in the grocery and vegetable trade, delivering to local areas, but a fire in 1929 completely destroyed the dwelling. Edward then moved to a newly-built bungalow at North Hill, or at the 'back of the village' as it was known in those days. In the early 1930s he built a wooden store for his merchandise alongside the property and he even had a 'Pool' petrol pump installed for personal use to supply his delivery vans.

Left: *A wonderful photograph, kindly supplied by John Simmons, of another of the lorries with his brother, Dennis, seated on the bumper. This vehicle was fitted out at Penroses of Truro. Inside was a central aisle with a flap counter and storage fitments along each side. The image dates from the war period – note the blinkered headlamps. During the war Dennis bought some ex-military DUKWS, four-wheeled amphibious craft, from Army surplus sales on Salisbury Plain. On their return, some of the vehicles were sold to the company which was involved in the dismantling of the battleship* Warspite *which lay stranded on the rocky ledges in Mount's Bay. The warship was taken apart for scrap. The other two vehicles were taken to Gyllingvase Beach, Falmouth to take tourists on trips around Falmouth Bay.*

Right: *Just returning from a trip around the bay, one of the Simmons' DUKWS. Dennis Simmons is the driver.*

Left: *At present this is our only photograph of the Simmons' garage at North Hill. In the late 1940s the large shed was built at the back of the bungalow, the steel frame and asbestos roof being purchased from Predannack Airfield on the Lizard. Dennis made the original roller doors for it. The filling station developed circa 1952–53, initially with two petrol pumps on the forecourt. By the early '60s the wooden store had been taken down. Peter Ella bought the garage in 1970 and soon afterwards a two-storey building was constructed, which included a domestic dwelling with an office-cum-store on part of the ground floor. By the early 1980s the garage had ceased trading, at which point the Richards family used the forecourt space to park the vehicles belonging to their tarmacadam business. The former office area was now incorporated into the ground floor of a second house. The large building behind the bungalow was then used by the Mrs Cooper who had a fruit and grocery round. At the time of writing it is a repair workshop for North Hill Motors, run by Terry Burrows since 1979.*

Mr and Mrs Speller resting outside their family-run business in Church Row.

THE SPELLER'S SHOE REPAIR BUSINESS

William Speller with his wife Graceta and children, Stephen, Frederick and Florence, moved from London to Cornwall, first living at St Austell then moving to No. 1 Chapel Terrace in the early 1920s. Their shop sold china on one side and they carried on boot and shoe sales and repairs on the other. Later on they transferred the business to Church Row where the family continued to do business right up until the early 1990s. When their parents died Fred and Stephen took over the workload.

BERT WOODLEY'S FISH-AND-CHIP BUSINESS

Mr Woodley had been running his mobile fish-and-chip shop since the mid-1920s. In those days he had a Model-T Ford to travel to tea treats, carnivals, shows and the seaside.

Above: *Herbert Woodley's fish-and-chip van in the 1920s. Betty Brooks is the young lady on the running-board. Before moving to Sparry Bottom, Herbert rented a shop in Ponsanooth. The next move was to Woodleigh in Fore Street where the high-roofed garage which housed his van still exists. No. 4 Church Street was their next home. To complement his fish trade he also acquired Nick Carbis' pop-making business in the late 1920s. This is dealt with in more detail in Chapter Six.*

TRELAWNEY, BROKENSHIRE'S CORNER WORKSHOP

At the time of writing the shed and buildings of Trelawney are a repair workshop run by Andy Richards which specialises in Land- and Range-Rover-type vehicles. Between 1986 and 1992 Peter Bullen's Impact Engineering Works was situated there. The previous owner, dating back to the mid-1940s, was Frank Penrose, a man of 'many hats': the village undertaker, a chauffeur of stylish limousines for that special occasion, local builder and decorator and respected bee-keeper. We can still remember visiting Frank and being shown around his 'wood store' – a long, low-roofed building attached to the house. Inside was a carpenter's utopia with many different types of well-seasoned wood, purchased over a long period from shipyard and farm sales, and lovingly kept, ready for the 'right project at the right time'. Joseph Charles Brokenshire, after whom the area is nicknamed, was the licensee of the Steam Engine Inn up until 1906 when he purchased Trelawney and started a coach-building and joinery business. This carried on until the Second World War.

Above: *Frank Penrose, on the right, in chauffeur mode with his cherished Rover limousine.*

THE SCRAPYARDS OVER UNITED

For many years following the war the area around United lay unused and barren. Then, in the late 1950s, Johnny Orchard bought some land and started up his scrap business site (in 1959). He lived in a caravan until a bungalow, built by Fred Nicholls and Sidney Albrook, was completed in 1967/68. The surrounding tree hedges were planted in the early 1960s with the concreted car base being completed in the mid-1990s. The Wares' business started in the mid-1960s with Malcolm Drew setting up a few years later. Malcolm's Pet Shop began in the late 1970s and continued for a few years, his coal retail outlet commencing around the same time.

Left: *This picture, courtesy of Mrs Kaskowski, shows the United area in the mid- to late 1950s, with what appears to be the beginnings of the Orchards' site. The Nissen hut seems likely to be the one still standing at the entrance to his yard in 2002.*

THE YARD AT FOXES ROW

This served as a coal yard for probably a century until the early 1990s when Jill and Ted Turner started an animal-feed store; this has now been taken over by Antony and Katie Ladd. Robert Stephens (local band and choir conductor), Ben Moyle, Percy Odgers, Cory and lastly the Williamses were the coal merchants using the place.

ALBION HOUSE & ADJOINING SHEDS

Mr Goldsworthy lived here during the 1920s. He possessed a Monarch bus which he used for postal deliveries and excursions and trips. The bus, either blue or green in colour, was quite small and only held about a dozen people. There were regular Friday trips to Redruth – ten o'clock from the village, returning at four from town. Summertime seaside rides to places such as Porthtowan were arranged. In the 1970s and '80s the business was extended and became the Albion Home and Ware Stores run by the Harrison family until the 1990s; it catered for everything from nails, paint, wines and spirits to clothes and food – an amazing range of produce for a village shop.

The two-storey structure on the right served two purposes back in the 1930s. The space below was a stable for Charlie Cann's horse, Violet. Above this was the space where Reggie Benbow, who was partially blind, made wicker baskets and chairs.

PROPRIETORS OF VILLAGE POST OFFICES

1862–73	Richard Champion	mid-1930s–'70s	Treloar/Odgers families, Old Post Office, Higher Albion Row.
1880s	Mrs Nannie Elizabeth Mitchell		
	James Wallace Towan	1970s–'87	Mr and Mrs Teather, No. 5 Church Street
1906–1920s	George Buzza, Elm Cottage		
1920s–'30s	Ernie Teague, No. 1 Church Street	1989–'97	Mike and Betty Nicholls from Bath, same site
1930s	Mrs Cock, Glenwood	1997–	Richard and Hettie Tye, same site

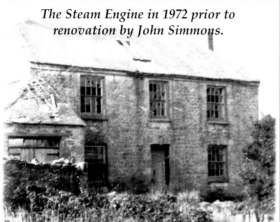

The Steam Engine in 1972 prior to renovation by John Simmons.

THE STEAM ENGINE INN

The Steam Engine Inn has been licensed since the 1840s when Thomas Tabb was in charge. It is very likely that it existed as an inn prior to this but as yet there is no proof. In 1925 the annual renewal of its licence was rejected. At that time it was run by William Couch on behalf of the Treluswell Brewery Company, the owners.

Right: *This postcard view, probably by Mr Govier of Chacewater, c.1907, shows the inn frontage with the steam locomotive 'Spitfire' and onlookers posing. The board over the doorway reads 'The Steam Engine, Joseph Brokenshire', the then licensee. He later moved to the Chenhale area and hence the area around was, and still is, referred to as Brokenshire's Corner. At one time the low building on the left of the inn housed a*

bowling alley. Following its closure the inn was the home of Charlotte Congdon until its renovation and conversion into separate dwellings by John Simmons in the late 1970s–'80s. Over the years Mrs Congdon saw fit to take many local residents to court concerning land possession and grazing rights.

Above: *This view by Govier, c.1907, shows the pub with its thatched roof. If the date is correct the family pictured could be the Thomases; if it was taken later in the 1910s they are possibly members of the Trestrail family.*

THE CARHARRACK STARS INN
(FORMERLY THE SEVEN STARS)

Thomas Reynolds is listed as the first licensee of the Seven Stars back in the 1850s and the business still survives. At the time of writing it is under the recent ownership of Steve Hooper who, in 2002, renamed it 'The Carharrack Stars'. For a period in the 1990s it was called 'Captain Blood's Tavern' by its then owners Terry and Linda Blood.

Below: *The Carharrack Stars Inn, 2002.*

Since the last war other licensees of the Seven Stars have been:

1940s	William 'Bill' Jory
1950s–'60s	Arthur Andrew
1960s–1985	Bernard and Anne Rogers
1985–89	Jim and Sandie Gulley

SIX

❧❧

CARHARRACK'S POP WORKS

THE DEVELOPMENT OF BOTTLES

Carharrack village is somewhat unique in that between the 1840s and 1970s it had six (possibly seven) ginger-beer or aerated-water 'pop' works. The probable reasons for this were initially the vast influx of people when the mines were at their busiest and secondly the availability of a local water supply,

A selection of village Codd bottles. Left to right: Nicholas Carbis, three Jory & Sons, two Goldsworthy's.

namely the shute. Before mentioning each family business, it is worth noting the development of ginger beer and pop bottles which, in some cases, provide the only proof that the manufacturers existed in the village.

Prior to the eighteenth century drinks were put into earthenware or stoneware containers but, after a short time, glass bottles were commonplace. In 1772 the art of manufacturing carbonised mineral water was discovered by Joseph Priestley. The main problem with storing the water was that the gas permeated the earthenware bottle's skin and thus made the contents flat. Mineral makers changed to using glass bottles with corks but these had to be stored on their side, so that the cork remained moist and swollen in the neck.

Between 1814 and 1870 the egg-shaped William Hamilton bottle (usually referred to as a Hamilton) was in general use. Surprisingly, a flat-bottomed version was not introduced until the 1870s. The year 1872 proved to be a watershed in bottle manufacturing because it was then that Hiram Codd of London devised his unusually topped versions – but at least they stood upright! The peculiar-shaped necks were a result of the type of stopper used. The neck was pinched inwards to hold a glass marble stopper

which was forced up against a rubber ring by the gas pressure created by the carbonised liquid inside. Many readers will remember smashing the bottles as kids in order to retrieve the 'marble' to play with. To force the marble stopper back down into its lug or holder a wooden cap with a plunger was supplied, either in the shop selling the product or to the customer.

Codd eventually took out 50 patents in order to improve his bottles, which included a 'spoilsport' child-reluctant oval marble. By the 1930s the Codds were superseded by crown-capped bottles. As a point of interest the term 'Codd's wallop', meaning an item of inferior quality or of little significance, originated from these mineral-water bottles, given that derogatory appelation by that intrepid band of connoisseurs, the beer drinkers.

Alongside aerated-water suppliers, the makers of ginger beer continued their trade and remained loyal to the clay stoneware bottles which were used well into the 1930s. The mouths of the bottles were later adapted to take screw stoppers.

The decorations on glass and stoneware bottles can also help to date them. Glass bottles tended to be adorned using embossing techniques whereas rival stoneware makers used incised marks. In the 1890s transfer labels became a feature and, despite sounding modern, they were merely found in a single colour – black.

Since 1986 the author has collected quite a few Carharrack bottles spanning 100 years and covering the many village works. Although not a common relic, they can usually be picked up at flea markets, second-hand shops and suchlike for a few pounds.

Henry Jory & Sons' delivery wagon at the beginning of United Road in the 1930s. Presumably the smartly dressed man is Mr Henry Jory. His father, usually referred to as 'Grandpa Jory', was renowned for the volume of his voice which could be heard as he was 'coming through Lanner'. He had an 18hh horse which was some size – a doorfull! There was once a ring at the Seven Stars where he would tie up the horse.

Left: *Nick Carbis' vehicle store in Railway Terrace, prior to becoming a dwelling in the late 1980s.*

Far left: *Three stoneware ginger-beer bottles. Left to right: Nicholas Carbis, Jory & Sons, T.M.P. Goldsworthy.*

The yard opposite Railway Terrace where Nick Carbis had his aerated-water works. Herbert Woodley took it over during the 1930s/'40s and, prior to development in 2001, it was last used by Frank Jory as a bottle store for his milk-round business.

THE CARHARRACK POP WORKS

The first mention of a possible works occurs in the census of 1841, when one Isaac Davey and his wife Mary Anne were brewers in the village. They were still resident here in 1851. At present there has been no firm information as to the whereabouts of their works, but there is a possibility, and only that, that it was sited at Little Carharrack and was later taken over by the Goldsworthy family. A relative may have taken over the business at some time because bottles exist which date from the 1880s to the 1890s bearing the name William Davey Carharrack, advertising his aerated water.

By the 1870s Thomas and Mary Anne Goldsworthy's herb and champagne ginger beer had appeared on the scene. Their works was in Farm's Lane, Little Carharrack and gave rise to the lane being called Pop Lane, a name remembered by some elderly residents. The following advertisement appeared in the *West Briton* on 20 August 1871:

Thomas and Mary Anne Goldsworthy have always on sale brewed ginger beer, three days in stock before tapped and as clear as gin. If anyone can prove that they do not use fruit, lemon and root ginger in the manufacture, T. and M. Goldsworthy are prepared to forfeit £100.

The Goldsworthys continued to be involved in ginger-beer making into the 1890s. Their daughter Harriet married Nicholas Carbis, a local farmer's son, and the name Carbis now decorated bottles. At the same time a Martin Goldsworthy of Ting Tang was engaged in ginger-beer making and may have worked with or for Nick Carbis. Number 16 Railway Terrace was the home of the Carbises and a vehicle store was adjacent to this. The actual works lay across the road in the old yard and continued there until the late 1920s. It was hoped that the business would be handed over to their son Tom but sadly he was killed during the First World War.

Ruby Wilton remembers Nick Carbis placing a bottle on a stand, pulling a handle and seeing the bottle fill with liquid, pushing the alley upwards. Mr Wilfred Bawden recalls:

Mrs Carbis would be making pop and a bottle would burst. The watching kids could go and drink from 'em – lovely lemon in small bottles – and then pick up the glass alley.

The 1890s must have seen cutthroat village competition. Besides the Carbis and Goldsworthy businesses the Jory name emerged as an aerated-water producer along with a William D. Jones and his wife, Louisa (although nothing else is known of the latter's business apart from it being noted in the 1891 census).

Rosewood Cottage appears to have been at the centre of the Jory pop and ginger-beer manufacturing. Two Jory families are mentioned during this period, Henry senr and Annie and Henry junr and Martha. The family name continued to exist in the brewing trade until the late 1930s.

At the time when the Jory business faded from the scene, the redundant Carbis works along Railway Terrace was taken over by Herbert 'Bert' Woodley, who carried on producing pop until after the war; the pop must have gone down well with the fish and chips sold from his mobile van business.

Synonymous with Carharrack pop is the name Jolly. In the 1891 census one John Jolly, aged 18, son of Harriet Jolly, a nurse, was listed as a ginger-beer assistant and several local residents who have been interviewed remember John working for Nick Carbis at the Railway Terrace depot. A serious disagreement between the two led to John moving out circa 1896 and setting up an aerated-water business of his own. In 1901 John and his wife, Mary Jane, and their son John were living in Foxes Row. By 1906 his business was well established and he had moved to an address in United Road where the business continued and prospered until the late 1970s.

When John Jolly died in 1938 the business carried on with first his wife then his daughter-in-law Teresa taking over the helm in 1947. Mr Dick Pelmear also helped out during this time. In the early 1950s Denzil, Teresa's son, took control of the firm at a financially difficult time but, principally through his effort and the support of his wife Patricia, trade picked up and they began to prosper.

By 1977 the firm's premises at 11 United Road were proving inadequate and it was time for expansion. This resulted in a move to Pool Industrial Estate. Denzil and Patricia's sons, Nigel, Ian, Robert and Roger, were now involved in the family concern.

Thus Carharrack's direct link with the soft drinks industry drew to a close. Over the years many local residents have found employment in the pop works. The Jolly name has now disappeared from the immediate locality as the company has merged with others over the years, but over the border in Devon a member of the family continues the tradition and so the name persists. Long may it prosper.

The making of aerated water and ginger beer requires several processes and pieces of technical equipment which were obviously more simple in the early days. Three basic ingredients are required to make pop: a good reliable water supply, carbonised gas in 'pop' making and flavoured essences.

As with many retail companies, promotional items were distributed by representatives to the customers. The address book shown overleaf dates from the 1960s.

Prior to the introduction of a piped supply, Carn Marth Shute was the main source of water. All the local manufacturers would have taken their horse-drawn wagons there loaded with tanks or barrels.

Above: *Just a few of the promotional items produced for the Jolly Company. A black jug, a pack of cards and an address book.*

Above: *A 'turnover filler' machine for Codd bottle filling as used by our local makers.* (Photographed courtesy of the Bath at Work Museum.)

Above: *An aerial view taken in the 1960s/'70s. Attached to the right of the house was the bottling plant, which had some storage area. Immediately behind this was more storage. The Bedford CA van in front was numbered MAR 254F.*
(Courtesy of Skyviews Aerial Archives, Leeds, www.skyviewsarchives.com. Ref. No. BA77306)

A selection of Jolly bottles. **Left to right:** *a Codd, a Corona-type one, a crown top of the 1950s.*

The carbonised water was created by the action of dilute sulphuric acid upon pieces of crushed marble but it now comes delivered in pressurised metal containers. It is difficult to know exactly what set-up the early village manufacturers had, but the Jolly's gas in the 1940s and early-'50s came supplied in miniaturised bell-jar systems. The mixture of flavoured essences were the individual trademarks of each maker and were much prized and jealously guarded by their owners. Since the 1940s Jolly's had purchased essences from three sources, Duckworths, Barnett and Foster and Nardens (a Dutch firm). Cyril Hitchens, who helped out in the evenings along with his brother Artley, recalls:

Granny would put syrup in a bottle, place it in a machine, turn a handle and the essence would mix with the pressurised carbonised water which entered via a pipe. This was a dangerous time because there was a possibility that the pressure inside the bottle would burst it. To protect yourself you wore a leather apron.

They only had Codd bottles in Cyril's days; in actual fact Jolly's were one of the last manufacturers to use this type of bottle. Another job Cyril performed was bottle cleaning. After washing, the bottles were placed inverted onto nails protruding from a wooden base, the nails pushed the marble stopper out of the way to aid drainage.

Ted Woodley, son of Bert, remembers the process:

The gas container was connected to the machine in which you placed a bottle, then you turned the handle [and] the bottle rotated. Syrup would be drawn up into it from a pan. You could regulate the mixture in the pump; it would push the liquid into the bottle and the rest was finished off with gas and water. You used loads and loads of sugar.

In the late 1940s and early 1950s George Pellowe, like Cyril, helped out at Jolly's. He said Denzil mixed the ingredients – essence plus tap water – in a large vat which was then stirred with a wooden spoon. George, who also sometimes accompanied Denzil and Dick Pelmear on their deliveries, was there when they purchased a labeller:

Mr Pelmear would mix up the glue and paste it onto a table. I would lay the labels in the glue and then pick them up by means of a tab and slap them onto the bottles.

BIBLIOGRAPHY
Bottle Collecting and *Antique Bottles*, Edward Fletcher
Bottles and Bottle Collecting, A.A.C. Hedges [Shire Albums]
Mainly Codd's Wallop, Ray Morgan
The Bowler Aerated Water and Ginger Beer Collection, at the Bath at Work Museum

Mr John 'Jack' Jolly, John's son, pictured alongside one of the delivery lorries, circa late 1930s.

Above: *Lansbury and Giew House which constituted Edwards' Commercial School. The library was housed in the right-hand dwelling. In the early 1990s the porch was rebuilt according to its original design with the stained glass also being retained.*

Left: *This is a photocopy of the certificate presented to John Veall for passing his autumn term exams at Edwards' Commerical School in 1879.*

Right: *This photograph was taken by Mr Govier, the Chacewater photographer, c.1903. Left to right, back row: Simon Mills, ?, ?, ?, ?, ?, ?; middle: Eddie Enstice, ?, Charlie Allen, ?, Sam Brown (Four Lanes), ?; front: ?, ?, ?, ?, ?, Charlie Penrose, ?, Tommy J. Allen, ?. Mr W.C. Edwards and wife Annie appear on the right of the picture.*

SEVEN

❧◈❧

EDUCATION IN THE VILLAGE

The year 1870 proved a watershed in the education of children throughout England, Carharrack being no exception. The Education Act of that time made it compulsory for every child within a certain age group to attend a school for formal education. In due course board schools were set up in Gwennap Parish at Lanner and St Day and were opened by 1878. The majority of Carharrack's children were catered for educationally at one of these establishments.

Prior to this the children of the poor and labouring classes had little or no opportunity to attend school, most positions were only available on a payment basis. The parish boasted several common day schools which provided a basic knowledge of the three Rs and no doubt some village children attended. Fees amounting to a few pence a week were required.

Since 1814 National Society schools had existed at St Day and Gwennap Churchtown and these catered for the whole parish, so some Carharrack offspring must have been educated at one or other of them. Some basic reading and writing skills were taught during Sunday school at the same time as instilling religious doctrine and knowledge. These schools had begun just prior to the turn of the nineteenth century and presumably those attending local churches and chapels would have received such teaching.

The following article appeared in the *West Briton* on 3 May 1850:

Gwennap Ragged Sunday School
The 19th anniversary of the school was conducted by Alexander Vivian in the whispering and reciting system held on Sunday last at Great Deliverance Chapel, Carharrack. Two sermons were preached on the occasion by Revd Hocking, Bible Christian, after which a number of children recited pieces in a very satisfactory manner.

The Revd Hocking preached an additional sermon on behalf of the school on Monday evening after which several pieces were again recited by the children.

At each the chapel was completely filled by an attentive congregation, who very liberally contributed to the funds of the institution. The collection exceeded those of last year. The school at present is attended by one hundred and fifty children and the most remarkable success has attended the labours of its benevolent conductor Mr Vivian and his assistants.

Thanks to Mr Vivian's great-granddaughter, Elizabeth 'Jill' Page, for providing this report.

For the more affluent professional families, the Trevarth House Grammar School for boys offered a good basic education with a technical slant in the syllabus linked to the requirements of an industrial mining county. There were three schools within Carharrack's boundaries, the Commercial School for boys run by Mr Edwards in the 1870s, Miss Johns' School from 1885 until the mid-1920s, and Miss Kathleen Gay's School which ran from the late 1920s until its closure in around 1945.

The village Men's Institute, which was built in 1841, supplemented the need for adult education. The Institute was a centre and source of learning for those beyond school age from Carharrack and other Cornish villages. Regular meetings and talks took place throughout the nineteenth century and during the 1900s the adult facilities at the Institute took on a more sporting bias with the provision of billiards and snooker.

EDWARDS' COMMERCIAL SCHOOL FOR BOYS

The Commercial School was run by Mr William Carah Edwards and his wife Annie and was active from the 1870s until about 1904. The school stood on the site now occupied by Lansbury and Giew House, Railway Terrace. Originally these two buildings were one dwelling; Lansbury contains the original staircase, while the school library was in Giew House. The rear section of Billy Bray's Chapel Sunday schoolroom, which is situated at the back of the schoolhouse, was used as a classroom. There was

Left: *Earliest known photograph of Miss Johns' School. This was taken in 1897 after the school had recently been established in the village. Left to right, back row: ?, ?, Reecie Nichols, Millie Dower, Miss Johns, Nellie Penrose, Lily Penrose;* middle: *Mildred Martin, ?, ?, Ida Penrose, ?, Minnie Martin, ?, ?, Isobel Dunkin;* on laps: *?, Charlie Penrose, ?, ?;* front: *Annie Penrose, ?, Maud Martin (Minnie's sister), ?, ?.*

Right: *Miss Johns' School, 1907/08. Left to right, back row: Laura Davey, Kathleen Rowett, Elsie Penrose, Ivy Tregonning, Dorothy Kellow; third row: Miss Johns, Geraldine Saundry, Dora Hooper, Adeline Annear, Maud Hingston, Hilda Sims, Thetis Morrish; second row: Ada Pelmear, Ann Cleave, Linda Vine, Ruby Dower, Maisie Kellow, Lily Cleave, Kathy Penrose, Gwendoline Tonkin, Olive Annear, Irene Pelmear; front: Hilda Penrose, Dorothy Brown, Esmi*

Brown, Dora Pelmear, Mildred Martin, Lucy Bray, Rosie Francis, Gwenny Brokenshire, Lilian Francis.

Left: *Miss Johns' School, pictured in the early 1920s. Left to right, back row: Miss Kitty Sedgeley, Doris Goldsworthy, Ester Watson, Daisy Ward, Averil Hitchens, Mary Richards, Miss Johns; third row: Cynthia Carlyon, ? Shemeld, Hazel Strutt, Beatrice Barrett, Hilary Saundry, Elsie Rowland, Barbara Enstice, Margaret Sedgeley, Phyllis Read; second row: Sylvia Shemeld, Emma Jenkin, Sylvia Carlyon, Hazel Barrett, Freda Jory, Maimie Manley, Doreen Odgers, Doris Manley, Irene Loam, Voilet Vinnicombe, Hazel Bear, Miriam Enstice, Sylvia Martin, Hilda Pelmear; front: Henry Vinnicombe, Joe Mills, Sydney Dunstan, Harvey Christopher, Douglas Carlyon, Arthur Marks, Audrey Trethewey, Sybil Roberts, Betty Babbage, Nora Richards.*

School group, early 1920s. Left to right, back row: *Isobell Southcott, ?, Barbara Enstice, Irene Carbis, Millicent Chinn, Margaret Sedgeley, Miss Johns;* middle: *Ester Watson, Phyllis Gould, Dorothy Mounce, Daisy Ward, Phyllis Carbis, Murial Pearce;* front: *Enid Cornish, Lucy Burrows, Mildred Chynoweth, Doris Manley, Maimie Manley.*

School group, early 1920s. Left to right, back row: *Miss Johns, Doris Goldsworthy, Ester Watson, Daisy Ward, Murial Hitchens, Mary Richards;* middle: *Doreen Odgers, Miriam Enstice, Beatrice Barrett, Hilary Saundry, Elsie Martin, Barbara Enstice, Margaret Sedgeley, Phyllis Read, ?;* front: *Freda Jory, Maimie Manley, Doris Manley, Irene Loam, Violet Vinnicombe, Hazel Bear.*

a seven-form teaching range and the syllabus covered a wide subject base. English included dictation, grammar, reading, essay writing and spelling skills, and arithmetic, history, geography, drawing, music and French were the other subjects mentioned in reports. Standards at the school seem to have been very high and on numerous occasions pupils' work was exhibited at local functions and society events, winning the entrants many prizes and much praise from the organisers.

Numbers attending the school seem to have been in the region of 20 to 30 at any one time, judging from the only surviving photograph of the school. As the picture shows, the pupils seem neatly turned out in their varying styles of single-breasted jackets and starched collars and caps. Mr Edwards hailed from Crowan and his wife from Gulval. Pupils also boarded at the school although only a couple could be accommodated along with the house servant.

MISS HELEN JOHNS' SCHOOL

Helen Curnow Johns was born in Carharrack in 1856, the daughter of George Johns, a mine agent hailing from the Roseland district, and his wife Eliza. In the 1881 census Miss Helen Johns was noted as being a schoolmistress, but she didn't open her school until four years later. She started with eight pupils and this number grew to 30 within the first month. The school occupied the meeting-room of St Piran's Church. The age of the pupils ranged from five to eleven for girls and five to eight for boys. Ruby Dower, a former pupil, thought the fees were in the region of five shillings per month in the early years of the twentieth century.

Infants would gather around a large wooden table, while the others worked at four desks-cum-tables. It was only in the late 1980s that the infants'

table was removed from the church room. The syllabus concentrated on the three Rs and spelling but other subjects were included during the school day. At the rear of the schoolroom was a small yard which served as a play area, in one corner of which was an earthen closet. Miss Johns' School continued to serve the village until 1925 when she retired; she moved to Lee-on-Solent seven years later. During the late-nineteenth century and early-twentieth she lived in Chapel Terrace with her widowed mother.

The following account reflects a typical day at Miss Johns' School. It is written by a former pupil, Elsie Hughes:

Off we go, me with my packed lunch in a little box. We have spelling lessons today, also arithmetic and multiplication tables. It is my turn to fetch a pitcher of water from the pump by the Wesley Chapel; it will be used for drinking, washing hands, etc. It is rather cold today and we are allowed to take our turns and warm our hands at the coal fire; Miss Johns' clock sits there warmly wrapped in flannel otherwise it refuses to work when it is cold.

Playtime! We go outside and play simple games such as Nuts in May, or tig. There is not much space. Then on to more lessons until lunch time, some go home, some stay at school for lunch. We sit around the fire, nice and cosy, and enjoy our lunch.

This afternoon we have lessons in sewing. I am making a bag for my father to carry his pasty in, when he goes to work at South Crofty Mine. I must do my best stitches or I shall have to pick them out and start again. The vicar of Gwennap, Mr Parker, is coming today to give us a talk about the scriptures.

When school finishes for the day, some of us go across the road to the shops to spend our halfpennies, some go to watch the smithy shoeing the horses. Then home for tea.

MISS KATHLEEN GOLDSWORTHY'S PRIVATE SCHOOL

Mrs Gay (née Goldsworthy) appears to have taken over from Miss Johns' School in the mid- to late 1920s. The schoolroom was within the Wesley Chapel and she used the room connecting the main chapel to the Sunday schoolroom. On occasions when there were small numbers or the weather was particularly cold she had lessons in her own home, Wingfield House (now called Alma House). The school was referred to as Wingfield House Private School.

As a pupil Roy Leah remembers starting lessons promptly at nine o'clock and continuing without a break until twelve, whereupon an hour and a half was taken for lunch. Afternoon sessions lasted until 4p.m., except on Fridays when 3.30p.m. was the closing time. It was soon after this time that Miss Goldsworthy caught Martin's bus for town with several of her class waving her off.

Miss Goldsworthy took in both male and female pupils ranging from 5 years to 15, teaching without the aid of assistants and the use of a blackboard. A few ex-pupils have expressed their surprise when attending state schools later on at the existence of this 'new-fangled teaching aid' which the teacher wrote on in chalk! Pupils were not placed into sets or groups for learning but instead progressed at their own pace, or not as the case may have been. Text books were purchased by the pupils – Roy remembers paying a shilling for his arithmetic book at WH Smith's when it was situated under the town clock in Redruth. Former pupils state that Miss Goldsworthy was fair but very strict. A favourite place for wrongdoers seemed to be under the organ in the chapel – a suitable spot to meditate upon your misdemeanours no doubt! The school closed in 1945 due to the impending marriage of Kathleen to a Mr Gay.

BIBLIOGRAPHY.
Lt Cdr Joe Mills' research when preparing the 'Education in Gwennap Parish' board in St Day churchyard

Seemingly the only photograph of pupils at Mrs Gay's 'Wingfield House School', taken just prior to the Second World War. Left to right, back row: *Esme Williams, Emmie Mills, Sylvia Hold, Margaret Simmons, Jean Stephens, Nancy Williams, Margaret Read, Eric James, Douglas Thorncroft, Cyril Jenkin;* middle: *Eugene Mably, Peter Collins, Sylvia Mitchell, Bryan Bickford, Kathleen Leah, Mrs Gay, Mary Beer, Dorita Thomas, Margery Mitchell, Alec Williams;* kneeling: *Reg Simmons, Roy Leah, Pat Longman, Kathleen Davies, Ann Young, June Lewis, Russell Mably;* front: *Margaret Downing, Betty Downing, Doreen Jay, Pamela Mably. Interestingly, Kathleen Davies, one of those kneeling, was an evacuee at this time.*

EIGHT

REMINISCENCES OF A CARHARRACK GIRL

Ruby's mother, Emily, aged 12 with her brother, 1869.

Ruby, daughter of William and Emily Dower, was born in 1899 and died in June 1993, aged 93. Her parents ran a grocer's shop from their cottage in Foxes Row from the early 1890s until the mid-1920s. Her father, who was born in Carharrack in 1854, worked as a miner in Pedn-an-drea, Poldory, Parc-an-chy and Tresavean mines. His father (Ruby's grandfather), John Dower, was also a miner and emigrated to the Australian goldfields in 1865 but sadly died two years later. Mary Ann, John's wife, ran a grocery business in Church Street up until the late 1880s. Ruby went to Miss Johns' School until she left in 1914, at which point she took a job in a Redruth shop. She lived in the village until her marriage in the early 1920s from whence she moved to Cardinham Farm in the Bodmin area, later moving to a property in the Mithian area. Carharrack always had a place in Ruby's heart and she still had contact with her childhood friends from the village. It was some time in the 1960s/'70s that she put pen to paper and gave us a priceless insight into her village life during the early years of the twentieth century.

My parents, William Dower a miner and Emily Brown, both of Carharrack, were the first couple to be married in St Day Wesleyan Chapel and were presented with a hymnbook and bible combined. I had three brothers and one sister. One brother died at six weeks old. I was born on 27 November 1899 and christened in the Wesley Chapel. When I was four years old I went to Miss Johns' School in St Piran's Church schoolroom. A boys school was at the back of the village called Edwards Hill (now called North Hill). In those days we had to make our own fun, the highlights being Anniversary on Whit Sunday and the Gwennap Pit service on Whit Monday. Then there was the tea treat on the nearest Thursday to 24 June when we would parade around the village headed by the band. One in particular I remember, the Illogan Brass Band conducted by the Revd Harry Oxland. After the village parade we would do the serpentine walk to the field where we all carried our mugs, had saffron buns and sugary tea out of pitchers. There were all sorts of games such as Three Old Bachelors, Nuts in May, Jolly Old Miller and numerous others, I could go on for ever.

There were many quaint personalities in the village. One in particular was called Lizzie Sherdy (Mrs Dunstan) who always carried a covered basket which no one was allowed to look in. On one occasion a girl was passing and Lizzie shouted, 'Come here chield, the bailies are after you.' This was a small bramble hanging from her dress and Lizzie stepped on it and pulled it off.

In the village there were ten grocers' shops, one drapery, three shoemakers, two wheelwrights, one blacksmith, two carpenters, a Post Office, a coal yard and two pubs, the Steam Engine and the Seven Stars.

When I was a girl a van brought bread from the workhouse. The relieving officer, the late Mr Johns, would distribute it to the poor. He also handed in slips of paper to my parents who kept a shop so that the poor of the village could collect 2 ozs of tea, 2 ozs of sugar, 2 ozs of lard etc.

We had to fetch our water from the Carn Marth Shute, beautiful clear water it was. We would fetch it in pitchers or anker and barrow. The anker was a barrel with a large hole into which they would put a funnel and fill it with a bucket. The barrow would have three narrow strips of iron so that the anker could rest on it to enable it to be wheeled.

We also had a Band of Hope and were always busy arranging concerts and a yearly trip when we would go to the seaside in Jersey cars and waggonettes which were horse-drawn. There was also a bus drawn by horses which went to Truro on Wednesdays and to Redruth on Fridays driven by Mr Kinsman of St Day;

it was sometimes necessary to walk up a steep hill but we thought it fun.

In the early 1890s many of our young men went to Africa and some years later returned to the village suffering from phthisis or silicosis from which some were dying rapidly. At these funerals and others I can remember the bodies being carried from Carharrack to Gwennap churchyard by relays of men who sang all the way. A man in front would have a time watch to tell them when to change over. They would go down Comfort Hill if there was a hearse drawn by horses.

People used to say there was a White Stile ghost (White Stile is at the entrance to the Trevince Estate at the top of a rise on the left, before the road descends to Comford). One moonlit night some of us girls dressed up some boys in white old-fashioned nightdresses and put bells on their arms and waists. We hid behind the hedge and waited for passers-by. We heard someone say, 'Did you hear that?'... 'What?'... 'Ringing'... 'Oh quick! Run! It's the White Stile ghost!' We were laughing up our sleeves; it was never found out who did it.

We had two chapels and one church in the village. A Wesleyan Chapel was built in 1815 and I can remember the Sunday School being built in 1906. My father and Mr Robert Stephens were secretaries. After it was opened there was a concert presided over by the Revd W. Hill and his daughter sang:

Pasties and cream, tin in the stream,
Herrings and pilchards all glisten and gleam.
Tho' we may roam, Cornwall's our home,
The dear old county of Cornwall.

I remember the chapel being lit by oil lamps and Mr Buzza would start at 5.30p.m. to get them all lit for the 6 o'clock service, upstairs as well as downstairs and in the pulpit. At anniversary times the chapel would be packed and seats had to be brought into the aisles. After Mr Arthur Moyle of Chacewater had painted and varnished the chapel it was reopened with a concert. There was a string quartet and Madame Jessie Strathern sang the 'Holy City' and our own choir finished with the 'Hallelujah Chorus'. We had a big

choir and a big Sunday School. A favourite hymn among the juniors was 'A little ship was on the sea'.

We also had our first band – a fife and drum one. When the band came out to play we teased the players and said they had driven all the rats away singing 'Driven from home'. Our real band was formed in 1913. Credit for this band goes to the Allen family who did so much for it. I remember one occasion, King George V's Coronation, we had a large decorated sign saying 'Long Live the King' with flags on top. Miss Sophia Hancock, a well-known character in the show world, was coming through the village on her way to St Day Feast and couldn't get through. She was going to cut it down, but a wisecrack came on stilts and showed her how he could walk over. The air was blue. Eventually she got through with her caravan and animals, all walking to St Day.

I was three years old when Queen Victoria died. I can remember King Edward VII reigning and when he died we all wore black armbands to go to the memorial service in 1910. At the Coronation of King George V our houses were decorated with flags and bunting, coloured fairy lights lit the front of our houses and the trees. I still have one of the fairy lights. Our closets (lavatories) were all whitewashed for the occasion and the houses painted over with lime, everybody being proud of their abode. I have lived in six reigns. We had a carnival and the children were given mugs and buns, then we went to Trevince House and had a torchlight procession through Squire Beauchamp's grounds. He was a wonderful gentleman and at Christmas time would give the poor joints of pork.

I remember once walking Ting Tang Road and saw what I thought were little chickens. I gently picked them up and took them home and said, 'I have got chickens'. My father said they were pheasants and we must take them back to the gamekeeper. I showed him where I had found them, so he put one back until the mother came. They had fallen out of the nest. When the next shoot took place the keeper brought me a pheasant.

I can remember all the names of the people who lived in Foxes Row, Shoot Row, Albion Terrace, Croft Row, Squire's Lane and Sparry Bottom. Nowadays these names are all altered and where there were United

This sampler was completed by Ruby's mother in the 1860s. It is typical of so many made by schoolchildren at that time.

Downs for quite a stretch, new bungalows have gone up. Many of the old names are still there such as Allen, Kellow, Pelmear, Kinsman, Evans, Teague, Brown, Williams, Jory, Penrose and Pascoe and their descendants.

We had a dear old soul who used to wash for my mother for a shilling a day and then take it home for mangling, to be done at a penny a flasket. Her hands were all soft and wrinkled with washing clothes all day. I used to stand at a box at the sink and wash my hands to see if I could make my hands as soft as hers. We always used wood trays with a place at the corner to put the soap. The clothes were boiled in a boiler on the Cornish stove and we used a dolly to push the washing up and down. Then the ironing was done – we heated the iron on the fire and taking it up with a poker, put it in the iron box. Another iron would be getting ready to change over. All the shirts were starched and my father used to wear a 'dickie'. It was something like a child's bib but very stiff with two buttons that could be buttoned to the shirt. We had old-fashioned clothes pegs made by the gypsies. There were always bussas (ceramic containers) in the house for salting tongues which were two shillings each; they were kept in brine for two weeks then boiled. Smashing with hot potatoes! A big shin would be about two and six. One part would be used for brawn, another part for soup and the middle to make a lovely pie. We used to go on Thursdays to Mr Penrose's killing house, the entrance was opposite the coal yard near to where Mrs Kent's shop used to be (Alma Stores), have 6d. worth of liver and bits to make pasties, this consisted of liver skirting. My, my, those were the days with real juicy pasties. When the pasties were baked ready I used to walk to Tresavean mine, where my father worked, with his pasty and my own and we would have them together sitting outside.

My father worked at Pedn-an-drea, Parc-an-Chy, Poldory and Wheal Damsel where there was a terrible accident years ago. There was another mine working I can remember, Wheal Bassett. There were stones being spalled (broken up) by the wayside. They used to do so many yards a day and put them in a lay-by in layers about 4 feet high and 9 to 10 feet long, all the same size. When they were wanted, a horse and cart would collect them. One dear old chap, Mr Henry Rawlings, was always there spalling stones and ready for a chat. These stones were used for the roads.

There was a train that went through Carharrack to Redruth where they took tin to be smelted and materials for the mines. There were gatekeepers all the way and as a child I loved to open the gate when the whistle called and close it again, they would whistle back 'Thank you'. Some distance up the line there was a

Ruby visiting Carharrack village exhibition in the summer of 1990.

feeder which filled the train with water. The railway ran at the back of my home, the ornaments on the mantelshelf would rattle as the train went by. The trains were called Smelter, Miner and Spitfire.

In my home we had an old-fashioned Cornish range. Every week my father would take out the oven and carry it into the garden and sweep it off. There was a granite surround around the fireplace and at night my mother would lay sea sand and in the morning she would sweep off the sand and then scrub it to make it sparkling. Our table was white wood and it had to be kept perfectly clean, scrubbed twice a week. Out of this humble cottage have come three BAs, three BScs, a doctor of medicine and a barrister; all grand-children of worthy grandparents. It makes me think of a poem 'Memories are golden but we can all share in them by doing one little task of love a day.'

The year war broke out, 1914, I can remember we were going to walk to Porthtowan, a party of us, and as we were passing the Steam Engine pub, there was a Naval reserve man saying goodbye to his golden retriever dog saying, 'I shall never see you again, Lassie.' Not knowing anything about the war this made a great impression on us. It was August Bank Holiday but we went not feeling like pleasure. Then the time came when the government wanted horses for the war effort and bringing them outside the coal yard to be picked out, oh how sad the owners were. In 1915 my brother enlisted in Canada and came across and was stationed in England for some time before he went to France. One morning I was walking down Alma Place, Redruth, going to work, when I saw a soldier talking to Mr Chapman and suddenly he rushed across. It was my brother. It was Thursday, we went to the shop. My employer said, 'It's only a half day, would you like to go home?'... 'Yes please.' So we walked the three miles back home, but what joy when we arrived there. He went back and was at Vimy Ridge and Passchendaele but came out without a scratch and was married in Truro in June 1919.

At Christmas time there was a lot of merriment. Men dressed up with masks would come from other districts and as a child I was very afraid of them. On Christmas Eve I was always ready to go to bed and wait for Father Christmas, and having older brothers and a sister I always had plenty. One night in particular I wrote a note, 'Hang up the baby's stocking, be sure you don't forget, but I've put a pillow case to hold the lot!'

On Christmas Day there was another note on the still empty pillow case, 'Selfish little girls don't get all they want, but please look down the stairs and see if Santa had another kind thought.' There was a hessian sack, but I never did that again! We had a very nice bazaar

Left: *A rural scene at Ruby's farm near Cardinham in the late 1920s where she moved after her marriage in 1925. Ruby is on the right.*

on Boxing Day (my mother called it 'Morrow 'pon Christmas Day'). All the children took part in the plays and concerts. We had hoop drill, fan drill and a children's stall which we all loved. My first recitation at the age of five was as follows:

Jappy was a happy land the maidens living
  there
Have dainty robes and tiny feet and flowers in
  their hair.
On cushions placed upon the floor they sit and
  take their tea
And all the time they use a fan and wave it
  merrily.
They love the little English girls who live across
  the sea
And should you visit Jappy land right welcome
  you will be.

At the bottom of Tresaddern Hill is a village pound. The man impounding stray cattle had to state the amount required for damage which the keeper would collect from the owner of the cattle before release.

No doubt it will be interesting to know that my mother used to buy 25 pilchards for 1s. and salt them in a bussa for winter use. The bussa would take 75, they were lovely boiled with hot potatoes. She used to marinade them and scrowl others with vinegar or butter. Also she would buy a bream and stuff it with parsley and breadcrumbs then bake it in a roasting dish with butter or dripping. Another nice dish was tatty cake. Boil the potatoes and when they are cold, mash them. Have a pan with 5 ozs of flour, 3 ozs of suet or margarine, a pinch of salt, tablespoon of sugar, handful of currants. Mix the flour, suet (or margarine), sugar and salt together and add the cold mashed potatoes. It should be moist enough to mix (add no milk or water), roll out 1 inch thick, put on a floured baking sheet, bake for 30 minutes. It can also be made a savoury dish using bacon cut up into small pieces.

I started work at Redruth for the Pope Brothers on 1 January 1914, a bound apprentice for five years for £20. My first pay day was 2s.6d. for a quarter. I left home at

7.30 in the morning to commence work at 8.30, walking the three miles in all winds and weathers. Our closing time was 7 o'clock Monday, Tuesday and Wednesday, 1 o'clock on Thursday, 9 o'clock on Friday and 10 o'clock Saturday. On Christmas Eve and Whit Saturday we worked until 11p.m. and then had to walk home. We did a lot of business after the pictures were closed. Prices in the shop were as follows:

cotton	1d. per reel
calico	2d.
materials	6d. and 11d. per yard
thick material	1s.11d. per yard
mending wool	1d. per card
knitting wool	2d. per oz.

Instead of giving a farthing change we used to hand out hair pins, a packet of pins or needles.

There was a dressmaking staff and millinery where everything was made if required. We had to dress in black with black sateen aprons, with a pocket to hold our scissors and pencil. In those days there were sovereigns and half sovereigns. When we made out our bills we had to stamp down the coin with our fist so that it could be duplicated (the reason was to make sure which coin it was). We were about 40 in staff and those that had left still kept in touch. We had an old-fashioned telephone, one that held the phone to the side on a crook. Also we had a tube that went from the ground floor to the milliners department. It had a stopper in it and there would be another at the other end. It would whistle. They would remove it. You would talk to them. Once finished you would replace your end and they would theirs, it was convenient. We had wonderful employers and had a very happy working time.

This was the year that the war began and I well remember a miners' strike taking place when they wouldn't allow the farmers to come in the town with their goods. They raided the traps and threw all the butter and eggs down the street and entered some of the shops and pulled bolts of material to wave as flags. The shop we worked in was the old manor house of Redruth, there is a painting on the cob wall and it is now in the occupation of Stead & Simpson. We were a wholesale firm. I remember when one of the staff of Messrs Anderton & Rowlands was killed on the way from Truro Fair to Redruth, I had the privilege to go and take an order for mourning. When we went to deliver it, we were shown the magnificient flowers and caravans; a thing I shall never forget.

The mourning orders consisted for a widow, a crape collar and cuffs, a hat with a veil made of tease with a white frill called 'widow's weeds'. One day during working hours I was sent by the assistants to go to Meadowside, West End for apples. I took a hat bag. All was well until I was coming up the street. I saw the boss coming, the bag broke. Smiling he said, 'Been robbing the orchard Miss!' I couldn't reply.

Each year we used to have a trip and go to St Ives in Jersey cars, [we] walked up little hills and always had a lovely tea of strawberries and cream. We also had other socials. I worked in the same business until I was married in 1925.

Market day was Friday at Redruth, sweet stalls and butchers in the street and a lot in the market-place. Then there was a butter market, the farmers' wives with their butter laid out on lovely white cloths with fancy decorations on them like the rose and thistle, also baskets of eggs and handmade bonnets 6d. each in one of the corners. On Saturday evenings the stalls in the street would be lit with gas lights and many times I have had a lift home to Carharrack with Mr Penrose, the butcher, and sometimes a lift in in the mornings with a donkey and shay. I had to ride with my back to the donkey and my feet dangling.

Another highlight was the Redruth two-day show when the Grenadier Guards Band would be playing, conducted by Lieutenant Col Miller and Miss Sylvia Spooner with her horse jumping and all the cattle. It was a wonderful show and a sad day for Redruth when it finished. There were lots of great names associated with it, especially Mr Lean who was the secretary. I think my husband was the last judge to judge the Ayrshires in the 1960s.

During the Great War lots of Australians were in Redruth, it was great fun when they used to come in to the shop and ask us to pick out presents for their wives and girlfriends at Christmas time. They always had plenty of money to spend so it was no trouble and some of the Aussies married Redruth girls, one I still keep in touch with. We were always helping out at concerts and getting things for the troops – socks, pullovers, mittens.

On Fridays all the farmers met at Tabbs Hotel and we loved to get a mirror and get the sun to shine on them from our shop window. They would be darting here and there. Luckily we never got found out.

I well remember seeing a Zeppelin. It looked like a pig and caused great excitement. It seemed as if it was passing over Falmouth. Then there were the troops marching through the town singing, 'It's a long way to Tipperary', then off to the station at Redruth not knowing where they would go. There were munitions factories at Redruth, Pool and Camborne where many of the older girls worked and of course there was the tram from Redruth to Camborne. It used to be grand to ride on the top. Those were the days, but we had to work and be happy. The enjoyment was helping one another.

What joy it was when Armistice was signed on 11 November 1918. We were outside the shop shouting and full of joy. The shop was closed and we went home thankful that all the fighting was over and our boys, we hoped, were coming back. At the time I wrote a little verse as follows:

God bless our soldier boys
Our navy and our airmen too.
Bring them safe home.
May they return again
Free from all wounds and pain
Forever to remain.
Bring back our boys.

Ruby was married to Mr Norman Wilton at Gwennap Parish Church on 27 December 1925 by the Revd A.H. Thorold, and following her honeymoon She moved away from Carharrack but always maintained a strong bond with the village. We would like to thank the Dower family who gave their kind permission to reproduce these reminiscences – a lasting memory of a grand old lady. Thanks Ruby.

Left: A postcard view commemorating the reopening of Carharrack Wesleyan Chapel after refurbishment in August 1907. Mrs Verran is seen standing at the door with Ruby, then aged seven, in the foreground. This postcard, dated 1907, was sent to Richard James Cock, East Rand RA Transvaal, South Africa and was just happened upon by our Old Cornwall Society recorder during a rummage through countless others at a Truro flea market. On the reverse it read: 'Ruby Dower is standing up and Mrs Verran in doorway. Ruby is a little better and they hope that she will recover from chicken pox.' Ruby Dower passed away in June 1993, aged 93… She must have recovered from the chicken pox!

Left: *Church Street. Note the shop fronts, they all resemble the style of the present fish shop. At the time of this photo, c.1907, the first one on the left was a grocery and tea dealer's store run by Joe Webster. On the wall above the window are two Venus Soap signs. Rooke's Drapery Store, right of centre, seems to be fully stocked.* (Courtesy of Paddy Bradley, Redruth) *Most of the postcard views of the village were from the Argall series of photographs, and they all seem to have been taken c.1910.*

Higher Albion Row, c.1910. Richmond, Newsham and Mulberry House are in shot. At the turn of the century the Stephens family lived in Richmond and the Pelmears next door; perhaps these people belong to those families. The blocks and holes for the railings are still visible in some of the walls at the time of writing, but the pillared porch is no more.
(Courtesy of Paddy Bradley, Redruth)

Right: *Albion Row, looking east. This is a rather relaxed occasion featuring a good few residents, presumably of the Row itself. The word must have travelled pretty fast on that afternoon. Whenever it was it must have been a day without schooling, or perhaps all the children are truants! Two people can be named: the tall*

man with the pony and cart is 'Long' Joe Odgers, who ran a shop close to the playing-field. He is also reported to have owned the first motor car in the village. The hatted gentleman is thought to be Charlie Treweek, a local builder and undertaker, who likewise had a shop, this time just down from the Seven Stars Inn. Just visible above the heads of the group of people on the right is Walter Locke's blacksmith's shop.

NINE

VILLAGE VIEWS

Left: *Church Row, c.1907. Little appears to have changed since this picture was taken apart from the mode of dress, the trees and the pace of life, although the little girl on the right seems to be on a mission. The two children, centre, are resting on some kind of four-wheeled dandy.*

Left: *Chapel Terrace, c.1910. An excellent view showing off the hexagonal structure of the Institute; such a shame it is no longer part of this scene.* (Courtesy of Paddy Bradley, Redruth)

Right: *Alma Terrace, c.1910. Once again apart from a covering of tarmac and the presence of two modern bungalows at the other side of Alma Cottage there has been little change to this view.* (Courtesy of Paddy Bradley, Redruth)

Left: *North Hill from Railway Terrace, c.1960. The main changes have occurred in the background. Bungalows have been built at the end of Railway Terrace on the left and the large barn, which served Laurel Cottage (the white-ended house, centre of picture), was demolished to make way for the entrance to Polkerris Road estate.*

Alma Terrace. This photograph was also taken c.1910. There is a predominance of youngsters in this picture, which could have been taken in early spring because the leaves appear to be opening. A council road-sweeper poses with his broom just in front of the building on the right. It still puzzles many people as to why the two houses on the right were constructed so close together, with side walls only inches apart. The farthest right was the home of Miss Kathleen Gay's school in the 1930s. Next door was the home of the Sedgeleys from the early 1920s until the new millennium and had not been modernised at all, without even electricity being installed.

Left: *Pop Lane at the end of Chapel Terrace. This 1960s view taken from Railway Terrace looking north-west has altered drastically. Parc Stenak housing development now covers the fields and the old buildings have been demolished. They have served several purposes – at one time they were the killing houses of Mr Simmons, the Chapmans kept poultry there and Bill Lewis, a keen local pugilist, used to run a boxing club from there. Why was it nicknamed 'pop shop'? We can only surmise that either the Davey Aerated Water Works or the Goldsworthy Pop Works were situated somewhere along this lane – it is possible to locate the other manufacturers' sites.*

Left: *Grove View, c.1910. If you have ever wondered why these properties along Grove View on the Trevarth Road resemble each other in construction and style, it is due to the fact that they were all designed and built by members of the Allen family. Joseph, a Truro-born mason by trade, and Matilda his wife, came to live in Carnmarth Cove in the 1870s. They had six children, including five boys, four of whom followed in their father's footsteps to become masons. The first house, No. 1 Grove View, was built in 1891 and, as the family grew and prospered, another dwelling was added to the row. Another collective feature of the Allen family is the number of them who have been band members: Thomas John, Joseph, Leonard, Willie, Clifton, Ronnie, Tommy, Harry and John Charles come to mind. Even in the late 1990s another family home was erected by Wesley Allen.* (All images this page courtesy of Paddy Bradley, Redruth)

Right: *Another postcard showing Grove View and the Allen-built houses on the left with the Carnside dwellings built by another village family, the Kinsmans. Above the castellated arch is a board which reads 'Allen Builders'.*

Left: *A view of the village from White Stile Hill along the Comford Road, c.1910. The conifer plantations were probably planted at the turn of the century by the Beauchamp Estate on the vast waste mine burrows of Ting Tang and Wheal Squire. Some of the former mine's dumps can still be seen centre left; they were not 'broken in' until the late 1930s when the Andrews family toiled hard to reclaim the waste grounds. The houses built by the Allens and Kinsmans are just visible above the spoil tips.* (Thanks to Richard Tye for his computer enhancement of this view and the one at the top of the page.)

Higher Albion Row, c.1910 (above) and 2002 (right). The only real differences in the buildings are that Rookes Drapery store on the left has been replaced by Henry Treloar's motorcycle building, the shop fronts are different and the railings have been removed.
(Above image courtesy of Paddy Bradley, Redruth)

Albion Row, c.1910 (above) and 2002 (right). Structurally little change has occured, most road-facing walls have been altered to accommodate vehicular access which is a trend that started in the '80s. In the older view the girl in the gateway is Miss Dora Pelmear.

Brokenshire's Corner, c.1910 (above) and 2002 (inset). The name for this corner dates back to the 1920s and 30s when Joseph Brokenshire had a coach-building and undertaker's business behind the dominant house in the picture. This large dwelling was at one time called Chenhale House and later Bendigo Villa, named after an Australian mine. It is interesting to note that the builder of the house, for the sake of artistic symmetry presumably, decided to include two false windows to the left of the front door.
(Both 1910 images on this page courtesy of Paddy Bradley, Redruth)

The photographer has managed to get most of the children to smile in the earlier view. The properties on the left housed the Edwards' Commercial School, which closed in 1905/6. In the centre of the picture, just before the street disappears around the corner, are the crossing gates for the railway. Most of Railway Terrace was erected between 1820 and 1840. To the older villagers this area is still referred to as the 'back of the village', dating from the 1800s when the main route, Fore Street and Albion Row, served the mines.

Railway Terrace, 2002.

Railway Terrace, c.1910.

Lower Albion Row, c.1910 (above) *and 2002* (right). *Albion Row looking towards Higher Albion Row showing Billy Bray's Chapel and the schoolroom annexe that used to jut out into the road until 1926 when it was cut back. The motorised tricycle AF 98 must have been one of the latest models at the time. Was he a travelling ice-cream salesman? We doubt it! To the left of the boy is one of the granite stones which designate the boundary between the manors of Carharrack and Cusgarne. A few still remain further up, near the public house.* (Top image courtesy of Paddy Bradley, Redruth)

Left: *Railway Terrace, 2002. There is an earlier photograph dating from 1910 on page 40. This shows the Terrace when the Williams sisters were the gatekeepers. They lived in Railway House, 11 Church Street, and were noted for their punctuality. Although the railway gatepost is no longer in position, one is still in situ across the road with its metal hanging bracket.*

Right: *Thorn Cottage, early 1900s, a superb view of the cottage along United Road with the then occupiers, the Pelmear family, posing for the camera. The gentleman is John Pelmear, born in 1854, who worked as a gardener. The ladies are likely to be his sisters Elizabeth and Susan. Although the house still exists, the gate and field have altered over the years due to road-widening schemes. A bungalow now stands in the field.*

Above: *Vine Cottage, Sparry Lane. This view was taken in the 1970s prior to the house being demolished and a new dwelling erected by Roy Leah, a local builder and decorator. Jessie Andrew lived there before the Leahs.*

Above: *Elm Cottage with The Elms adjacent and the farm buildings beyond. In the 1950s the then owners, the Leathams, enlarged and renovated the house. At one time it was a Post Office run by the Buzzas, a brother and sister.*

Left: *Alma Terrace. Another gem from the archives, this photo shows Miss Margaret Sedgeley and her sister outside their home in Alma Terrace during the 1920s. Margaret only moved out of the property in 1999, and had managed to cope without electricity throughout that time.*

Left: *Lyndhurst, North Hill. This bungalow was built by Joe Odgers for Edward Simmons and family in the early 1930s after their Ting Tang property had been severely damaged by fire. The photograph was taken soon after completion.*

Right: *Little Sparry Farm, the Francis family home captured in watercolour by a local artist, Stephen Speller. This vibrant painting was finished some time just after 1945. In the 1970s the property was badly damaged by fire when Jenny Penna resided there; today it has been replaced by a Woolaway-type bungalow.*

Left: *Well Farm, Trevethan, c.1960. Between the late 1940s and 1960s this was the home of the Homer family. One of the daughters, Jean, described the house when she lived there:*

There was a verandah on one side full of perfumed flowers. We had a walk-in larder – used for incubating the chicks. From there they were transferred to the loft, which was entered by outside steps. A well was the only source of water; it doubled up as our fridge – it kept the milk and ice-cream cool. There was a Cornish range in the living-room and in the ceiling was a coffin hole for access. Electricity arrived in the mid-1950s.

The pound, 1970s. Built c.1830s, it is situated at the junction of the manors of St Day and Carharrack in the former's parish, although it is now controlled by Carharrack Parish Council. Stray animals were locked up until claimed and payment of a small fee was made for release. During the late 1940s/early '50s Peano Knowles, a well-known local sportsman, taught Cornish wrestling in the adjacent field. If you lost, or were not paying attention, 'he'd throw 'ee in the stream'.

Left: *A busy scene outside the Miners Arms, c.1910. The sign reads 'The Miners Arms – William Osborne'. The two older men in the cart seem to be enjoying their drinks. Mr Hingston of Woodbine Farm is the man in the centre on the cart.*
(This view was supplied by John Kellow.)

Above: *Although not a village view this 'gem', courtesy of Clive Benny's collection, shows our own Bert Woodley serving a helping of fish and chips to a little girl at Porthtowan.*

The Miners Arms, now a private dwelling called Tregarlands Farm, United Downs, c.1910/'20s. The public house was serving its wares back in the 1820s under its then proprietor Thomas Tabb; he was also in charge of the Steam Engine Inn until the 1840s when he moved to Bodmin. (Courtesy of Paddy Bradley, Redruth)

The village casualty-centre nurses who were trained and ready to offer help and assistance during the Second World War. Left to right, back row: *Lilian Daniel, Lilian Moyle, Mary Jory, Elsie Woodley, Gwen Murton;* middle: *Mrs Jory, Alma Cocking, Nurse Pascoe, Minnie Pengelly, Bessie Hitchens;* front: *Josephine Peters, Katie Williams.*

Left: *The nurses parading along Alma Terrace during a Hospital Sunday in 1942. It is a possibility that this photo is of a Hospital Sunday mentioned in the* West Briton *on 5 October 1942. The paper states that this event was organised by Mr O. Richards and Mr A. Hocking under the auspices of the Carharrack and St Day Silver Band. The band led a procession through the village, which later assembled on the playing-field to listen to guest speakers. The gathering included: ARP Wardens, St Day Red Cross and Junior Link, WVS members and Sunday school members. These 'Sundays' were regular occasions before the war and were organised to raise funds for local hospitals and health-care projects. Left to right as they parade: Lilian Cock, Nurse Pascoe, Mrs Longman, Lilian Moyle, Elsie Woodley, Katie Chinn, Mary Bailey, Mrs Swithenbank, Minnie Pengelly, Mrs Hugh Jory (schoolmaster's wife) and Barrie May; he was dressed in Air Training Corps uniform and was attached to the ARP wardens group.* (Photograph courtesy of the West Briton *archives*)

TEN

✧✦✧

WARTIME CARHARRACK

THE FIRST WORLD WAR 1914–18

The speed at which this war began and escalated, thus involving Great Britain, surprised the whole nation, not just a hard-working community like Carharrack. Several people have mentioned that at the time everything seemed so distant: 'How could it affect us!' The expectation of the village people was that, 'We're Great Britain; we've got the Empire behind us, and the Territorials; we're the best.' 'It'll be over in a few weeks!' As we now know this was not the case and gradually Carharrack realised, along with everywhere else, the enormity of the situation and the effect that it would have on village life.

August 1914 witnessed Great Britain's official declaration of war on Germany. Because of the expected brevity of the conflict several local men enlisted, thinking that their involvement would not last long. Apart from families where loved ones rushed to Lord Kitchener's call for volunteers, the first major impact remembered by locals was the gathering of horses to be commandeered for action at the front. On a Tuesday afternoon in mid-August nearly 200 animals from Gwennap Parish were assembled outside the Steam Engine Inn near the top coal yard to be inspected by Captain Tremayne and Mr Forbes, a Truro vet, on behalf of the military authorities. A number of animals were purchased and Mr Jory from Sparry was seen crying when some of his horses were selected for shipment.

Wartime price guides were listed for food and each village was to have its own price values. Even Carharrack's close neighbours, Lanner, had differing charges. Some of the prices in Carharrack were:

Coal	1s.6d. per cwt	29s.6d. per ton
Flour	2s.6d. per 17½lb	39s. per 280lb
Sugar	2d. to 3d. per lb	
Butter	1s.1d. to 1s.2d. per lb	
Eggs	1s.2d. to 1s.3d. dozen	
Pork	9d. to 10d. per lb	
Beef	9d. to 10d. per lb	

Fowls	1s.1d. per lb
Ducks	1s.2d. per lb
Lamb	9d. to 10d. per lb
Lard	8d. to 9d. per lb

At this time troop ships from the Empire, such as the 50 or so transporting the members of the Canadian Expeditionary Forces, began to arrive at Plymouth and other ports in the South West en route to Europe. Recruitment to this regiment and others, such as those from New Zealand and South Africa, attracted more local men. A War Committee was formed for St Day and District with three main aims:

To provide relief for the families of servicemen.
To help those deprived of their work.
To provide materials for the Red Cross and men at the front.

Later on in August a meeting was held in the church schoolroom to form a working party. Both church and chapel were well represented and a ladies committee agreed to meet regularly to make under-clothing and bandages for the sick. Mrs Edwards, widow of the former school head, was appointed treasurer. The village and district were canvassed for subscriptions to help with the war effort. Within three months regular shipments of Red Cross parcels containing pyjamas, bed jackets, nightshirts, aprons and socks were being sent.

As the war effort increased General War Notices began to appear in the district emphasising concentration on certain aspects of need. Included were the following:

Increase home garden produce
Recruitment posters at fairs and shows
District war relief funds
Support the Belgium refugee and relief fund
Help Cornwall's patriotic fund

Early in 1915 there was a great national requirement

Charlie Penrose on horseback somewhere in France during the First World War. Prior to joining the Army as a 17-year-old he worked on his father's Trevarth Farm.

for more recruits and, in the words of one news item at the time, in some villages the male population seemed to 'vanish'. In Cornwall the St Michael Penkevil Parish's recruitment figures were impressive. Out of 165 inhabitants, 24 men had enlisted and two others were rejected on the grounds of being too young. The death toll at this time was sickening and recruitment drives became commonplace. William Barrett, Wilfred Bawden and Harry Tredre all have vivid recollections of the day the 'men in skirts' paraded through Carharrack's streets – they were the Scots Regiment.

On a Wednesday evening in August an open-air meeting of the National Patriotic Society took place in Carharrack Square. G.S. Bray presided over a large gathering, the aim being to conjure up government support. The brass band was present and played martial airs concluding with the National Anthem and three hearty cheers for the King. Throughout the hostilities the band had sufficient numbers to be present at many fund-raising events.

January 1916 brought tragedy to one family living down Sparry. Harry Tredre, aged 93 in 2002, lived two doors from the family and can still picture Mr James Gleed proudly sporting his uniform prior to his departure for the war which claimed his life. The Military Service Act came into force in June 1916 and men between the ages of 18 and 41 were enlisted.

One major problem in any war situation remains the difficulty of continuing businesses when a number of employees are commandeered for duty. During the First World War military tribunals were set up to deal with any applications for the exemption of personnel by businesses and suchlike. All local cases were dealt with at Redruth. Applicants had to provide sound reasons as to 'Why it is in the national interest that they themselves, or their employee, should remain in employment and not tender themselves for recruitment?'

The following extracts are taken from newspapers in 1916 and all deal with local inhabitants' cases:

A farmer and egg dealer applied for exemption for his horseman aged 25. The claimant stated: 'It was in the national interest that he should remain on the farm.'

Mr Shopland, the military representative: 'It is not in the lot of certified occupations however.'

Claimant: 'You would not find the Prime Minister's job there!'

Mr Shopland: 'He is over military age: he is an old man.'

Clerk of the court: 'Mr Chairman, I object to men of 60 being called old men.' (Laughter breaks out in court.)

The application was refused.

1 June

A miner, aged 37, working at Poldory for wolfram applied. He stated that he, along with his brother, started the mine four years ago and have struck a goodly lode that branches into three. One on tin, one on copper, one on wolfram. Forty pounds weight of wolfram per ton of ore being extracted. We are hoping to sell the concern to East Pool Mine. The application was refused on the grounds that the concern was considered to be too small to come into the category of 'national importance'.

July

A mineral water manufacturer and road contractor applied. The claimant stated that there were three generations: his father, himself and his son.

Chairman: 'The Father, son and holy ghost are applying.' (Laughter abounds.)

Claimant: 'I require time to complete the summer trade.'

Chairman: 'Has he had time before?'

Thurston Peter for the military: 'No, he's had two years opportunity.' (Laughter again.)

Application refused.

As the war progressed some food items became more difficult to obtain and in 1917 the government imposed regulation orders that were enforced on produce. Order No. 372 on cakes and pastries stated 'No ornamental ones'. This applied to such delicacies as jam tarts. Order No. 317 stated that traders were to keep a watch out for hoarding and order No. 439 that horse food be regulated.

In August a local man called W. Douglas Sadler, 2nd Lieutenant, died from wounds received. In 1917 very severe cold weather in early February through to March hampered soil preparations for future crops and ponds were frozen over for the first time that century. No doubt local children made the most of this situation. In the same month a Carharrack farmer and butcher received exemption for six months on the condition that one-fifth of his holding was planted with corn and potatoes.

In January 1918 *The Cornubian* reported that Private William James Rowe, aged 21 of Albion Row, was home on leave whilst sadly that same month saw the death of Tom Carbis, son of Nick and Harriet, whose family ran the aerated-water business in Railway Terrace. Wilfred Bawden said in an interview in 1990 that he and Tom were great friends and got up to many laddish pranks in their youth. Another casualty from Carharrack was Gilbert Pelmear, aged 30, whose family had a smallholding behind the Steam Engine Inn. He died in September.

At the conclusion of the First World War celebrations were widespread. Harry Tredre recalls the building of two decorated arches, one outside the Seven Stars Inn and the other at the Steam Engine end of the village. A carnival was organised with sporting events in a local field. During 1919 the possibility of erecting war memorials at Gwennap and St Day was discussed – the latter eventually being unveiled in late November. A Carharrack Peace Celebration Carnival visited St Day on a Saturday evening in July 1920 headed by the brass band with decorated jingles, traps, carts and bicycles following. The procession numbered hundreds and it is supposed that this entourage toured Carharrack as well.

THE SECOND WORLD WAR

Unlike the First World War, the Second was to involve the village people more directly. Since 1918 the governmental and military authorities had got their act together. Conscription for men of 20 or more began in April 1939 and with the advancements in aerial transport and weaponry the conflict was brought closer to home. The war zones were no longer distant fears and improvements in communication such as radio made the villagers much more aware of goings on. The BBC nine o'clock bulletin was a magnet for all and was an opportunity to discover the present state of affairs and 'gen up' on the latest government directives.

Government and civil defence information leaflets, plus blanket coverage in the press, led to the locals enjoying better knowledge and understanding of the situation. As early as August gas masks were issued in the Gwennap area. Margaret Sedgeley, the only female member of the ARP, was responsible for issuing the masks to children. She stated that during the war some children returned for several fittings as they outgrew their kits so quickly. As the war lengthened black-out precautions became necessary for each family, simply to ensure that they had some plans in the event of air raids. Only a few Anderson shelters appear to have been constructed in gardens and some are known of in Railway Terrace and Alma Terrace. Brian Saundry's neighbour in Railway Terrace had an indoor Morrison shelter. From talking to many of those who lived through these fretful times, it seems that most villagers stayed inside when the enemy planes passed overhead. Improvised black-out curtains were made, with some people preferring to erect shutters. One inhabitant along Albion Row recalls their black-out shutters being 'removed' by an assailant. Any chinks of

escaping light would summon up the call 'Put out they lights, pull down that blind' from the likes of Harry Jory, one of the wardens out on patrol.

Few local folk were affluent enough to run a vehicle and so there was little difference on the roads around the village. Yet there was a notable depletion in the quantity of 'passers through'. Such vehicle owners as there were – principally the tradespeople and carriers, like the Simmonses of North Hill, Ben Moyle with his coal wagons and Bert Woodley with his chip van down Sparry – were instructed to adapt their lights to conform with black-out regulations. In the case of masking cycle lights several residents said that it made life on two wheels at night perilous. Those moonless nights were not made for cycling!

In September the first evacuees arrived at St Day School which acted as a distribution centre. Homer Row RC School and Marylebone Grammar provided the 41 boys. Whether they were found placements in the village is not certain. Land Army girls were being organised and began to appear in the district. Kay Bush was attached to Lower Trevethan Farm, which the Pearces worked.

With the fall of France in 1940 Cornwall became more vulnerable on two fronts: as a route for German bombing missions on strategic areas further into Britain, notably the industrial prizes of South Wales; and, more locally, in the vicinity of attacks on the harbours of Falmouth and Plymouth. July saw raids on Falmouth for the first time. The noises and flashes of exploding bombs and lines of tracer bullet fire were witnessed easily from the village. Indeed many took to walking up Carn Marth in order to view the spectacular if frightening and distressing scenes. Enemy planes were now being heard and seen above the skies of Carharrack en route with their deadly cargoes intent on destroying industrial and military sites. In the early hours of 11 July, the locality echoed to the sound of machine-gun fire when the Crofthandy area was strafed. The same attackers also sought out the RAF's directional light site at Porthtowan.

Midsummer saw the arrival of another batch of 85 evacuees from the London areas of Limehouse, Hornsey, Leyton, Tottenham and North Islington. Mrs Minnie Pengelly was one of those who helped to organise their dispatch. Gerald Brown remembers well one evacuee, George Reed, because he attended Redruth Grammar with him. George was placed with Peano Knowles and family. Phyllis Nicholls had a young Russian Jewish girl who, with special permission from her parents, was allowed to attend Billy Bray's Sunday School. She was supposed to have no white meat to eat, but due to the rationing and shortages, Phyllis used to 'disguise' other meats to comply with the request. Mrs LeRoy Gumma took care of two girls, Gwen and Evelyn Sidell, for two years. Mrs Longman, who lived in Albion Row, took in three: John Plant and his brother, and a young girl, Kathleen Davies, who attended Miss Goldsworthy's School. Mrs Cock, who ran a village shop, had the daughter of Harry Leader, a well-known band leader of that time.

In the summer food and clothing rationing was introduced. Living in a rural close-knit community like Carharrack helped to alleviate many of the problems emanating from limited food supplies and shortages. The bartering of foodstuffs was widespread. Many a gallon of spuds was swapped for other desirables. The large number of people who kept fowls would trade their poultry ration for beef or other produce, maybe chicken feed. Mr Luty down at Sparry Farm sold produce such as potatoes. Waste not want not! Mrs Teague in her grocery used to cut up the butter ration into sections, weighing it precisely and using the scrapings from the knife to balance out the scales. Digging for victory was evident throughout the locality in garden plots and so-called rough patches. Milk could be obtained from the likes of Mr Blamey at Tresaddern, Mr Odgers from Goongumpus and Mr Prophet 'over' Lanner.

Three Second World War village evacuees. The Sidell sisters, Gwen and Evelyn, are on the left; they were living with Mrs Leroy Gumma. The other young girl was with Phyllis Nicholls.

Villages' fund-raising activities centred on supporting the Mills' Hall, the band and the war effort, with the latter taking precedence. Metal and salvage collections, clothing exchanges organised by the Women's Voluntary Service and numerous events to raise money for such worthwhile causes as the Spitfire, Warship and Aid to Russia Funds, Christmas gifts for the Forces, the Red Cross and the local Nursing Association, plus the Camborne and Redruth General Miners' Hospital and Royal Cornwall Infirmary were well patronised. Salvage dances on Thursday evenings, usually organised by Eddy Enstice, were regular features at the Mills' Hall. Apart from providing light relief amid the tension the dances must have resembled a scrapyard scene. Everyone was encouraged to bring something suitable for the right to purchase a reduced priced entry ticket, i.e. 3d. plus 5lb salvage. People in smart casual clothes carting old tyres, pieces of metal and bundles of paper conjure up an amusing sight.

At a meeting of the trustees of the Mills' Hall in the autumn of 1943 it was mentioned that:

... for nearly three years Saturday night dances at the Hall have provided entertainment for servicemen and women, and during the last year in particular, including US personnel, £1,000 had been raised. There is no charge for members of the forces – a voluntary gift being asked for.

There was no end to fund-raising ideas. Later on in the proceedings (March 1943) a lemon given by a gentleman who had recently returned from South Africa was auctioned at a Mills' Hall dance. It raised 28 shillings for the Merchant Navy Fund. Also active throughout the proceedings, raising funds and offering support, were the three places of worship: Wesley, Billy Bray's and St Piran's Church.

In 1941 military activity in Cornwall was reaching panic levels. St Eval was the only airfield offering air cover at the war's outset but within four months RAF Portreath and Trevellas aerodrome (RAF Perranporth) were operational, with St Mawgan soon to follow. Portreath had fighter squadrons of Spitfires and Hurricanes whose main role was to escort bombers on raids. It also served as an advanced base for French raids using Beaufighters and Blenheims. Trevellas housed day-fighter squadrons. It is hardly surprising that activity in the air over Carharrack increased. Enemy raiders crossed the skies with greater regularity during March when Germany made a determined effort to obliterate the threat of Plymouth's naval bases. The frightful sight of the north-eastern sky awash with flames and smoke still lingers in people's thoughts and memories. Over Falmouth barrage balloons broke up the horizon, being floated higher for greater disruption when raids were expected. Exploding shells and tracer fire littered the skies. Several incendiaries fell in the Hale Mills Valley early on 14 April; luckily no casualties and little major damage was reported. Redruth air-raid sirens could easily be heard from the village. 'Little real panic was caused, anxiety maybe,' recalls Margaret Sedgeley of the ARP:

Nine thirty was the usual call-out time for us. This was the time of the up trains from Penzance and it was thought that the German planes tracked these evening services in order to locate targets such as Holman's factory.

The Battle of Britain victory the previous year was beginning to have an effect; British air supremacy resulted in fewer enemy raids and routings about the county. By mid-1941 such sorties ceased to be a daily occurrence.

Unfortunately the slight let-up in the air conflict was not reflected at sea where, from 1941 onwards, the Atlantic conveys were suffering badly from U-boat attack which greatly disrupted the importation of much-needed foodstuffs and materials. The planting and growing of vegetables became of paramount importance. Margaret Sedgeley, who worked at Banfield's Nursery along Pennance, states that 'Banfield's did produce a few flowers during the war, but overwhelmingly concentrated on vegetables and the like.' With the American presence in the area, British methods of packaging were challenged. Workers were puzzled with the US orders for produce. Banfield's were required to package items by weight, for example 1 cwt of lettuce. 'Does the order really mean what it says?' was one question posed.

Everything was about to change drastically over the next few years. As the early days of 1942 approached, Japan's attack on Pearl Harbour the previous December and the subsequent entry of the United States into the conflict had far-reaching effects, in particular parts of Britain including the Carharrack area. US troops began to arrive on British shores and by the spring of 1943 were in several places in the county. Overnight, or so it seemed, tented villages sprouted up at Wheal Busy and on United Downs. For the next 12 months or so these once much-utilised areas would echo not to the sound of Cornish voices and the pounding and grinding of mining machinery – symbolic of the time in the mid-1800s when men, women and machines struggled to make a living from the mineral deposits below – but to the transatlantic drawl of black and white American troops and their accompanying motorised giants preparing themselves for the invasion of Europe and hoping for future victory. Cornish hymns and harmonies were replaced by the strains of men whistling the tunes of Artie Shaw and the Glen Miller Band, and gospel/spiritual music was performed by American servicemen at concerts in both the Wesley and Billy Bray Chapels. A musical service performed at Wesley by black American troops was entitled 'Kingdom Chorus'.

CARHARRACK'S US CONTINGENT

The US forces which were eventually stationed on United Downs formed part of the National Guard Units, the personnel hailing from Maryland, Virginia, Pennsylvannia and the District of Columbia. Two of Britain's most famous ships, the *Queen Mary* and her sister ship, *Queen Elizabeth*, ferried the 'blues and grays', as the members of the 29th Infantry Division were nicknamed, to British shores, arriving at Greenock on the River Clyde in Scotland on 3 and 11 October 1942 respectively. The title 'blues and grays' derives from the colours of the two combatants in the American Civil War.

The 'blues and grays' comprised: 115th, 116th and 175th Infantry Divisions, and the 110th, 111th and 224th Field Artillery Battalions, the divisional commander being Major General Charles Hunter Gerhardt. Initially they were all stationed at Tidworth Barracks, on Salisbury Plain, where routine training and manoeuvres were carried out. In

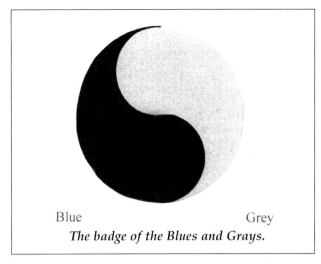

Blue   Grey

The badge of the Blues and Grays.

late May plans were made under the code-name 'Operation Bolero' to re-deploy the troops in various areas of the country, a proportion of the 29th moving into the Exeter and South Devon Districts. This move, code-named 'Exercise Hanover', involved the troops in four days of walking and riding until they reached their desired destinations, 160 miles away on the Cornish border. At the end of the summer of 1943 a further reallocation saw the 175th Combat Troop move from the Torquay area to the west of Cornwall – around Redruth, Camborne and St Ives – the 115th Infantry were stationed at Bodmin Barracks and the 116th stayed at Plymouth.

From the author's research, although without definite proof yet, it seems that the forces on United Downs who arrived in the late summer of 1943 were units of the 175th Infantry Division. From observations of local people at the time it would appear that the first foreign inhabitants arrived probably as an advance force whose tasks involved preparing the site and setting up for future units. Billy Penrose and Gerald Brown remember seeing heavy, multi-wheeled engineering vehicles in the area. These motorised monsters, the likes of which had never before been witnessed in Carharrack's lanes and on the streets, probably included four-ton, six-by-six wheeled Diamond-T dump trucks, caterpillar-tracked Allis Chalmers tractors and GMC Studebaker six-by-six wheeled water carriers plus trailers. Several of those mentioned would have incorporated winch equipment.

The actual camp sites were as follows: the present go-kart track was home to the white unit members, with the black members housed in fields just across the road. Parallel to the Pulla Cross Road, just skirting the village side of the shallow valley leading down to the sewage farm, was the possible site of more permanent structures such as stores and/or two canteens which they were known to have. Until recent landscaping and infill (circa 2000) two large rectangular concrete bases were visible. The front meadows of Trevince House had a tented complex and the road linking Gwennap Church and Comford was often the scene of traffic confusion caused by American water carriers charging their tanks with local stream water. Overhanging foliage acted as perfect camouflage.

As the summer of 1944 approached, the local US Forces were increasingly busy preparing for that final 'push' across the channel which was initially set for May but was put back a month. 'Operation Overlord', the code-name for the assault on the Normandy beaches, began on 4 June when a great convoy put to sea after dark from Falmouth and the surrounding waters. Unfavourable weather developed and a decision was made by General Eisenhower to delay proceedings for 20 hours. So on 5 June the separate conveys set sail from the havens along the South Coast – the 29th Forces leaving from the Fal and Helford Rivers – for an initial concentration off the Isle of Wight. The US Forces in the Carharrack area were apportioned part of the Omaha Beach to assail. The sands there sloped gradually for 300 yards out from dominating bluffs and cliffs which reached a height of 170 feet above the surf.

The 29th Forces were faced with heavy defences which included an elaborate system of underwater structures – a series of steel gate-like menaces 10 feet high known by the invasion planners as 'element C obstacles', with mines attached to these constructions as an added 'bonus'! In shallower waters beachside, sunken poles topped with the obligatory mine awaited the unobservant troop barges. The 'American tourists' of 1943/44 deserve the gratitude and thoughts of all residents of Carharrack. The total casualties incurred during the European campaign by the 29th Infantry Divisions numbered 19,184.

Everyone living in Carharrack at the time has their own reminiscences and comments about the American visitors, the vast majority of these being favourable ones. Village streets bustled with American accents, jeeps dashed to and fro and shopkeepers did well from the custom. Carharrack residents were brought face to face with a different lifestyle and culture that most of them had only read about in print, or seen on visits to the nearby cinemas. This was the first viewing of 'dark-skinned people' for most villagers and to small children their presence and that of the whole US contingent plus accessories must have evoked feelings of excitement and wonderment.

Dances for the troops were held regularly at the Mills' Hall on Saturdays with Mr Conquest usually the master of ceremonies. Win Jewel, along with her sister-in-law Betty, recalls them both walking over from Betty's home on United Downs and singing at such dances. Phyllis Nicholls and Mrs Enstice often served the refreshments. In 1943 several of the dances were run by Joe Martin, a London band leader. He introduced 'Do as you please contests!' – sounds fun! Although most of the occasions were incident free, Brian Saundry does remember one

event that frightened him at the time. Just prior to one of the evening dances Pearl Webster and himself (they were aged about eight or nine) were attending Mr Conquest's dancing club when an altercation broke out between the US troops. The children were ushered under a table by Mr Conquest and more tables were stacked above them for protection. Eventually the local bobby, PC Dale, dealt with the incident, much to the relief of the two youngsters.

Roy Leah, a mere youth then, has nothing but praise for the US brigade. He recalls:

At the bottom of the lane down to Sparry and Poldory there used to be a rifle range practice ground with a trooper on duty. Tommy Roberts and myself strolled down there and were greeted by the guard who said, 'Would ya care for some candy, boys? Go home and get a large box and I'll fill it up.' We rushed back and I got a small shoebox, returning as fast as I could.

'Ain't ya got anything bigger than that! Get a bigger something.' Back we went. Mum didn't have anything larger so I emptied a Shreaded Wheat packet of its contents and took it. Needless to say I returned home for a second time with the box filled to the brim.

At Christmas the Americans invited local children over for a party. Roy can still taste the delicious canned beans served up as if it were yesterday. Indeed the very young village children had never seen the likes of bananas prior to the arrival of the Americans and for the adults it was the likes of coffee, margarine, lard and certain meats such as hams and corned beef that endeared them to the visitors. Exchanges between the inhabitants and the troops were commonplace. Many a copper full of servicemen's washing was tackled in exchange for a quota of such 'luxuries'. One local delicacy that the Americans lacked was fresh eggs. Carharrack was a poultry cornucopia.

The tide was turning rapidly when 1943 arrived and Germany's army were defeated at Stalingrad in

These concrete foundations, believed to be the sites of stores or canteens, are all that remain of the US encampment at United Downs. This picture dates from the 1980s; the area has since been covered with waste material.

February. In May the Dam Busters Raid took place. Summer saw preparations for the invasion made nationwide, and as stated in the US section of this article, Carharrack saw a great increase in military activity in the vicinity. Roads were busier and troops were active. There must have been some weaponry in existence at the United Downs site because some long-remaining mine buildings were utilised for target practice. Loam's engine-house on the Poldory sett overlooking Trevince and Hocking's house at the entrance to the present waste disposal yard were demolished.

The American departure was sudden and total. One day they were everywhere and the next, history. Machinery, structures and all other items and materials were dismantled and removed overnight and the remaining items disposed of in the numerous shafts surrounding the downs. Reports of large quantities of cycles being dumped down them proved correct and when Mount Wellington mine workers were cleaning out an old shaft in readiness for reopening, many rusting two-wheeled discards were unearthed. However, not all was lost – Roy Leah's father used to make farm wheelbarrows during the war, but was restricted by the shortage of hooped iron. Scouting around the downs after the departure of the Americans, behind one of the derelict sheds, he discovered a pile of the desired stuff – a product of crate wrappings. Several troops visited local homes with 'windfalls' – foodstuff that was no longer required for consumption. One resident welcomed the jars of coffee, tins of fruit and hams. 'Take it or we dump it' was the maxim.

In October '42 metal railings were to be commandeered unless they were required for safety or security, used as an enclosure for animals or of special artistic or historic merit. Walls along Alma Terrace, Higher Fore Street and beside the chapels and church were stripped of their metalwork. These removals proved unpopular at first and became more so when most of the iron proved to be of the wrong type. The metal was stockpiled on the Hayle dockside and, to add insult to injury, after the war it was possible for a person to visit the site and reclaim their boundary fence albeit at their own expense.

Throughout these difficult times two wartime organisations were omnipresent in the village: the Air Raid Patrol and the Home Guard.

The ARP went on duty whenever an air raid was expected or had occurred. Tommy Allen was the senior warden and had a telephone installed in his Grove View home. The headquarters was in the schoolroom where they met once a month. Margaret

Miss Margaret Sedgeley at the village exhibition in 1990 alongside the ARP uniform she wore in the ARP photograph overleaf.

Sedgeley was the telephonist. Warning of an air raid came from Penventon HQ. She would receive a call and contact the members, usually on foot. Each person worked one day or night in three. Margaret recalls:

One night Penventon control rang up fretful about the presence of artillery fire over Carn Marth, thinking something was happening that needed backup. It turned out that the artillery units in the Higher Trevethan area were having a practice session. Suffice to say HQ were none too pleased.

The anti-aircraft unit along the Trevethan to Busveal Road was run by the Army and a large contingent of men in tents was stationed there. One of those present was Bombadier Daniel Saundry from Plymouth whose family lodged for a while at Carndene Farm.

The ARP's weaponry consisted of a whistle; three blasts for danger, one for all clear. When they were issued Charlie Treweek stated, 'Well the one with most breath will blow the loudest!'

That person turned out to be Margaret, who is not exactly of 'boxer-like' proportions.

On one occasion, late on in the conflict, the call to action caught a certain member off guard. There had not been a 'shout' for ages and everyone was a little rusty in procedure and preparation. The call came during the night and one male member, who had dutifully rushed in to attend, surfaced on parade minus his 'gnashers', much to the humour of the rest.

Carharrack never had its own Home Guard and the village members combined with St Day. The Commanding Officer was Mr O'Brian, an ex-Army man, the 2nd Lieutenant was a Mr Edwards who was from Carn Marth at Fairview. When the Home Guard began there were no uniforms available and the St Day base was not ready, so they met at the Drill Hall, Chapel Street, Redruth. They later moved to Mr O'Brian's courtyard in St Day and held indoor meetings in one of the side buildings, on average a couple of times a week. Ben Moyle, the local coal merchant, had a half-ton flat-bed truck for deliveries which was driven by his son, Leonard 'Champ' Moyle. He was in his early twenties (our very own Pike) and used to pick up his fellow members and ferry them to St Day.

Richard Kinsman, who farmed at Carndene along the Pennance Road, spent many a night session at the observation outpost at Carn Marth. It was kitted out with a field telephone and bunks. The ruinous bungalow-type building still survives at the junction of several paths just on the Carharrack side of the top quarry. Each night the area was covered by local

Carharrack ARP wardens. Left to right, back row: *Stevie Daniel, Owen Bray, Freddie Heblich, Dick Jacob, Willie Allen, Bill Lewis, Charlie Treweek;* middle: *Matt Moyle, Willie Gay, Tommy Allen, Bert Phillips (Divisional Warden of St Day and Lanner), Margaret Sedgeley, Mr Banfield, Henry Treloar;* front: *Roy Mitchell, Willie Penrose.*

Left: *The remains of the observation building on the track from Sunrise Hill to Carn Marth summit which was used by the Lanner and St Day Home Guard units.*

Right: *This Nissen hut, which stood along the Pennance Road opposite the Shute Hill junction, was used as an ammunition and materials store from 1939 to 1945 by the Home Guard. It was demolished in the late 1990s.*

Home Guard units; Lanner was one of the other users. The group on guard would have someone patrolling outside up the Carn while the others slept. Richard can picture now Tommy Kent from Scorrier Farm diligently searching the skies for enemy paratroopers during a raid.

Richard remembers the following Carharrack Home Guard members, and apologies to any who have been omitted:

Bert Woodley, Stanley Chapman, Willie Webster, Mr Pellowe, Mr Andrew, Ben Moyle, Leonard Moyle, Mr Cleave, Mr Knuckey, Mr Carlyn, Mr Hicks, Mr Pelmear, Mr Draper, Albert Godwin, Steve Vigas and Mr Vinson.

There were only two, or possibly three, occasions when enemy bombs fell in the proximity of the village. One late summer's evening, as the weakening rays of the sun appeared after an earlier shower, the drone of engines could be heard deepening from the Trevince direction. Witnesses saw the plane low, almost too low, skimming the chimney tops along Alma Terrace. Margaret Sedgeley, at home in the terrace, felt the vibration as it passed overhead. Billy Penrose saw it almost brush the treetops in front of the chapel. It was so low that both he and Richard Kinsman, who was in his five-acre field at Carndene checking his crop of oats, remarked that they could see the front observer studying maps or suchlike. The plane then banked sharply to the left and headed for Trevarth. Almost straight after its manoeuvre it unleashed a fearsome load of incendiaries in Tommy Allen's field along Grove View. On hearing the explosions Phyllis Nicholls' father grabbed his bike and rode over to help out. The auxiliary fire brigade from Redruth attended, but luckily little damage was done, the conditions underfoot averting the possibly of setting the trees and ground alight.

On another occasion a returning marauder decided to rid himself of his weaponry, or else decided to shoot at Willie Penrose's livestock. The 'Zip! Zip! Zip!' of gunfire was heard down Squire Lane at the back of Elm Farm in one of Mr Penrose's fields, and then there was the noise of an incendiary exploding. Again little damage was reported apart from a pit in Willie's meadow.

The next device, which is the mysterious one, did not explode but merely made a fair-sized hole in a field behind Richard Kinsman's Carndene home. He awoke one morning to find this hole in his field; no crater, just a deep hole. Thomas John Allen, the ARP warden, was sent for. 'Oh my goodness, that's a bomb!' Notices were quickly erected proclaiming 'Danger keep out!' The Plymouth bomb-disposal unit was sent for. Later that day a jeep containing several chaps arrived to deal with the aerial intruder. They excavated quite a large pit around the device before extracting it. This took a few hours. It appears

that a stray anti-aircraft shell from the Falmouth area was the culprit.

Sadly, a major part of all warfare remains the human sacrifice and tragedy that befalls families in the community and Carharrack was not spared. Two members of the Stephens family were victims. Edward J., who served on the *Courageous*, was lost when it was torpedoed. His nephew, Robert, died on duty with the RAF, and Lance Corporal Eric Lawry, aged 20, who lived in Shute Row/Hillside Terrace was lost in action in Italy. Prior to enlisting in the Hampshire Regiment he was a miner, he was a keen and talented athlete and came first out of 300 entrants in a marathon race held in London. Harry Tredre, who left the village before the war, was on a tour of British War Cemeteries several years after the cessation and came across Eric's headstone – Harry recognised the name from his village days. Albert Wills was another victim. In September 1942 the *West Briton* reported the death of Edgar J. Martin, aged 51, youngest son of Mrs Martin of Ash Villa. In 1909 he emigrated to South Africa as a blacksmith and later served as a mechanic in the Royal Flying Corps, spending four years in France. John Bailey, a gifted musician, whose home was along United Road, failed to return.

With the conflict over, Carharrack's community looked to the future with an awareness of how fortunate it had been to live in a village somewhat distant from major happenings. Memories of that distressing time remain vivid for those who lived through it.

VE Day and VJ Day were occasions of wonderful celebrations. Brian Saundry lived in Railway Terrace and as a child remembers a street party at the end of the war. Stanley Pope was a new recruit in the band and among his first musical outings were VE Day walkabouts in Carharrack, Lanner, St Day and Cusgarne. Services of thanksgiving were held at the two village chapels and St Piran's.

A village committee was formed to promote such celebrations and afterwards continued as the Carharrack Sports and Carnival Committee with Mr Albert Pengilly as chairman, G. Pelmear as vice-president, LeRoy Gumma as treasurer and Sylvia Mitchell as secretary. Subsequent committees arranged the annual carnivals and other village entertainments that continued for many years into the 1950s.

BIBLIOGRAPHY
Operation Cornwall, Viv Acton and Derek Carter
The *West Briton* and *The Cornish Post & Mining News* 1914 to 1920, and 1939 to 1946
29 Let's Go; A History of the 29th Infantry Division in World War Two, Joseph H. Ewing
The Staff of the DCLI Museum, Bodmin

Left: Carharrack's earliest rugby side, 1907. Left to right, back row: *?, ?, Mills Barrett, George Pelmear, Francis Cock, Eddy Enstice, ?, ?, Joe Brokenshire, LeRoy Gumma; middle: ?, John C. Treweek, ?, Mr Dunstan (capt.), Mr Martin, Thomas John Sims; front: Peano Knowles, ?, William Brown, ?, Sparry Verran.*

Right: *The first rugby side after the Second World War, outside the old Redruth changing hut in 1946/47. Left to right, back row: Telegraph engineer at Truro, 'Chippie' Stanley Chapman, Bill Lewis, ?, Phillip Pill, Arthur Richards, Jack Ryder, LeRoy Gumma, Harold Parminter, Redvers Richards, Ronnie Ryder, Ivor Hancock, Jack Eddy; front: Lesley Dunstan, Bill Whitburn, Alec Young, Frank Parminter (capt.), Owen Richards, 'Manna' Ford, Edgar Swan.*

Left: *The 1948/49 side. Left to right, back row: Matt Swan, Jack Eddy, Ken Pill, Harold Parminter, Redvers Richards, Ivor Hancock, Bill Downing; standing: Ray Townsend, Joe Roberts, Bill Whitburn, Courtney Butler, Arthur Richards,*

Artley Hitchens, George Gill, Des Downing, Denzil Jolly, Owen Richards, LeRoy Gumma; seated: Len Crabtree (kneeling), Donald Lear, Ronnie Ryder, Stanley Chapman, Charlie Parminter, Tom Peters, Frank Parminter, Bill Lewis, Peano Knowles (referee); front, seated: Ted Woodley, Arthur Mills, Jack Dunstan.

ELEVEN

SPORTS CLUBS

RUGBY

It is possible to trace three village rugby sides which have lasted for a period of time since 1900. The first one dates from 1907, which is confirmed by the fact that there is a dated photograph of the team. Unfortunately, little is known of where the side played or of the duration of their existence, although there is a photograph from c.1910 of a rugby game being played in a space at the start of United Road.

The next rugby side was formed following the Second World War by, amongst others, the Parminter brothers and Alec Young, ably encouraged by Roy Gumma. Alec, who moved to Primrose Farm in 1936, had played for Cornwall's under-15 side before the conflict started and had just been demobbed from the Navy. Albert Pengelly's three cornered field at the junction of United and Consols Roads served as a pitch, although a few years on the team did play down Sparry Lane. George Pellowe helped out on Saturdays at the Youngs' farm, one of his tasks being to rid the playing surface of bovine deposits.

The 'Blue and Whites' continued to play regularly against local sides until the early 1950s. Luckily there are several team photographs which cover their reign.

Carharrack's next 15 started up in the late 1970s, playing for only a couple of seasons. It seems Charlie Parminter and Roy Gumma helped set up the club which had its headquarters at the 'old' Carharrack Sports Club, built on as an extension to the hexagonal Institute structure. Home matches were played in Gould's field, on the right along United Road just after the entrance to the lane serving Rosewood Farm. They shared the use of the field and prefabricated changing shed with the soccer team. One avid follower states: 'They played 'friendlies' in the loosest sense of the word!' Playing members included: George Pellowe, Willie Webster, Melville Woodley, Chrissie Matthews, Bernard Mably, Billy Chown, G. Curnow, Phil Grant, Owen Richards and Rufus Williams. Billy Wright worked hard behind the scenes and made the occasional 'guest' appearance when they were short on numbers.

A photograph taken c.1910 of, presumably, a Carharrack rugby team playing a home match on a pitch opposite the beginning of United Road. Note the complex of sheds and buildings in the background prior to the erection of the Mills' Hall.

Left: *The 1952 side. Left to right, back row (in doorway): ?, Max Phillips, Ronnie Ryder; second row standing: Gerald Phillips, ?, Tommy Burley, Alec Littlejohns, Bill Matthews, Tommy Chapman, Des Downing, Barrie May; seated: Courtney Butler, Owen Richards,* Stanley Chapman (president), Rufus Williams (capt.), Roy Gumma (secretary), Stanley 'Manna' Ford (?); on floor: Jack Ryder, Peter Dale.

The cricket team, 1977. Left to right, back row: *Sid Richie, Trevor Burrows, Charlie Streat, Donald Tangye, Robert Dawes, Roger Harding;* front: *Rod Mitchell, Bernard Pearce, Gerry Gimson, Phil Grant (capt.), Billy Chown, Colin Dower.*

CRICKET

The nucleus of Carharrack's only cricket side that spanned the years 1975 to 1985 began as extras, or guest players, for the Truro *West Briton* team which played local sides in evening fixtures. Over two or three seasons the Carharrack boys became pally with the *West Briton* lads and it was decided to organise a team to play in the Western Division Four League.

A field down Sparry Lane, already owned by the council and earmarked for the rugby side, was to become their home pitch. A dividing hedge had previously been demolished by the rugby boys, thus creating a larger playing area.

As it turned out the rugby team elected to play elsewhere so the cricketers moved in. Although initially the square was rough pasture it was possible, after a lot of effort, to cut out a couple of playing strips. At the mention of a village team several locals, such as Jack Eddy, Bernard Pearce and Bernard Mably who had been playing 'abroad' for Lanner and other villages, joined the group.

The team managed to purchase a small green caravan which served as a changing room, pavilion and tearoom. Summer afternoons and evenings were enjoyed by spectators and players alike, and the cricketers received good support from the villagers with numbers swelled by passers-by out for a midsummer stroll. One handicap of the Sparry location was the proximity of the allotments, some of which were not always in a manageable state. Their jungle-like features often thwarted efforts to retrieve well-struck or slashed sixes.

Bernard Pearce's 129 runs against Goldsithney, Donald Tangye's 8 wickets for 9 runs in 69 balls against Gulval and D. James' 9 wickets for 31 were the best batting and bowling figures recorded in the scorebooks. One highlight of the club's existence was when their one and only entry into the National Village Cup Competition took place. 'Everyone was keyed up for the contest,' recalls Billy Chown. They lost against Lanhydrock, not by having a weaker run rate, or succumbing to superior spin bowling. No, they lost by the toss of a coin in St Columb Minor car park. Due to the abandonment of the game because of bad weather the rules at that time decreed a coin toss was to decide the outcome.

The Rhondda, Wales, was the location of one 'world tour' by our intrepid touring side. The opponents had a very, very useful fast bowler. Legend has it that the Carharrack captain asked his opposite number if it would be possible for the 'Fred Trueman' character to bowl at a slightly reduced pace so that the Carharrack players would have a chance of glimpsing the ball, let alone hitting it.

After ten enjoyable years, family and work commitments among its members made it more difficult to field sides, so it was decided to disband the club.

TENNIS

In the early 1920s Edward Tribble, a Falmouth dentist and chemist, had recently moved to the village following his retirement and wished to do something for the youth of the area. He duly financed the building of two tennis courts at Ting Tang, plus a members' pavilion with changing facilities that was large enough for social functions. At either end were smaller sheds for the storage of equipment. At present a bungalow which incorporates one wall of the old pavilion, plus an adjacent derelict building plot, mark the site of the courts, which were close to the main Comford Road just prior to the track linking the Comford and Trevarth Roads. The opening ceremony on Thursday 1 May 1924 was performed by Mr C. Beauchamp, after which a set of doubles was played between the president and vice-president and Misses Bailey of Lanner. Carharrack brass band attended under their new conductor, Mr T. Allen.

The 1920s saw a lot of activity by club members during the summer. Numerous matches were played against the likes of Cusgarne and Ponsonooth. Team players included L. and W.F. Ellis, Mrs Bailey, H.E. Strutt, H. Curnow and ? Sedgeley. Officers were the president Revd Thoroid, vice-presidents Revd Paul Ellis, C. Beauchamp and Captain A.H. Moreing MP, Nick Carbis was honorary treasurer, Mr W. Darlington honorary secretary and Miss E. Parkinson assistant honorary secretary. The committee members included Mrs Enstice, Misses Parkinson, P. Gould, P. Ellis and Messrs A. Teague, ? Tribble, J.C. Treweek, ? Cornish, H. Curnow, L. Ellis and W. Gay. The Enstice sisters, Margaret Sedgeley and Kathleen Goldsworthy, were keen playing members.

Many social events were organised during the club's existence and one detailed article in the *West Briton* in July 1925 noted:

The previous Thursday a Moonlight Dance took place at the Carharrack Lawn Tennis Club. The hard courts were carefully prepared by the secretary, being prettily illuminated. Mr Conquest was the MC with music supplied by Miss Mordaunt on the piano.

The facilities at the clubhouse were made available to the Carharrack and District Sports Club and, in the late 1930s, to the Horticultural and Fanciers' Society, both groups taking full advantage of this offer through the years. At an AGM of the District Sports Club in 1934 it was maintained that the newly-constructed putting green was proving very popular, but sadly the tennis courts were nowhere near fully used. By the start of the Second World War the Tennis Club seems to have ceased and the courts lay neglected for many years. Subsequently, a wooden dwelling, the Pines, was constructed on part of the site and later a modern block bungalow was erected by John Simmons alongside.

BADMINTON

Mr Albert Pengelly with the Treweeks and a few others started the Badminton Club in March 1935, which survived until the outbreak of war. Mr H.G. Swithenbank was the first chairman and games were played on Tuesday evenings while matches took place on other nights. Practices and home games were all played at the Mills' Hall. Phyllis Osborne, née Chapple, recalls:

On one of the away matches we travelled by Bernie Martin's bus to Breage and play was in the church hall. The court was short and the markings extended a foot or more up the wall where the fireplace stood. The suppers there were particularly good; a definite plus for a hungry teenager like myself. Another time the 'bus' found a hill too steep and all the men had to get out and push!

Playing members included Mr and Mrs Pengelly, Mr and Mrs Swithenbank, Mr and Mrs E. Longman, Mr R. Bawden and his brother, Mr and Mrs Bernard Honey, Mr J. Mills, Mr Stanley, Gerald Martin, Patrick Batty and Dorothy and Phyllis Chapple.

CARHARRACK & DISTRICT SPORTS CLUB

This club, organised and run in order to raise funds for the brass band, was up and running in the early 1920s. It held annual sports days, usually in August, most of which took place in Charlie Penrose's field just behind Alma Terrace. The field was reached by using the track almost opposite the Chapel Terrace junction. After the sporting activities, which included some gruelling and technical events, such as the two-mile run and high and long jumps, a carnival took place when all the competitors toured the village headed by the band.

It was at one such sports day in August 1930 that the band were presented with new instruments by Mr Joseph Mills, Mr W.J. Mills being incapacitated. In the same month two years later the Carharrack Draughts Association was formed with regular tournaments being held at the Tennis Club, Ting Tang. The new organisation was linked to the District Sports Club as, it appears, was the Tennis Club by the mid-1930s when the new putting green was opened. The impending war saw the demise of these groups.

BILLIARDS & SNOOKER

The years just before the outbreak of the First World War saw the first mention of a village billiards side. They played in the Gwennap League which included Stithians, Lanner, Four Lanes, Chacewater, Carharrack and St Day. Playing members were R. Odgers, George Pelmear, Charles Treweek, S.E. Trengove, Ernie Teague, W. Pelmear, Francis Cock,

Above: *Carharrack Billiards Team, 1914.*
Left to right, back row: *Francis Cock, Charles Treweek, W.G. Pelmear;* seated: *S. Trengove, R. Odgers, G. Pelmear, Ernie Teague.*

Below: *The all-conquering team of 1959.*
Left to right, back row: *Charlie Gay, Mellie Annear, Ronnie Moore, Dougie Thorncroft, Roy Leah, Johnny Chynoweth;* seated: *Horace Pelmear, Clifton Allen.*

W. Webb, Gordon Beckerleg, H. Webb, Horace Pelmear, T. Triniman, A. Rowe, John Jolly and S. Eade.

By the 1920s no league teams existed and this situation continued for many years. The probable reason for not entering any sides at this time was that the league rules required playing on a full-sized table and Roy Leah recalls mention of purchasing a full-sized one in 1930. There is a report of an exhibition match of billiards at the Institute in May 1926, when Gordon Beckerleg, a member of our early league sides and listed as an ex-county champion, met a Mr Williams of Redruth.

An Institute billiards team joined the Mining Division Junior Section, Eastern Area in 1930. Regular team players were Redvers Richards, Fred Penrose, Ernie Teague, Willie Gay, Clifton Allen and Horace Pelmear, with W. Simmons, Jack Combellack, Roy Gumma, Harry Tredre, W. Martin, Alf Burrows,

Left: *Gwennap League Champions in the 1930s, the Carharrack Institute team.* Left to right, back row: *Horace Pelmear, Redvers Richards, Leonard Allen, Clifton Allen;* seated: *Arthur Mills, Ernie Teague, Johnny Chynoweth.*

Below: *Mining Division Champions, 1950.* Left to right, back row: *Johnny Chynoweth, Dougie Thorncroft, Redvers Richards, Reggie Barrett (Lanner), Len Moyle;* seated: *Clifton Allen, Ernie Teague, Horace Pelmear.*

Left: *Falmouth and Penryn Division Two winners, 1979/80.* Left to right, back row: *Terry Harry, Terry Chynoweth (capt.), Alan Repper;* front: *Roy Leah, Desmond Harry.*
(Photograph courtesy of Eric Parsons)

Right: *Mining Division Two winners, 1981/82.* Left to right, back row: *Terry Simmons, J. Anthony, Mike Tregenza;* front: *Desmond Harry, Roy Leah (capt.), Terry Harry.*

J. Wakem and G. Burrell supporting. Soon after, Carharrack entered a team in the newly reconstructed Gwennap Billiard League.

League billiards and snooker teams continued until the 1934 season and L. Verran, Albert Swan, Willie Penrose, W. Treloar, A. Mills, J. Ash and W. Penberth became regulars.

Roy Leah, himself no novice at both codes, looked up to Leonard Allen as his hero in postwar days. Leonard was a left-hander, always smartly dressed with hair neatly parted in the centre. Roy thought he was the bees knees and tried to emulate him, even by having the same hair style, the problem being that Roy's hair was curly!

In the late 1950s the side won all the major trophies possible which included the Mining Division Shield, County Team Billiards, Senior Billiards and Snooker Titles. That team was made up of Charlie Gay, Mellie Annear, Horace Pelmear, Johnny Chynoweth, Clifton Allen, Roy Leah, Dougie Thorncroft and Ronnie Moore, who also doubled as their transport manager because he had the use of a bakers' van.

One of that all-conquering side deserves extra mention: Douglas 'Dougie' Thorncroft. He began playing for the Institute side in 1946 as a 17-year-old and went on to become a village legend in his own time. In 1960 he won the County Amateur Billiards Cup outright, after winning it every year since 1956. That same year, 1960, he won the County Snooker Cup. He repeated this double in 1963 and 1967.

The Carharrack Club still encourages both billiards and snooker, although in 2002 the latter is the dominant game. In more recent times Carharrack have been winners of the Falmouth and Penryn Division Two in 1979/80, the Mining Division Two in the 1981/82 season and in 1992/93 the Mining Division Four League.

SOCCER

There is no record of any soccer side existing in Carharrack prior to the 1930s. In December of that year a Carharrack Association Football Club was formed and at the inaugural meeting C.H. Beauchamp was appointed president with Harry Tredre as the secretary. Over the next few years the club held many fund-raising events, but they do not appear in any fixture lists within the local newspapers. Presumably the team merely played friendlies against local opposition.

In September 1931, in order to raise some funds, the club organised a gala day at which they had a push-ball contest involving five local sides. The referees were Carharrack's own Mr C. Treweek and Mr H. Swithenbank. The winners… Lanner!

After the Second World War, Roy Leah remembers schoolboy 'pick-up' sides playing in the fields opposite Simmons' garage, North Hill.

Inside view of the old Carharrack Institute, c.1915. Charlie Treweek is about to attempt a cannon at billiards while Francis Cock looks on, with Ernie Teague in the background.

Gregory Collins, who lived in the large house in Chapel Terrace, used to draw caricatures of the players with large heads on small bodies, and it is said that they were very good.

The present soccer team dates back to 1965. At that time several lads were the nucleus of a Trewirgie School side which was run by the PE teacher Mr J. Thomas. The team, which played on a pitch by the cemetery at Trewirgie, were a good mix of talents for a youth side and, under the guidance of Mr Thomas and later Michael Nancarrow, soon acquired Junior League status. In the 1965/66 season the club became Carharrack AFC, and by 1970 the football club merged with the Men's Institute to become part of the Carharrack Sports Club set-up, using the club as their headquarters.

Since those early days there have been many 'highs and lows'. Winning 72 matches in succession, being elected to the Cornwall Combination League in the 1970s and winning that league were early 'highs'. During that impressive winning streak the team played in so many end-of-season cup matches that the county footballing authorities had to make special provision for the Carharrack team to play the Dunn Cup Final at the beginning of the next fixture season. The team, still in the Combination League, continued playing on their rented pitch with its prefabricated changing rooms and goalposts donated by Roy Wales. A change of ownership of the field on United Road led to problems for the team as no other venue was available. The Ting Tang pitch was at that time being developed and was not ready. Many villagers probably remember barbecues being held there, inviting parents and children to collect stones for 50 pence a bucket whilst munching a hot dog. There was no soccer team for a couple of seasons and then a side was started up which re-applied to enter Junior League Football. One of the council-run pitches at Clijah was used for a few years until the Ting Tang venue was ready. In 1999, the same year that Manchester United achieved their noted treble, Carharrack's lads did the same, winning the One and

The village Youth Club football team before a match with Camborne in October, 1965.
Left to right, back row: *Dudley Bawden, Terry Chynoweth, Russell Curnow, Phil Grant, Tommy Ware,*
David Andrew, Alec Hancock, Trevor Burrows; kneeling: *Ronnie Annear, Micky Burrows, Jack Eddy (capt.),*
Terry Simmons, Bernard Mably.

Moon Shield winners, 1965/66. Left to right, back row: *Michael Nancarrow, J. Thomas, Terry Chynoweth,*
Billy Chown, David Andrew, Phil Grant, Ronnie Annear, Tommy Ware, B. Ware; front: *Russell Curnow,*
Terry Simmons, Micky Burrows, Dennis Woodley, Jack Eddy, Clarence Ware (mascot), Trevor Burrows.

Left: *Combination side, 1970s. Left to right, back row: Arthur Burley (manager), Pat Pearman, Mel Edwards, Jeff Burley, Phil Grant, Tony Potts, Terry Simmons, Kevin Rundle; front: Graham Hart, Roy Davey, Gordie Hawke (capt.), Brian Davey, Dixie Devlin.*

Right: *Mining League team, 1969/70. Left to right, back row: Alan Jenkin, Peter Davey, Jeff Burley, Phil Grant, Terry Prisk, Trevor Burrows, Russell Curnow; front: Terry Simmons, Paul Tidball, Roy Davey (capt.), Micky Burrows, Billy Chown.*

Left: *The 1987 team. Left to right, back row: Tony Pascoe, Bernie Pellow, Colin Dower, D. Williams, Kevin Drew, Robert Job, M. Burns, Trevor Burrows; front: Gary Trevena, Kevin Rundle, Michael Dawes, John Williams, Johnny Webster, Michael Jones.*

The 1991 team. Left to right, back row: Kevin Rundle, Joe Vargus, Paul Ivey, Martin Trestrail, Paul Caddy, Kevin Drew, Gary Giles, Robert Dawes, Johnny Webster; front: Michael Jones, Ian Curnow, Shaun Wills, Treve Ivey, Roy Peters, Michael Dawes, Tony Pascoe.

All Sports Mining League title (their third league title running), the Dunn Cup and the Torch Cup Final – statistics of which to be proud.

Three principal venues have been used by the soccer team over the years. Firstly the pitch in Gould's field, United Road, and secondly the council pitch complex at Clijah, South Downs. After great efforts by the Carharrack Soccer Club and with help from other village organisations and businesses, a piece of land at Ting Tang was cleared and prepared as a playing surface. It was later officially named the Howard Beauchamp Recreation Field.

THE CARHARRACK INSTITUTE & SPORTS CLUB

The hexagonal structure of the Mechanics Institute, built in 1841, stood prominently in Chapel Terrace for some 140 years until its collapse and subsequent demolition in the early 1980s; its demise still saddens many a villager. The Institute was funded by public subscription at a time when the local adult male population required a place of refuge, relaxation and learning. It contained a large well-stocked library and an area for reading. During winter evenings readings and lectures took place and indeed the subject matter for the talks, given by eminent people of the time, was of a topical and at times highly technical nature.

As can be seen from the rules of the Institute in 1898 *(overleaf)*, there was a strict etiquette policy and bad behaviour was not tolerated. By the time of the First World War billiards was being played and the club was developing and broadening its sporting activities. In February 1925, through the generosity of Mr H.T. Halse of Trevarth, a member since 1865, a reading room was built adjacent to the Institute by Mr Eddy Matthews of St Day at a cost of £100. In donating the gift he expressed a desire that the villagers would make a real use of it and support it in every way they could. It was opened by Capt. H.P. Peters of Newquay, who hoped the young members would derive much good from the reading matter supplied. Mr Darlington thanked Capt. Peters on behalf of the members. A brass tablet was to be placed in the reading room by the members of the Institute as a token of their appreciation of the gift.

Card games, darts, snooker and billiards seem to have been the main preoccupations until well into the 1960s. The club soon became known as the Carharrack Sports and Social Club, and in 1972, at a cost of £4,500, an extension was built onto the hexagon. Over the next few years the club's sporting and social life blossomed. In December 1980 storm damage caused the partial collapse of the old

Institute and it was at this time that the then committee of eight members decided to have a larger clubhouse with modern facilities built on a site a little further along Chapel Terrace at an original cost of £60,000. With the help of a loan of £18,000 from Usher Breweries and a remarkable amount of work put in by a nucleus of 15 stalwart volunteers, local firms doing the blockwork, plumbing and providing some furnishings, the new Carharrack Club and Institute was opened on 18 December 1981. The committee at the time comprised Roy Leah (chairman), Terry Chynoweth (vice-chairman), Margaret Lewis (secretary), Mr and Mrs Billy Chown, Phil Grant, Trevor Burrows and Brenda Moore. The following helped out with the work: G. Harvey, T. Freeth, K. and B. Lewis, D. Tucker, D. Dunn, A. Williams and R. Annear. In the autumn of 1990 an extension was built onto the social club, with a large room-cum-dance area equipped to cater for top-class entertainment and private functions. On the adjoining wall between the old lounge bar and new function room Mr Eric Rabjohns painted a mural depicting an underground mining scene.

THE HOWARD BEAUCHAMP RECREATION GROUND

In the summer of 1994 work began on the provision of changing facilities at the Howard Beauchamp Recreation Ground at Ting Tang, the land having been leased to the Carharrack Social Club on very favourable terms. The club obtained several grants for the work which was carried out by the local firm of W.J. Ladd and Sons (builders), the site foreman being John Uren of Carharrack. The services were brought up to the site through the woodland.

October saw the grand official opening, which was a special occasion for those members of the Sports Club who had planned for the event so many years before. Although the weather was not the kindest it did not rain. The procession left the village headed by the Carharrack and St Day Silver Band, club committee members and the Parish Council. It proceeded to the recreation-ground site where the opening ceremony was conducted by Harley Lawer, Sports Editor of the *Independent* newspaper. The whole occasion was a great success with a number of children and adults assembled. Bouncy castles, stalls, commemorative photos and reminiscences were the order of the day. A representative combination team played the 'boys'. Later on in the day a buffet was held in the Sports Club and amid the speeches the amenity was officially named in the presence of Mrs Vanessa Stone, daughter of the late Howard Beauchamp.

Left: *The hexagonal Institute building standing proud in the 1950s with the reading room, built in 1924/5, just visible to the left of the entrance.*
(Photo courtesy of Mr Donald Bennetts)

Below: *A 1980s view taken at the rear of Chapel Terrace showing the 1972 extension to the club. The site now contains two Ladd-built houses and part of Parc Stenak Estate.*

Below left: *The Carharrack Social Club built in 1981. This view shows the new function room on the right-hand side, under construction in the 1990s.*

Rules to be Observed by the Members of the Carharrack Institute

1. That persons over 15 years of age be eligible as members and that the subscription of one shilling and sixpence per quarter be paid in advance.
2. That the secretary post in the room the names of all the members in arrears for more than one month, after one week's notice to the defaulter.
3. That the directors elected for the time being, with the treasurer, shall be called a committee of management, invested with power to expel any member or members who wilfully break the rules.
4. That any members called to order the second time for breach of rules, and refuses to obey, shall be summoned before the committee to show cause why he should not be expelled from the Institute.
5. That no profane swearing or disrespectful language be used in this room, and also no obscene pictures or illustrated matter of any kind be placed on the walls of this Institute, or any kind of play which may lead to unpleasantness.
6. That no written matter, offensive or pertinent, in relation to the order of business or otherwise of this Institute, shall be allowed to be posted without the name of the writer.
7. That half of the double table nearest the fireplace shall always be reserved for the exclusive use of the readers, with the papers thereon.
8. That the committee shall meet monthly unless disturbed by the half-yearly meeting.
9. That three members of the committee, with the secretary, be constituted a quorum.
10. That any member may introduce a stranger for the evening without payment, but if a resident in the village, he must pay a penny for each visit.
11. That no member may retain any paper, or any part of the same, beyond twenty minutes, if it is required by any other member.
12. That no member be allowed to play more than three games, if the games be required by any other member; and that no gambling be permitted.
13. That no member be allowed to introduce any game or paper without the sanction of the committee.

signed John R. Rooke (Secretary) Carharrack, 20 January, 1898.

Left: *Setting up for the grand opening of the new changing rooms in the centre of this view.*

Below: *Billy Chown thanking Harley Lawer after the cutting of the ribbon to open the changing rooms.*

Below left: *Ladds team of builders who built the new changing facilities at the Howard Beauchamp Recreation Ground. Left to right: Barry Moyle, Paul Matthews, John Uren (foreman), Tim Uren, Mark Sweet.*

Members of the Social Club Committee and guests at the opening day. Left to right: Johnny Chynoweth, David Tucker, Paul Matthews, Kevin Rundle, Melville Woodley, Barry Paterson, Jeff Burley, Willie Webster, Trevor Burrows, Mary Webster, Roy Leah, Roy Ladd, Vanessa Stone, Joyce Chynoweth, Rose Brown, Terry Chynoweth.

Left: *Preschool playgroups. Left to right, standing adults: Carol Cupples, Luke Hanson in Lena Daddow's arms, Sonia Holbroke, Teresa Leah, Julie Rasheigh, Maureen Allen, Lynn Webb, Brenda Moore, Helen Bates with Simon Hanson;* fourth row (children at the back): *Luke Snell, Liane Morford, Andrew Coad, Leah Richards, Lana Bleik, Laura Evans, Tegan Williams;* third row: *Michael Stanforth, Madeleine Fliss, Laura Pedley, Ben Greening, Jennifer Pentecost, Kirsty Webster, Mark Leah, Carly Jones, Morwenna Pooley;* second row: *Adam Stone, Donna Williams, Rebecca Mulkeen, Chantal Holbroke, Sapphire Hodges, Jemma Rundle, Morna Wanell, Samantha Matthews;* front row: *Mark Ashman, Thomas Jones, Simon Harris, James Macfarlane, Hannah Pring, Hannah Schotel, Joss Brown, Sam Keverne, Adam Brooks.*

Below: *Organisers and helpers at the 'Spring Fayre' held in aid of the Carharrack Horticultural and Fanciers' Society in 1939. Photographer Mr Hankins of Redruth.*

Above: *Just some of the displays which made up Carharrack exhibition in 1990. Altogether there have been five village displays.*

TWELVE

❧❀❧

VILLAGE SOCIETIES & GROUPS

THE PRESCHOOL PLAYGROUPS

In 1973 the first playgroup was opened in the Wesley Chapel. Dot Turner and Sally Pooley were the supervisors with a team of helpers including Brenda Moore and Judy Rashleigh. In 1976 Dot Turner moved away and the group was closed. In response to requests from the young mums of the village, Brenda Moore opened a new one in 1978:

In 1978 I opened a playgroup at the Wesleyan Chapel for 15 children. I had the help of three staff who stayed with me for the following 17 ½ years: Judy Rashleigh, Maureen Allen and Lena Daddow. We increased in numbers over this time; 30 children for four mornings a week being our largest total. Our main aim was to prepare children for the large step of going to the 'big' school when they were five. Mostly we had them for two years and were able to teach them basic learning skills, knowledge of the colours and shapes, etc. and above all to learn to share and interrelate with others. We saw a whole generation grow up, literally hundreds of children, most of whose names I can still remember. When we closed in 1995 we had a second generation,

The committee members of the village Old Cornwall Society pictured at Carharrack village exhibition in 1996. Left to right: Barrie May (president), Betty Dunn (secretary), Eric Rabjohns (recorder) and Pam Thomas (treasurer).

offspring of the original playgroup members, in our care. I shall remember those busy days as some of the happiest of my life. Brenda Moore, August 1996.

A month later a new Preschool Learning Alliance Group was set up. It was run by a management committee including parents. Carol Cupples was the preschool leader. After a few years it was amalgamated within the Carharrack and St Day community school-run playgroup, which started in 1999/2000.

THE CARHARRACK OLD CORNWALL SOCIETY

The society was inaugurated in the summer of 1987 at a meeting at the Carharrack Club to seek support. The day, 24 September, saw the first indoor meeting at St Piran's Church Hall and Eric Rabjohns (the society's recorder) gave an illustrated talk on Cornwall's mine engine-houses. The venue changed during the following year to the Methodist Sunday schoolroom. Besides providing a series of regular meetings with a local, or Cornish, theme, the society's principal aim is to record for prosperity anything relating to the development and history of the village and the county in general. Since the inception of the society information of amazing depth has been amassed through photographs, memorabilia and recorded interviews concerning the community. On several occasions the society has held village exhibitions displaying the collected material. These events have been well supported and have been successful in generating great interest. During June 2002 an event took place in the Cornwall Centre, Redruth, in a bid to reach ex-Carharrack people who might have had that 'odd memory or photo' which would prove priceless.

The society has been involved in several projects over the years. In the early 1990s the group took it upon themselves to re-erect the old village pump as close to the original site as possible – it had been removed many years before for road widening and the site itself was partly built over. The society has

Left: *Pop star and entertainer Frankie Vaughan on his visit to Carharrack Boys' Club in 1962. Auriel Taylor is being presented with her autographed disc by the star; she won the raffle prize. Barbara Nurhonen, one of the instigators of the club, looks on.*

Right: *The founder members of the WI cutting their 25th Anniversary cake at the society's party in 1993. Left to right: Pam Thomas, Bertha Keats, Betty Dunn, Jean Youlton, Margaret Osborne.*

Left: *Taken at a WI bazaar held at the Mills' Hall. Left to right, behind the stalls: Betty Dunn, Hazel Moyle, Mary Kirkbride, Jenny Dyer.* (Photo courtesy of Peter Hughes, Camborne)

Right: *Presentation time at the allotments in the early 1990s.* Left to right, back row: *Stanley Pellow, Nigel Turner, 'Sid' Sidney;* front: *Simon Snell, Brenda Moore and Dennis Morris.* (Allotment photos courtesy of Colin King)

Left: *The allotments in the early summer of 1994; the plants look to be in a very healthy state.*

organisation, visited the club premises in the Mills' Hall back in 1962 – quite a coup, because at the time he was at the height of his popularity as an entertainer and pop star.

THE WOMEN'S INSTITUTE

In 1968 the village was developing quickly and the formation of a WI came about as the result of an influx of newcomers. Mrs Fullman, a WI member, moved to Carharrack and decided to join the local institute. To her amazement there wasn't one, so she canvassed her neighbours and, encouraged by the interest shown, she contacted the county headquarters in Truro to set the wheels in motion. In November of 1968 the first meetings were held and a WI with 36 members was formed. Mrs Fullman was elected president and for more than 30 years the members of Carharrack WI played an active part in village life, raising funds for many causes. A Christmas tea for local pensioners became an annual event and entertainments for the children were a feature of the spring and autumn fayres. We particularly remember the Halloween Fayre where all members present dressed as witches so realistically that one little boy had to be taken home by his mother. Another was the Strawberry Fayre, one of several held in the playing-field, which was opened by Brenda Wootton, renowned for singing Cornish songs and broadcasts on Radio Cornwall, who thrilled all those present by singing a few of her well-known songs. Brenda was a member of Canonstown WI who were twinned with the Carharrack institute.

The WI was involved in many projects including tree-planting, a survey of rubbish illegally dumped in the vicinity, the Silver Jubilee and royal wedding celebrations and the presentation of an inscribed tankard to each male in the village who took part in the Gulf War. Members also helped with village shows and carnivals, entering both with good results. The Women's Institute are proud that they play a part in national matters and have lobbied parliament to good effect in many cases. It was a sad day in 1999 when Carharrack WI held its last meeting.

also designed and printed leaflets and booklets concerned with the history of various aspects of the village's past. During 2000/2001 notice-boards telling the history of certain village features began to appear. These were part of a wider Mining Village Regeneration Scheme to publish pamphlets relating to village walking trails. The communities involved were Carharrack, Lanner and St Day. Again the society provided much of the information.

THE VILLAGE ALLOTMENT ASSOCIATION

The allotments were originally set up in the 1960s by the Camborne-Redruth Urban District Council and since April 1991 the Carharrack Parish Council have managed the allotments on behalf of Kerrier District Council. Before that time the whole area was quite neglected and wild with about six tenants working a few scattered plots. However, interest was revived and this number soon rose to 35 plots being worked by 22 tenants.

Two types of plot are worked: the larger one of two rods and the smaller bed of about half that size. Rents for the year are quite reasonable. There are several water points available for use throughout the field and a tunnel exists which tenants can make use of. Competitions have been held on a regular basis with Kerrier and Carharrack village Parish Council providing prizes. During the 1990s barbeques were a feature of local prize-givings and shield presentations. Thanks to Colin King for providing the above information.

CARHARRACK BOYS' CLUB

In 1957 Dennis and Barbara Nurhonen started up a branch of the Association of Boys' Clubs in Carharrack. Terry Mankee and Raymond Hole were the leaders and indoor meetings were held in the Mills' Hall. There was a wide range of activities offered to its members including canoeing on the River Fal and participating in the Duke of Edinburgh's Award Schemes. The club continued for several years into the late 1960s. Frankie Vaughan, who was a great believer and supporter of this

THE CARHARRACK PLAYERS
~ LINDA WILLIAMS ~

The Carharrack Players celebrated their 30th year of pantomime production in February 2002, when they presented an original pantomime, The Lamp and His Aladdin, *written and produced by one of its members, Beccy Thomas. As has been the case ever since its formation back in 1971 and its first production in February 1972, this was a sell-out and yet another resounding success for the players.*

Right: *Jeanette Dunstan (wardrobe mistress) adding those final touches to the Blue Fairy costume worn by Pat Hope in the 1986 production of* Pinocchio.

Below: *Programme for the production of* Puss in Boots.

Above: *Young dancers in the 1988* Cinderella *production.* Left to right, back row: *Rosemary Richards, Sarah Pellow, Amanda Blanks, Cheryl Richards;* front: *Gemma Pooley, Gayle Jolly.*

Above: *A few members of the 1995* Frankenstein *cast.* Left to right, back row: *Leila Mole, Andrew Trebell, Anita Matthews, Cheryl Richards, Diana White, Gary Thomas, Margaret Rowe, Pat Trevethick, Margaret Dawes;* front: *Pat Williams, Graham Alded, Tamsin Williams.*
(The 1986, '88 and '95 photos were taken by Richard Thomas.)

Left: *The programme for the Players' production of* We've Got Rhythm.

As a founder member, who has been in every pantomime and all the other shows staged by the society excepting one summer show in 1994, I look back with pride, pleasure and enjoyment on the continuing success and growth of this fun-loving group of players, whose talent, enthusiasm and, above all, teamwork has made our pantomime group, in my opinion, one of the best around.

It all actually began way back in the summer of 1971 during the Carharrack and St Day band's carnival week, when Raymond Wherry produced a variety show for two nights of that week as a fund-raising event for the band. This event was so successful that Raymond was prevailed upon to present a pantomime as a winter show. On hearing of this proposed venture I immediately volunteered to become a member of this fledgling society and I'm very proud to remain so to this day.

Back then the hall was a far cry from the bright and warm venue it is today. There was no kitchen at all and it only had two toilets, each of which was situated adjacent to the back of the two rooms on each side of the hall behind the stage. The annexe contained a small coal-burning fire in the far-left corner which, when lit, emitted belching smoke across the room, and though burning hot to the touch seemed to give off little if any heat from three feet away – at least not until the end of the performance when it was time to leave. Opposite the entrance door of the annexe was the only sink in the building with one cold tap, and from beside this door across to the sink hessian sacking was strung to provide a 'wall' for a dressing room. There was a tin roof above, which, as the room gradually warmed, caused continual condensation which then fell on the cast below in cold droplets!

Our first show was Sinbad the Sailor, for which the ladies were dressed in bolero tops and flimsy baggy trousers, needing body make-up applied to legs, arms and midriffs by means of a wet sponge from the cold water tap, which was in direct line with the outside door, and consequent cold arctic wind each time

someone entered! Nevertheless, this first show was a resounding success; initially staged for three nights, but sold out so quickly that a further two shows were staged the following Friday and Saturday too. There was, however, a snag in that at that time there was a miners' strike in progress and on the second Friday, just as we were collecting the costumes from the producer's house, we had a power cut and had to perform the first half under two headlamps and a 100ft beam torch. Changing rooms were lit only by candle and torchlight. But even under these austere conditions we had an almost full house, and at least finished the show with the electricity restored at half time.

Today, of course, especially since 1996 when the central heating was installed, the hall has been far more comfortable to work in. The initial improvements, the kitchen and toilets, were built by Raymond with Charter Thomas who also built our first wardrobe where one of the original toilets had been.

Raymond was our producer for the first six pantomimes: Sinbad, Tom Thumb, Dick Whittington, The House That Jack Built, which featured our first pantomime cow, and Mother Goose. The following year no production was staged. This was because, due to various reasons, several key personnel on the committee and production team were unable to serve and as our AGM at that time was held in September one month was not long enough to find replacements in time to begin rehearsals.

During the interim a new producer was found in Ivor Bray who joined the society in 1978. His first production was Sleeping Beauty, in which was featured our first pantomime horse, Penelope. I say 'our' in a more personal sense, as this was the first 'animal' that my husband Keith had made and in fact is still upstairs in my collection of various props, etc., made over the years. Keith actually joined the society from the outset, initially to ensure that the audience would have a cup of tea in the interval, by borrowing a large boiler for the back of the hall! However, this single act resulted in him becoming stage manager and

The cast of Sinbad the Sailor, the first production in 1972. Left to right, standing: Aubrey Basset, Baynard Braddon, Francis Hall, Alan Richards, Heather Richards, Sheila Braddon, Sheena Woodley, Valerie Wherry, Marilyn Richards, Joy Richards, Raymond Wherry, Charter Thomas, Raymond Strathen, Maud Jory, Colin Pellowe, Pete Goldsworthy, Elaine Strathen; front: Linda Williams, Debbie Williams, Sharon Pellow, Vanessa Bennett, Hazel Riley, Michelle Youlton – Janice Pellow, Carol Pellow, Sarah Goldsworthy, Lynn Gay, Cathy Dawes, Anne Riley, Ian Bennett.

devising various special effects and props used in the subsequent productions.

Ivor produced the next two shows, Polly Flinders *and* Goody Twoshoes. *In the first of these we had a scene containing a working, lighted windmill, made by Keith and Barry Munday. This was the first time that the scenery alone received applause, even before any of the cast entered the stage.*

As Ivor was unavailable the following year, 1981/1982, we recruited the services of David Williams who produced The Queen of Hearts *for us. This show was a lot of fun to do and some of the audience enjoyed the extra delight of eating the stolen jam tarts.*

Ivor returned the following year to produce The Man in the Moon, *which is still one of my favourite productions. We were very lucky to have the services again of Arthur Marks to paint our scenery, which was so colourful and realistic and his moonscape was genuinely 'out of this world'. Keith had fun with some special effects including moving stars, a star which shot a moving shooting star, sometimes into the audience, while three of the cast had to actually 'catch a falling star' as they sang the song. The following year Ivor produced* Puss in Boots *which featured one of our funniest slapstick wallpapering scenes, where the cleaning of the dowager's portrait reduced her neckline, a huge spider climbed up the wall, and the dame was left hanging from the chandelier.*

The next two pantomimes, Humpty Dumpty *and* Pinocchio, *were produced by a fellow cast member, John Trebell. The latter caused a few headaches for Keith who had to construct a boat large enough for six people and a whale large enough to swallow boat and cast, all on a stage only 15 feet wide at the back, with wings of only 3 feet! Ivor was producer again for the next show* Red Riding Hood *and began the production for* Cinderella *the following year. Unfortunately he was unable to continue after Christmas due to the ill health of a relative, and I was asked to step into his shoes so that the show could go on. Radio Cornwall featured this production and Duncan Warren came out during rehearsals to witness the final preparations. The 1989 production, which I produced, was* Ali Baba *and featured a pyramid and camel. Keith and I, with help from a neighbour, spent many hours trying to create a realistic camel only to have one child in the first night's audience exclaim 'Oh look, a giraffe!'*

In 1990 Annette Hillman took over production with another version of Dick Whittington. *This she followed with* Goldilocks. *Margaret Dawes then produced our next show* Aladdin, *which was entered in the Calor Gas Village Pantomime Competition where it proved an enormous success, winning third prize overall, first prize for choreography and first prize also for comedy male lead. Annette produced our next show,* Mother Goose, *and the following year Simon Sweet, our hilarious 'dimwit' from previous productions, made his debut as producer with a totally new kind of panto, a rock'n'roll* Frankenstein.

In 1996 the hall was refurbished so no show was staged, but the panto planned for that year, Babes in the Wood, *was presented the year after, produced by Margaret Dawes, who also produced the next two,* Beauty and the Beast *and* Old King Cole. *The latter production was a little different from usual in that it featured a storyteller on stage throughout the show. The millennium year provided another first for the players when Annette produced a pantomime which she had written herself,* Jack and the Beanstalk. *This year also marked another milestone, when Margaret produced our first stage musical,* Oklahoma. *This was our most ambitious production ever and the players proved their undoubted talent with a first-class show and excellent performances to packed houses. Some 12 months later Annette produced a reprise of* Dick Whittington *and this brings us back to this year's (2002) hilarious show written and directed by Beccy Thomas.*

In between the mainstay of our pantomimes, however, we have also presented very successful summer variety shows, produced by Raymond, Margaret and also Marilyn Richards, our first principal girl. These have been a selection of song, dance and comedy items, with occasional guest appearances too. Marilyn's first show in 1997 was a little different, being set in a coffee bar and taking us back to the rock'n'roll era. Then in 1999 she gave us all a party in On the Beach. *The set for this was one that Keith was most proud of featuring waving palms, sand banks and a beach pagoda.*

For every show that has been presented throughout these past 30 years, our society has been blessed with a wonderful team of volunteers, who are not seen by the audience. I refer, of course, to the backstage crews, scenery painters and designers, lighting technicians, raffle and programme sellers, front-of-house personnel and especially our wardrobe mistress.

Our backstage crew members have changed over the years as, with the exception of Keith, many have been bitten by the lure of the footlights and subsequently joined the cast on stage. However, their hard work in silent scenery changing, storing props and furniture and ensuring the curtains function at the right time, are essential to the smooth flow of every production. What appears to the audience to be a simple matter, is in fact tremendously hard work, especially when the society started. We only had four backcloths plus six 3ft wide wooden flats, which had to be manoeuvred into position avoiding the fluorescent lights on the ceiling. The backcloths themselves had, and still have, to be rolled up and down by two crew members climbing ladders at the back of the stage, while the cast continue the action in front of the curtains and have to squeeze past them in the process. For the first production of Mother Goose, *the stage props were so many and large, including a 'nest' and 'wishing well' both big enough for the dame and others to climb into (to disappear), that the second half's props were stored in Keith's van outside the hall, and were exchanged during the interval for the first* half's equipment, since there was insufficient space to store both lots in the wings! In those days, to provide us with some storage space for props at the sides of the stage, one of the first jobs that had to be done before the dress rehearsals was to erect platforms over the wings made from trestle-table tops, nailed to wooden supports attached to the stage, which then had to be dismantled again at the end of the week's performances.

Once the kitchen had been built it was often used for access to the annexe for props too large to store in the wings and the tea ladies assisted by opening the hatch doors at the right time so that the props could be passed on to the stage. When you consider that the small passage between the kitchen and stage is also the only access to the toilets, you can understand the difficulties sometimes encountered during the manoeuvres!

We have been extremely fortunate over the years to have the services of some wonderful artists for our scenery. Our first shows, and some of our later ones too, were painted by Mr Arthur Marks and during rehearsals our cast were always amazed at his transformation of a previous backcloth into a new scene, appearing under his capable hands while we watched. Other productions have featured the talents of Mrs Sue Szepitowska who is more affectionately known simply as Mrs Sue. In one production she and her colleague appeared in the jungle scene where they performed a gorilla dance for us, as did Neil Allen whose stage debut was in our 'camel' for Ali Baba, during the night of which he 'sprouted' two extra legs while Ali was singing 'A Four-legged Friend' to him. More recently two newer members of our society, Becky and Gareth Thomas, have provided our props too.

I come now to our most hard-working member who is never really seen by the audience, except as a raffle seller. I speak of course of our tireless wardrobe mistress, Jeanette Dunstan. From the first day of rehearsal she begins sewing. Together with Margaret Dawes, they plan the colour scheme, style and number of costumes needed for each production and then proceed to measure and fit each member of the cast. The costumes she provides for us on stage are perhaps the most memorable part of the productions, adding colour, elegance and character to the whole show. We also owe a debt of gratitude to Annette Hillman and Margaret Dawes who design, create and decorate various hats and headdresses as well as all the extra touches to the costumes themselves, plus help with overall design and supervision.

When the society was formed, we had an equally talented and hard-working wardrobe mistress in Ella Strathen who, together with Sylves Wherry, began the design and creation of our now extensive wardrobe. Initially, all the costumes were stored in their homes, but once the annexe wall had been built and a false ceiling installed these costumes were catalogued, boxed and stored in the new 'loft'. It was a tremendous improvement when our first actual wardrobe room was built instead. And now with our recent wardrobe we are at last able to store these wonderful and colourful clothes on hangers!

No show could ever take place without the invaluable contribution of our unsung heroes, our musical directors. Like the cast, they attend each rehearsal to teach us new songs, advise and assist us with harmonies and tempo, and supply the added mood and movement which is vital to any production. A special mention must be made to our first and long-serving musician, Mabel Thomas. In our first productions when the hall was sometimes cold enough for a fridge, while the cast at least had the opportunity to move as they rehearsed, poor Mabel was obliged to remain seated continuously at the piano. How she managed to still play so well for us during the coldest evenings I'll never know! Others who have also served as our backbone for various shows and to whom we sincerely express our thanks are Sally Carpenter, Graham Homer, David Turton and Tim Briggs. Each of these talented musicians has ensured that every one of our shows, be it pantomime, musical or variety, has always been a delight to listen to as well as to watch.

Last year a new venture was undertaken when several of our younger members established a new group especially for the children of the area, called Carharrack Young Entertainers, and in September their first highly acclaimed show, Kidz, produced by Neil Allen, was staged. With up-and-coming talent like this, the future of both this new associated group and the Carharrack Players can only continue to flourish, and their audiences can look forward to ever more enjoyable family entertainment in the years to come.

THE CARHARRACK & St DAY SILVER BAND

First mention of a band being formed occurs in the 'Carharrack and District Coronation Minute-Book' dated 28 April 1911. To quote:

On the motion of Messrs J. Brokenshire and E. Enstice, Messrs J. Odgers and E. Pascoe be asked to try to get young men of the village to form a Fife and Drum Band for the occasion, some instruments being available.

At the same meeting a request was made as to whether funds would be forthcoming to buy new fifes in some instances.

The band was duly set up, being called the Carharrack Coronation Band, but was usually referred to as the Carharrack Fife and Drum Band. The band's activities, relating to the events on the Coronation Day of King George V and Queen Mary, 22 June 1911, are well documented in another chapter of this book, suffice to say that a note in the minute-book states that 'The band performances were most praiseworthy.'

Evidence that the band played at other functions and events, and that their programmes were not limited to instrumentals, is shown by the following

Left: *The band with Mr Fred Bray as leader, c.1920. He was previously bandmaster at Twelveheads. Left to right, back row: T.J. Allen, ?, H. Hugo, W. Evans, ?; middle: ?, ?, W. Murton, Harry Allen, Willie Tonkin, ?; front: ?, ?, Freddie Bray (leader), Bill Tonkin, ?; seated: Willie Allen.*

Above: *This photograph is of the presentation of new instruments to the band, c.1930. On a later occasion, 23 March 1933, Mr Joe Mills presented instruments on behalf of his great-uncle, W.J. Mills, who had kindly donated them but was unable to attend due to ill health. Mr Joe Mills well remembers the event held at the Wesley Chapel because it was his maiden speech in public. The instruments were inscribed, 'Presentation made in memory of Mr T.R. Tripp late president of the band.' Left to right: ?, Nick Carbis, Mr H. Beauchamp, ?, Mrs Quinlan, Tom Tripp, Tommy Allen, ?, Charlie Treweek.*

Above: *The band performing at the Stenalees contest in 1948 under the guidance of Clifton Allen. They won two first prizes in the third section. Soft drizzle did not dampen our lads' spirits.*

Left: *The first photograph of the Carharrack Brass Band taken in 1913, sporting their newly purchased uniforms.* Left to right, back row: *W. Evans, T.J. Allen, W.J. Murton;* middle: *E.J. Williams, W.T. Allen, G. Pelmear, H. Hugo, George Cann, G. Bray;* front: *Joey Allen, J. Charles Allen, R. Stephens (bandmaster), Harry Allen, W.G. Pelmear, Leonard Allen. Note that six members are from the Allen family.*

report taken from the *Royal Cornwall Gazette*, dated 3 August 1911:

Gwennap
The Church Sunday Schools of Carharrack and Cusgarne had their tea treat on Saturday afternoon at Trevince. The attendance was late on account of the storm, but a pleasant time was had. Carharrack Fife and Drum Band gave some excellent singing as well as instrumental music.

It appears that by 1912 this inaugural group had disbanded. It is curious to note that in February 1912 there is a report in the *Royal Cornwall Gazette* of the decision to form a Fife and Drum Band in Chacewater; one of their early engagements was in our village in May of that year.

The formation of the village brass band began circa 1912/13, no doubt being inspired to some degree by the fife band although only two members of the former group, Messrs W. Murton and E. Williams, appear in the new set-up. The Allen family, in particular Thomas John, played the major role in instigating the new band. On purchasing a second-hand cornet he sought tuition, duly finding the ideal person in John Williams of St Day, the bandmaster of Redruth Town Band. Five other Allen family members joined in Mr Williams' twice-weekly tuition sessions, at a cost of ten shillings per quarter each. Soon other local men joined the group which had swelled to 14. Now the pressing problem was finding a suitable practice room. Several places served this purpose during those early years; a barn at Tresithey Farm, a room at the coal yard between Crofthandy and Carharrack, Ting Tang count-house along the Trevarth Road, and the schoolroom of Billy Bray's Memorial Chapel.

The year 1913 saw Robert Stephens, who ran a coal merchant's business from the yard opposite the former Alma Stores, appointed as the band's first bandmaster. New uniforms were ordered at the expense of the band members and very smart they looked wearing them in the first band photograph taken in 1913.

Clifton Allen began his association with the band as an eight-year-old in 1916. He was to have a long and distinguished career, becoming the longest-reigning bandmaster until his resignation in 1960, holding that position since October 1937.

The following extract is taken from the band's *65th Anniversary Booklet* published in 1977:

Reminiscing recently, Mr Clifton Allen recalled the first contest in which the band took part. The contest was in Redruth, they were entered in the third section and played 'The Bohemians', but they hadn't the full complement, lacking soprano cornet; they were also without bass trombone and no BB. In spite of these handicaps, the adjudicator complimented them on their effort, remarking the gaps in instrumental capacity.

The acquisition of a BB was the next step forward. The next contest recalled by both Clifton Allen and Mike Martin of Crofthandy who joined the band in 1915, was to be at St Newlyn East, still under the baton of Robert Stephens. The band left Carharrack at 6a.m., travelling in a Jersey car drawn by three horses (Jimmy Chynoweth driving), on the way one of the traces broke and a stop was made at Zelah for both refreshments and practice, with Newlyn East being reached about midday, six hours after leaving home. Entered in the third section, the band was awarded First Prize on the March, playing 'Follow Me.'

On August bank holiday of the same year, the band entered a contest at Newquay, travelling up in a

Left: *Carharrack and St Day Silver Band, 11 May 1941. Left to right, back row: Donald Richards, Ainsley Sandow, Kenneth Pelmear, Leonard Allen, Rex Martin, Freddie Pope, Ronnie Penglaze; middle: Fred Pelmear, Tommy Martin, Denzil Trevithick, Artley Hitchens, Courtney Trevithick, Stanley Chapman, Alfred Bartle, Ronnie Allen, Joe Allen, Charles Allen; seated: Jack Williams, Luther Martin, Courtney Tresidder, Jack Buzza, Clifton Allen (bandmaster), Owen Richards, Michael Martin, Willie Allen, Sidney Bone.*

Right: *This picture was taken during Tommy Martin's reign as bandmaster in the early 1960s. Left to right, back row: Gerald Pellow, Sims Morris, John Morris, Lou Piper, Rodney Grigg, Bernard Pearce, Tony Richards, Colin Pellow, Dennis Pearce; middle: Roger Eddy, ?, ?, Sid Carter, Ronnie Symons, Eric Pearce; front: Guy Sanders, Roy Symons, Archie Richards, Ernie Pearce, Tommy Martin, Alister Pellow, Roderick Facey, Denzil Jolly, Alfie Opie.*

Under the baton of Clifford Bolitho, 1968. Left to right, standing: Bert Cook, Dick Penaluna, Howard Blee, Clifford Bolitho, Danny Madge, Alan Richards, David Lloyd, Dennis Lloyd, M. Jeffery, Michael Martin, Heather Richards; front: Leonard Adams, Robert Cook, Graham Bray, Lou Piper, Sid Carter, Ian Facey, Graham Joslin, K. Rowe, Robert Braddon, Ian Jolly, Terrence Blee, Barrie Trevena.

charabanc which was the first one run by the Great Western Railway in Redruth. The journey of 20 miles was this time accomplished in less than an hour. At this contest the band took second prize playing a selection called 'Recollections of England'.

Mr Clifton Allen further recalled that for many years the band played carols in the neighbouring district over Christmas. He clearly remembered the first Christmas under Mr Bray's direction when, as a boy of ten, he went with the band leaving Carharrack at 6.30a.m. They walked to Scorrier and played to the inhabitants there – one man threw open a window and shouted 'Go away! I hate music!' – then threw them a ten shilling note and slammed his window shut. A generous subscription in those days! They then walked on to Blackwater and played all their carols, thence to Chacewater to repeat the performance, and having played in the village centre, they walked up Chacewater Hill to play in that area. By about 5.30p.m. the bandmaster said, 'I think we'll go back to Crofthandy now boys, and then home to Carharrack.' So they walked on to Crofthandy, played there, and finally played at Carharrack. Clifton Allen, aged ten, at the end of a 14-hour day of walking, marching and playing, got home at 8.30p.m., fell asleep on the sofa and woke next morning to find himself in bed! On Boxing Day they walked to Trevince, thence to Gwennap Church Town, up the hill to Burncoose, down Rose Hill and on to Lanner! The good old days!

Also included in the *Band Booklet* are several reports taken from the *West Briton*:

West Briton, 3 January, 1918
Friends from Carharrack recently visited Skinner's Bottom Wesleyan Church and gave the following programme:

Duet (euphonium and cornet), Mr W.G. Pelmear and Master W. Tonkin
Euphonium solo, Mr W.G. Pelmear
Trombone solo, Mr E. Pearce
Duet (trombone and euphonium), Messrs Pearce and Pelmear

The *West Briton*, 2 January 1919, reports the Christmas Day activities as follows:

Christmastide, St Day... During the day the Carharrack Band under Mr R. Stephens visited St Day and rendered carol music at various places in the town.

Soon after this event Robert Stephens was replaced as bandmaster by Mr Fred Bray, who held the post through to the early 1920s when Mr T.J. Allen succeeded him. T.J. was in sole charge until circa 1928; Mr T. Hubbard then taking the role of musical director. In order to cover the fees of Mr Hubbard a 2d. weekly charge was levied on each member.

The beginning of the 1930s saw a need for the renewal of the instruments and an approach was made to Mr W.J. Mills for a donation towards them. A meeting between the interested parties was arranged, the outcome of which was that Mr Mills not only provided new instruments as an outright gift, but also much-needed new uniforms. It was at this juncture that, as part of the deal, the band was to be known as Carharrack and St Day Temperance Silver Band. At a concert held at Carharrack Wesleyan Methodist Chapel, 2 March 1933, the new instruments were presented to the band's trustees by Mr Joe Mills, W.J.'s great-nephew, due to his relative's ill health. Mr Joseph Odgers gratefully accepted them on behalf of the band.

With the provision of a superb new village hall for Carharrack by W.J. Mills in 1934, the band now possessed a place for practice and storage of their instruments, with the main hall being allocated for their use twice a week. The future of the band was assured.

Clifton Allen, who had joined the band as an eight-year-old in 1916, was appointed the new musical director in 1937 following the resignation of E.J. Williams who had taken over from Mr Hubbard some three years earlier. His reign as MD was to last 23 years until 1960, during which time the band matured musically, maintaining a consistent influx of young blood.

Over the years the band has entered numerous contests, both local and throughout the South West region, usually within the second section. Highlights of a playing career covering 90 years have been:

1948 – Two first prizes, third section, Stenalees contest.
1959 – Second prize in the second section of Bugle band contest.
1960 – First prize for the march at Bugle contest.
1969 – Second prize in the march and third prize for the selection, Bugle contest.
1969 – The band made its debut appearance on Westward Television.
1970 – Won first prize in the second section at Paignton Band Festival, which qualified it for the first section, for the first time.
1981 – Entered Pontin's Championship Contests in Somerset, qualifying for the finals held at Prestatyn, North Wales, where they achieved a creditable tenth place.
1986 – Penzance Band Festival, the band entered the second and third sections, winning them both. 'The outstanding band of the contest' was the adjudicators' comment.
1999 – The first time that the bass drum had been played by a lady at St Day Feast; Linda Williams was that lady.
2001 – The band recorded their first CD/Cassette.

The Parish Council logo designed by C. Davies. A competition was set by the Carharrack Parish Council in 1987 to design a logo.

The Parish Council at work helping to install new play equipment. Left to right: *Dan Gibbs, Kevin Bennetts, Raymonde Reeve.* (Photo courtesy of the West Briton)

The beginnings of a makeover on the Pennance side of the railway bridge. Filling in of the old track bed has started and planting commenced.

The same view in 2002; a good job done by all concerned.

Left: *The first Darby and Joan Committee.* Left to right: *Phyllis Kessell, Mrs Enstice, Phyllis Nicholls, Anne Harrison, Mrs Vincent, Mrs Dunstan, Mrs Woodley.*

Musical Directors since 1960	
1960–65	T. Martin
1965–66	C. Morris of Falmouth
1966–76	Clifford Bolitho
1976–84	Philip James
1984–86	David Pascoe
1986–89	Jim Richards
1989–90	Noel Harris
1989–94	Reubin Long
	Jim Wyatt
1995–2002	Roy Trelease

Acknowledgements: Thanks to Comdr J. Mills for permission to use information and sections from the two booklets published by the Carharrack and St Day Silver Band; namely the *65th Anniversary Booklet*, pub. 1977, and the *75th Anniversary Booklet*, pub. 1987. Thanks to Roy and Linda Trelease for more recent information. Also thanks to band and family members who have kindly loaned band photos to us for reproduction.

THE CARHARRACK PARISH COUNCIL

In 1972 an Act of Parliament was passed called the Local Government Act 1972. It required the District Councils to carry out a parish review in line with recommendations made by the Local Government Boundaries Commission of England.

Six years later, in 1978, Kerrier District Council advertised its intentions to carry out the review and invited comment. A Carharrack Village Association was formed and an application for parish status was made in December of that same year. In 1981 Kerrier DC published its draft recommendations and in 1985 the Kerrier (Parishes) Order came into being which approved the draft of 1981. Carharrack was to become a parish with a seven-member council.

In early 1985, Kerrier DC advertised for persons interested in joining the new Parish Council. Only two applied, Daniel Gibbs and Alan Harris. A further advert brought a better response and on Tuesday 28 May 1985, Garfield Stevens, the chief executive of Kerrier DC, summoned the first meeting at the Mills' Hall, the seven-member council comprising the following: Angela Chegwidden, Daniel Gibbs, David Hayes, Alan Harris, Susan Moor, Michael Sweet and Derek Williams. At the first council meeting David Hayes was appointed chairperson and Michael Sweet as vice-chairperson. The first clerk, Bernard Nankevil, was appointed in July.

Since its formation, the Parish Council has acted as a 'pressure group' to ensure that the viewpoints of the inhabitants have been heard by others. It has also brought pressure to bear on other local authorities, particularly Cornwall County Council and Kerrier District Council, to ensure that the village receives its

fair share of expenditure on the part of these authorities. It is possible that the following village improvements would not have taken place had it not been for the Parish Council's involvement:

The modernisation of the street lighting in Carharrack
The road improvements at Higher Railway Terrace
The provision of pavements in Church Street and Chapel Terrace
The improved road layout at Pound Crossroads
The provision of new equipment in the playing-field

In addition, the council has undertaken to carry out certain projects and ongoing works, including :

The restoration of the footbridge site
The management of the allotments
The provision of seats and notice-boards
The maintenance of areas where ownership is unknown
The issue of grants to worthy village causes
The setting up and publication of the Parish Newsletter, *which was first published in September 1985 and appears three times a year.*

(Redrafted from research undertaken by Alan Harris)

DARBY & JOAN CLUB

This group was started in about 1956 when most of the members of the WRVS who provided meals on wheels were asked by that organisation if they would consider forming a club to accommodate the elderly of the village. In the early days the original seven members of the committee were greatly assisted in fund-raising by Gertrude Bailey from Frogpool. Ever since then the club has been actively engaged in providing entertainments, visits and refreshments for its members. Several special parties have taken place to celebrate birthdays and anniversaries.

THE HORTICULTURAL & FANCIERS' SOCIETY

The Horticultural and Fanciers' Society was started in March 1935 and has managed to survive into the new century despite a disruption during the war years and a gap of about ten years from the mid-1950s. Charles Treweek was its first elected chairman, other officers being Albert Godwin, honorary secretary, with John Bailey as the honorary treasurer. Their first show was in August 1935 and proved very successful. Initially their meetings were held at the Ting Tang premises of the Tennis Club and later they moved to the Mills' Hall, which has since been their home venue. Several of their early schedules are held by local residents and our society has copies of them. They reveal a comprehensive range of classes for both vegetables and livestock.

After a break for hostilities, the annual shows began again in 1947 and continued until the mid-1950s. The initial post-war event staged in January was the society's first open show which attracted over 500 entries, including poultry, pigeons, bantams and caged birds. Charles Treweek was still the chairman with E. Stephens, T.R.B. Richards, W.T. Pellow and Mrs W. Gay filling other offices.

When the society was resurrected in July 1967 it was renamed the Carharrack Fanciers' Society and in 2002 it celebrated its 35th year.

THE GIRLS' LEAGUE

The Girls' League was formed in 1934 by Mrs and Miss Kellie, the wife and sister of the then minister, Revd Coburn Kellie. It was part of the Cornish Methodist District of Girls' Leagues and was formed mainly for the support of overseas missionary work. A group of girls from both Methodist churches in the village met on Friday evenings alternately at the Wesley and Billy Bray Memorial Chapels. On joining the Girls' League members were received at a dedication service and their pledge and aim was repeated at every meeting. There was a quarterly magazine entitled *The Lamp*. One of the conditions was that members should attend a place of worship.

During the winter months evenings were spent doing needlework and handicrafts in preparation for the annual bazaar held in December. The group would also put on the evening concert on that day with music and drama. Every year there was an outing, Christmas party and carol singing in the village to collect for charity. After several years the Girls' League became affiliated to the Youth Missionary Association and ceased. Those who attended thoroughly enjoyed themselves. Thanks to Sylvia May for researching this article.

MILLS' HALL TRUST

The Mills' Hall Trust, which today takes charge of the day-to-day running, maintenance and organisation of the village hall, developed from the trustees of the Carharrack and St Day Temperance Silver Band. These band trustees met in August 1933 with a view to forming the nucleus of a larger committee to arrange the opening of the playing-field and the band hall. This they did and part of their remit, as it were, was to administer the bequests of the Mr W.J. Mills Benevolent Fund, which included free tea for the elderly and Christmas gifts for certain village groups. Within the trustees' deeds it states, 'They and their successors constitute themselves into a Management Committee to oversee the Mills' Hall.' It has been many years since the trust had dealings with the W.J. Mills' Benevolent Funding side of matters. At the request of Mr W.J. Mills the band have certain privileges concerning the hall – they are permitted two weekly sessions for practising (with the option of other times if required) and the availability of a separate bandroom.

Above: *The Girls' League in 1945.* Left to right, standing: *Lilian Jenkin, Rachel Peters, Nancy Williams, Sylvia Mitchell, Ruth Daniel, Thelma Treloar, Rosemary Teague, Elizabeth Teague, Margaret Teague;* seated: *Patricia Treweek, Joyce Pelmear, Naomi Hitchens, Rhona Ryder.*

Left: *A Girls' League outing in 1953.* Left to right, back row: *Alastair Pellow, Joselyn Stephens, ?, Jeanette Trevethick, Rex Bray;* third row: *Rita Odgers, Janet*

Polkinghorne, Bridget Waters, Bill Wright; second row: *bus driver, Eric Richards (with pipe), Sylvia Mitchell, ?;* front: *Sandra Nichols, Shirley Gumma, ?, Jeanette Gumma, Marlene Pellow, Stella Mably, Joan Thomas.*

THIRTEEN

❧❧❧

FAMILY HOMES & VILLAGE PEOPLE

TRESITHNEY FARM

On the next page the farm is pictured in around 1910, whilst in the possession of the Tresidder family. The photograph depicts, from left to right, Mrs Tresidder, Thomas Henry and their daughter Mabel, who later became the second wife of Richard Kinsman (senr). They moved from Carn Marth after Thomas Henry retired – for years he was a coal merchant at Lanner. The Swithenbanks moved in during the 1920s and '30s and kept a poultry business. In the 1960s Mrs Porteous had the farm as a riding stables. When Tresithney Estate was being constructed the house was in a derelict condition so it was decided to demolish it and build a new house. The granite posts at the new driveway entrance are part of the old farm. One interesting point is that the original house faced southwards, but the new one faces north.

THE KINSMANS

The Kinsmans were a St Day family who, along with several other properties, owned the row of four houses on the bend of New Road, now called Sparry Lane. The last one was utilised as a builder's store. They moved into Carharrack and purchased land on the other side of the bridge and built Carnside 1 and 2. John Kinsman and his son Richard were the builders. Carndene House and buildings were erected in around 1900 and John bought the land,

LeRoy Gumma senr, c.1912.

approximately 20 acres, and broke it in. He then started building the house and his son later completed the structure.

The picture of Carndene on the next page shows the walled garden which was subsequently extended down to the Pennance Road. Above the house on the left can be seen the old barn, which is a small dwelling at the time of writing. Originally this building had two storeys, the upper one giving access to the top field. The premises were used to keep livestock and store foodstuffs. The chimney on the property served the great bussa (container) for boiling up the swill. Richard Kinsman (senr), a mason by trade, serviced the Wesley Chapel and was employed in the upkeep of buildings on the Trevince estate. Richard and his son, also called Richard, took over Carndene from the mid-1920s and they worked it until Richard junr moved away in 1965.

CHENHALE FARM

The farm is pictured overleaf at the time when it was occupied by LeRoy Gumma senr and his family, c.1907. LeRoy was born in Colerado in 1886 and came to the village when he was 11. On Christmas Day 1909 he married Hettie Jory at Stithians Wesley. Later they moved to Ivy Villa near Brokenshire's Corner where they started up a shop.

In the 1920s the farm was run by the Smitherams who operated a small boot and shoe shop there, and in the last 20 years it has been a riding centre.

Left: *Tresithney Farm, c.1910. Left to right: Mrs Tresidder, Thomas Henry and their daughter Mabel.*

Below: *This photograph of Carndene shows the walled garden and, above the house to the left, the old barn which is a small dwelling at the time of writing.*

Left: *Chenhale Farm, c.1907. At this time it was the home of the Gumma family.*

WOODBINE FARM

In the early to mid-1900s Woodbine Farm was home to John Hingston and wife, Caroline. They originated from the Grampound area. John was a cattle dealer and is shown as such living in Merril Place, Falmouth, on the 1901 census. It is known that he was a supplier of meat to the hotels in the Falmouth area. John had business connections with William Polkinghorne, butcher and slaughterman of Garby Lane, Southgate, Redruth, and through this connection John Hingston's daughter, Gertrude, married William Polkinghorne's son, William. William and Gertrude lived at Roseland, South Downs. A couple of their children would eventually live in Carharrack – Jack Polkinghorne, who had a fish-and-chip shop in Church Street in the late 1940s, and Emma Polkinghorne, who married William Benbow of Carharrack and lived in Albion Row.

Above: *The Hingston family, c.1905. This image and the picture taken overlooking St Day (below) were kindly loaned for copying by John Kellow, a great-grandson of John and Caroline Hingston. Left to right, back row: ?, ?, John Hingston; seated: ?, Caroline (John's wife); front: ?, Caroline Maude.*

Right: *This photograph, taken in a field behind Woodbine Farm, shows a view of the School Hill area of St Day. John Hingston is the man in the shirt, possibly Caroline Maude is on the left. Bearing in mind that he was a cattle dealer, perhaps they were setting up a purchase!*

JOE ODGERS OF ROCK HOUSE

This substantial house *(right)* was built c. 1907 on the site of an old blacksmith's shop with an orchard beside it. Mr Odgers *(left, in his undertaker's garments)* was a miner, carpenter and undertaker in his time. He was a real craftsman and made much of his own furniture, one villager recalls seeing Joe searching the woods for trees suitable for future projects. On

the village side of the property is an extension which served as a shop in the early 1920s. It was known as 'the *West Briton* and wallpaper store' for obvious reasons. Mr Odgers often mentioned that he had built his and his wife's coffins well in advance of them being required. They were stored across the roof timbers of an outside shed.

SYDNEY JAMES BEER

Left and below are two examples of fascinating views of the village in the late 1930s and early '40s, which were captured in watercolour by Sydney James Beer. Several local families have some of his works in their possession. Much of his subject matter covered the Carharrack and Falmouth areas. He was born in Paignton in 1874 and his early years were spent working for

the family business as a joiner/carver, but by the early 1900s he was described as a fine-art dealer. He set up 'The Little Studio' at No. 6 Arwennack Street, Falmouth, which he ran until moving to Heatherbank, United Downs, where he died in 1953. His Carharrack paintings comprised views of the village pump, Chapel Terrace, Elm Farm and Cottage, Church Street and Alma Terrace.

THE TREWEEKS

An attractive family photograph *(left)* of the Treweeks at the back of their shop in Fore Street. John William Treweek, born 1852, moved into the village in the 1870s. He left for a while but soon returned and by 1891 was running a grocery business with his wife Mary Phillippa *(pictured standing beside him in the photo)*. To the left of them is their daughter Evelyn, and on

the right their son John Charles. John Charles is remembered as a local builder and undertaker. Several future carpenters served their apprenticeships under him. He was also a talented runner.

THE CHINN FAMILY

William Henry and his wife Mary Anne moved into the Gwennap area in the 1880s and to Carharrack ten years later. They had 12 children, one of whom was Richard (Dick). He was employed by Cornwall County Council as a road foreman. He held every office in the United Methodist Church, of which he was a member for 30 years. Daughter Millicent was an organist for the Band of Hope and Sunday school. Katie Chinn's marriage to Edward John Williams in the 1930s was the first at Billy Bray's Chapel. The Chinns lived down Squire Lane prior to moving to the Newquay area in the mid-1920s.

Above: Local 'bobby' PC Charlie Dale outside Lansbury House, Railway Terrace, 1940s. Many children, mainly young lads (we cannot think why!), recall being ticked off for some misdemeanour by the PC.

Left: The Chinn family. Left to right, back row: Katie, William George Goodland (married to Mary Jane), possibly Selina, ?; middle: Mary Jane, Richard (born 1889), Mrs W. Chinn, ?; front: names not known.

Left: Charlie and Lily Hocking celebrating their 50th wedding anniversary. Charlie had a slaughterhouse at the bottom of the lane running from United Road to Poldory and sold scraps for animal feedstuff.

THE BROWNS

A photograph of Mr William John Brown *(right)*, plus animals, taken up at the junction of Chapel Terrace and Church Street, c.1910. He was a mine captain and moved into the village from the Vogue area. He and his wife Elizabeth had six children. Two of their sons went abroad to seek work, an action not uncommon in village families. Bennet went to South Africa and Arizona and California were two of William's ports of call.

Willie Gay holds the horse while Grandpa Jory looks on.

THE JORY FAMILY

Rosewood Farm was the Jory family home for many years. Henry and Annie Jory began as farmers in the 1880s and by the 1890s had begun an aerated-water business with their sons, Henry and William. They also sold fish locally and Grandpa Jory could be heard down at Lanner selling his wares. The sons would spend the night fishing from Newlyn and return home, selling their catch en route. In front of Rosewood, across the track, was an old disused cottage that served as a mowhay back in the 1920s. Next to it was a pond surrounded by rushes where the Jory boys would clean their baskets by dumping them in for a soaking.

THE PENROSE FAMILY

The Penrose family can be traced back through all the census returns to the birth of John Penrose in 1811. He married Eliza and they had ten children, six of whom were girls. One of the boys was William, the grandfather of William 'Billy' Penrose of Wheal Damsel bungalow. 'Grandfather' William and his wife Louisa outshone his parents, producing 13 children! Of those Willie John used to have Elm Farm, brother Thomas and Bessie (his wife) ran a shop in Church Street, Charlie was a butcher and had a smallholding behind Alma Terrace approached by a short lane which now lies between two bungalows, Nellie married Ernie Teague and ran a Post Office with him at 1 Church Street, and Fred ran a small-holding and lived at one time in Pelmear Villa.

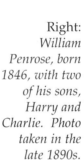

Right:
William Penrose, born 1846, with two of his sons, Harry and Charlie. Photo taken in the late 1890s.

Hilda Penrose's marriage to Jack Scholar, 1923. Left to right, standing: *Tom (bridegroom's brother from Plymouth), Ruby Dower, ?, another of Jack's brothers, Jack, Hilda, Kathy Penrose (Hilda's sister), ?, Tom Penrose (later emigrated to New Zealand);* seated: *Mrs Mitchell, Mr and Mrs Scholar, Bessie Penrose (bride's mother), Granny Lyne (bride's granny), Mrs Enstice (organist). The middle girl at the front is Nancy Teague.*

Right: *Trevince House, c.1900. The conservatory was built in the 1880s.*

Below: *Trevince House entrance in 1910.*

Below: *Vivian Sara, the valet and footman, as a young man. Vivian is wearing a cockade is his hat. It is thought that the Beauchamp family were the only family authorised to wear such an embellishment. (The photo is courtesy of Mrs Daisy Sara.)*

Above: *A family group, c.1878. Edmund Beauchamp and his wife, Louisa, with,* left to right, middle: *Edmund (junr), Charles Howard, Violet, ?;* front: *Geraldine, Luna with Hermana in front of her.*

Right: *The estate gardeners in 1894. The man in the centre is possibly the head gardener, Mr James.*

TREVINCE & THE BEAUCHAMP FAMILY

When Martin Beauchamp married Margaret Trevyns, daughter and heiress of Henry Trevyns, in about 1524, two long-established Cornish families were brought together. The earliest record of the Beauchamps is at Binerton near Crowan in West Penwith, in 1195. There is a record of Robert de Trefyns being a jury member for an ecclesiastical investigation in Gwennap in 1281.

At the time of the marriage, lands held by the Trevyns included Trevince, Cusgarne, Caskair, Pengreep, Gear, parts of Trebowland and Lannarth, Penstruthal and Chycoose. During the period 1550–1779 mining was carried on by successive generations of the Beauchamp family. In 1695 William Beauchamp started raising copper from Poldory. Joseph Beauchamp (b.1741) had an interest in Ting Tang where Watt erected his first engine. This was not the success that future Watt engines were to be, and it is believed that Joseph himself took no further interest in mining.

For many centuries the Beauchamps had married within the county, making alliances with the Tubb, Trefusis, Trehane and Enys families, among others. In 1729 Francis Beauchamp married Ellen Cranmer of Essex, and from that time the Beauchamps travelled further afield in search of spouses. The family lived at Trevince and at Pengreep, which was the dower house. In 1817 Henry, the only son and heir to the estate, was thrown from his horse at the entrance to Pengreep and was killed. It is said within the family that he was cursed by a gipsy after refusing to give her some money, thus leading to his accident.

In 1807, following the death of Elizabeth Beauchamp, Trevince was advertised 'To Let' and in 1811 Michael Williams of Scorrier took on the lease which he retained until the 1860s. Anne and Ellen Beauchamp, Henry's cousins, and now co-heiresses of Trevince and Pengreep, had wed and left Cornwall.

In 1866 Anne's grandson, Edmund Beauchamp Tucker, who was raised in Devon, returned to Trevince with his first wife, Maria Sadlier, and their daughter Matilda. Maria's diary records the welcome they received from the local people. She died in 1870 after several miscarriages and a stillbirth.

In 1873 Edmund, who was a keen huntsman in England and Ireland, met and married Gertrude Persse of Galway. She died, probably in childbirth, having had three daughters: Frances, Geraldine and Luna. Edmund then married his third wife, Louisa Longueville-Jones of Shropshire, and they had two sons, Edmund (who died aged 12) and Charles, and two daughters, Hermana and Violet. Edmund, like Francis Beauchamp (1755) and Joseph Beauchamp (1784), became High Sheriff in 1870. He was a JP and Deputy Lieutenant of Cornwall. He was also a keen sailor and Vice Commodore of the Royal Western Yacht Club.

Charles left Trevince and set up a small engineering works in southern England. He married Grace Eileen Bonner of Worthing and they had an only child called Howard. On the death of Edmund in 1921, they returned to Trevince. Charles was soon involved in local government and was a member of Cornwall County Council from 1922. He was particularly interested in agricultural policy. During the Depression he was responsible for the idea of providing seed potatoes to anyone who had a bit of ground. He was a trustee of the Mills' Hall, Carharrack, and, like all members of the family, took an active interest in local matters.

Howard and his wife and family were living at Trevince from the late 1940s onwards. Howard was market gardening and, on the death of his father, took on the running of the estate and made many improvements. He provided some land on Trevarth Common for Carharrack Sports Club to be used as a football pitch and gave Lanner Silver Band a hut in Lanner, which they later sold, using the money to buy the hall they use at the time of writing. He was chairman of the Rural District Council and, as well as his interest in agriculture, was extremely knowledgeable about minerals, being a founder member of the Minerals Group of the Country Landowners Association.

THE HOUSE & GROUNDS

While there is a record of an area known as Trevince (which appears with various spellings) from 1281, the earliest firm evidence of the house is a carved granite coat of arms, which was made following the marriage of William (1) and Joane Tubb of Gwennap. William died in 1616.

Until the 1970s there was a ridge-tile on the roof which depicted a horseman dating approximately from the 1620s. It was typical of many that were found in Cornwall and Devon and was probably made in the Looe or Lostwithiel area. This tile is now kept in the house to prevent further damage from weathering. Also on the roof is the Pisky Gow, a finial topped with a ball, round which the piskies could dance and not bother the inhabitants of the house. The earlier Pisky Gow had disintegrated and when the house was re-roofed in the 1990s a new one, covered in lead, was made by Wesley Allen of Carharrack.

Any early papers relating to personal affairs, other than leases, vanished after the death of Joseph (1819) at Pengreep, so there is no accurate record of the meeting between Francis Beauchamp and John Wesley. The latter was preaching at Gwennap Pit when he was arrested by Francis and taken to Trevince under guard. Another version of the story is that Wesley had angered his audience of miners and Francis had rescued him from danger. Whichever is the true account, it seems that the two men parted amicably and Wesley continued his mission in the parish.

When Trevince was advertised for letting, a description of the house appeared in the *Royal Cornwall Gazette* on 4 April 1807:

Desirable Residence
About 6 miles from Truro, 3 from Redruth, 5 from Penryn and 7 from Falmouth, all excellent market towns. To be let by private contract, for a term of 7 or 14 years, all that capital mansion house, called TREFINCE [sic], late the residence of Miss Elizabeth Beauchamp, deceased: comprising a small sitting room, with an office or study, a very good dining parlour, and drawing room, kitchen, back kitchen, servants hall, offices, 6 good bedrooms, with proper dressing rooms, 4 rooms for servants, china closet, apple chamber etc. etc. A coach house and a six stall stable, walled garden well stocked with fruit trees, green house, and shrubbery, 4 acres of orchard ground filled with choice table and cyder fruit trees, pound-house etc.

The taker may also be accommodated with 60 acres of land 40 of which is very good, with the barn, stable and outhouses, and have possession immediately.

The house stands in a dry warm and healthy situation, near the Turnpike road, is well sheltered from the cold winds, and within half of a mile of the parish church of Gwennap. The taker may also be accommodated with the household furniture, corn in the ground etc. at a fair valuation.

For further particulars apply, if by letter post paid, to Geo. Simmons, of Trevella, near Truro.

It is said that the house was a place of 'ups and downs, long passages and ghosts', and in the 1860s Edmund Beauchamp Tucker had part of the house demolished and rebuilt, with a second floor added. Ground plans for the rebuilding drawn over an earlier plan of the house give some idea of its appearance before 1866. The architect was Mr J.P. St Aubyn, and the builders were Messrs Olver & Sons of Falmouth. Mr St Aubyn was responsible for additions to Trelissick and there are obvious similarities in the gable windows of that house and Trevince. The Olvers also built the Pendeen lighthouse and Penzance railway station, among other notable buildings in West Cornwall. The arms of EBT and MST are picked out in cobbles under the porch at the front door with a dog-Latin tag 'Auspice Teucro' (thought to mean Lucky Tucker). In 1874 Edmund changed his surname from Tucker to Beauchamp. On his return to Trevince in 1866 the following article appeared in a local newspaper:

At Gwennap Church-Town
For the last two years a great many hands have been employed in draining, reclaiming the wastes, and otherwise improving the estate of Trevince. Upwards of 50 acres have been added to the farm, and a great part of Wheal Squire common enclosed and planted. The house has also been undergoing extensive additions and improvements by the firm of Messrs Olver & Sons, Falmouth: Mr J.P. St Aubyn being the architect. Thursday last being the day of Mr Tucker's removal from Greatwood in Mylor to Trevince, the villagers of the church-town, with the tradesmen and labourers employed in the building and premises, determined to give him and Mrs Tucker a suitable reception on their 'coming in'. On their arrival at the entrance to the village, about half past two, the six fine-toned bells of the old parish church struck out a merry peal, and on their coming to the entrance to the lawn, they were met by hearty rounds of cheering from the assembled villagers and work-people. Over the gate an arch was erected, spanned with the word 'WELCOME' in large letters, and overhung with a garland of evergreens… In the evening the employees of Messrs Olver & Sons (over 60 in number) were entertained by Mr Tucker at an excellent supper. The 'meet' was at the old-established house, the Fox and Hounds Inn, Comford, kept by Mr Nicholas Jory. The large 'meet' room, which was intended for a ticketing room (where copper ores were sold by a form of auction) was tastefully decorated.

The Fox and Hounds belonged to the Beauchamp family until the mid-1900s, when it was sold to the St Austell Brewery.

From the 1860s until the start of the First World War, Trevince flourished. As well as the family, there were maids, a footman called Mr Sara, Mr Blaker the coachman, Mr Treneer the gamekeeper and five or six gardeners. At dinner time the bell outside the kitchen window was rung to summon everyone from garden and fields for their meal. In spite of the advent of mobile phones this practice continues.

At the top of the house were the day and night nurseries and staff bedrooms. The children only saw their parents at set times of the day. The authors have notes and drawings sent by Charley to his father Edmund telling him about his daily activities. The children of Edmund's second marriage were great friends with the daughters of the Revd Saltram Rogers who lived in Gwennap Vicarage. They would signal each other across the valley from the upstairs windows of their respective houses.

When it became clear that there would be no more mining, Edmund started the Plantations, now known as Trevince Woods. Conifers managed to flourish on the mineralised ground, although it took some years for them to establish, and Edmund, like many other countrymen, used to take a pocketful of acorns on his walks and plant them in holes made with his walking stick. This practice was continued by Rosetta Beauchamp and the Society in the 1950s on Trevarth Common, from which the trees had been harvested for use in the Second World War.

In the nineteenth century it was fashionable to plant the pretty but invasive *Rhodendron ponticum* in woodland. This has become a serious problem, covering paths and disguising the old men's workings, which were so prevalent in the heyday of mining, but which were never recorded on maps.

In common with many other Cornish gardens, the area around the house was planted with trees and shrubs newly discovered by Lobb, Forrest and others. From the 1960s onwards, areas of laurel and *Rh. ponticum* have been cleared, and Howard Beauchamp started a collection of the big-leaved rhododendrons, as well as planting other shrubs and broad-leaved plants.

He had the foresight to start planting young trees before the old ones died or were blown down in gales. Trevince is now taking part in the Conifer Conservation Programme with the Royal Botanic Gardens, Edinburgh. This programme is dedicated to the preservation of trees and plants which are endangered in their own habitat. Seed is collected from temperate areas where, for various reasons, the plants are threatened, and when the seedlings are sufficiently well grown they are given to gardens where they can flourish undisturbed. The aim is to collect seed from these specimens and, when possible, re-establish trees in their native country.

Coffins had to be carried from Carharrack to Gwennap for burial and in 1837 the stile and resting stone at the entrance to Trevince top drive, known as Whitestile, was improved to its present state so that the bearers would have somewhere to rest. At that time the 'drive' was a track going down what is now the public footpath across the fields and through Green Lane to the Churchtown road. The top and middle drives were built in 1895/6 and completed at the time of the great blizzard of 25 March 1896, when the depth of snow was over four feet. Charles Beauchamp remembered standing on the snow and watching the workmen digging below him at the entrance to the top gate.

A leat was built from the Lanner end of Carn Marth to United Mines to provide water for the stamps. Part of this leat was in use before 1784, when it only extended as far as Comford and supplied a mill. It was extended (c.1817) across Comford Moor field, between two hedges with a path alongside, now known as The Ramparts. It then went across the park and through the walled garden of Trevince and the Inner Wood past Little Trevince, finally reaching the area of Wheal Cupboard.

A photograph of the leat passing through the Wilderness, dated 1894, shows a gravelled path and flowing water. It was possible to walk beside the leat from the Carharrack to Comford road to Arsenic Works Field, at the end of Inner Wood, until the late-1950s when *Rh. ponticum* and brambles took over. In the 1960s Howard Beauchamp had the open part of the leat in the park covered. The stretch through the shrubbery and walled garden was probably covered when it was built and is now collapsing in places.

Since 1888 rainfall and climatological daily records have been kept at Trevince. In the past, details of rainfall, temperature, barometric pressure and wind direction went to the Meteorological Office. More recently only the rainfall measurements are sent. The old 8-inch rain gauge has been replaced by a 5-inch (127mm) one. This is regularly inspected by someone from the Met. Office. The amount of rainfall is measured at 9a.m. each day, and the data sent monthly to the Met. Office and to the Cornwall Rainfall Association. Looking at the overall pattern of rainfall at Trevince for the past 114 years, there have been very wet periods (although what we are experiencing in 2002 are exceptionally wet months), as well as the glorious sunny days which everyone seems to recall from their childhood.

During the Second World War, Trevince was let to the Save the Children charity for evacuees from Plymouth. The furniture was put into store, and Charles and his wife rented a house in Restronguet, where they remained for the duration of the war. About 16 children and their carers lived at Trevince, sleeping on camp beds in dormitories. At that time there was only one gardener, Mr Facey, who had come to the garden in 1936. There is correspondence between C.H. Beauchamp and the charity recording the struggle there was to maintain the garden and supply the large number of residents with vegetables and fruit.

The Fourburrow Hunt used to meet once or twice a year at Trevince until a couple of hounds were lost down a shaft whilst pursuing a fox. It seems that the fox jumped onto a ledge in the shaft, but the hounds fell to the bottom.

Between the wars, young women from Carharrack helped in the house. Among them were Audrey and Hazel Thomas, and Nellie Teague who was the cook. Nellie stayed with the family until her retirement. Mr Facey also worked for the family as gardener until he was forced to give up in 1989 because of arthritis. He and Charles Beauchamp, and later Howard, managed to do the work of five men. He was followed by Andrew Cox, whose grandmother was brought up in Carharrack. Andrew was responsible for beginning the redevelopment of the garden. He was a talented propagator and an imaginative gardener. He died tragically young, but his legacy is evident in the plantings he made.

Each generation of the family has been active in Gwennap Parish and in the life of the church. Successive Beauchamps have been vicar's warden and, since the inception of Parish Councils, members of the family have been chairmen of Gwennap Parish Council which, until the change in parish boundaries in 1934, included Carharrack.

This section was written by sisters Vanessa Stone and Clare Page (née Beauchamp).

The Fife and Drum Band formed especially for the Coronation celebrations. The band did play a few other engagements later that year, but by 1912 seems to have disbanded. Left to right, back row: ?, ?, ?, ?, Charles Pelmear, Ernie Wills, Willie Trevithick, ?; middle: Jack Mills, Jack Kinsman, ?, Joe Odgers, Ernie Pascoe, W. Murton, ?, George Cann, ?; front: ?, Leslie Smitheram, Fred Tremberth, ?, ?. The band members present but as yet unidentifiable include: Messrs W. Bray, Clome, Teague, Williams, W. Mitchell, R. Chinn, L. Chinn, J. Chinn, Purdy, Pote, Collins.

Left: The afternoon parade moving along Grove View back to the village, headed by the Revd Broad, Mr C.C. James and Sydney Furze with the band in close pursuit and flag-carrying children behind. The arch in the background was the one built by Messrs Allen and Barnes.

Right: A second view of the festivities showing the people in the procession making up the centre and rear sections of the proceedings. Bedecked in all their fineries the ladies, gents and children certainly made the occasion one of special note in the village's history.

followed at four o'clock. Sports for the youngsters and other ages included such favourites as the egg-and-spoon run, sack and foot races for the children; adult interest was roused by the tug of war with the 'marrieds' versus the 'singles'; obviously the superior stamina and guile of the former won the day.

Evening proceedings continued with the carnival and even a downpour could not dampen spirits as the band made its way with the train of revellers en route to Trevarth via St Day. Motor cars driven by Mr Visick of Devoran and Mr Scotland, from Truro, formed the first and last items in the line respectively. Amid the gathering were W.G. Pelmear, the cycling clown, T. Carbis, the equestrian cowboy, W. Chinn, Miss K. Chinn, E. Jowles, K. Mills, D. Daniell, L. Chinn and J. Mills dressed as fairies, and Hugh Jory clad in Red-Indian gear. Some 55 individuals entered the carnival categories. At 10p.m. the bonfire was lit by Mr Beauchamp of Trevince House in a field located between Martin's Quarry and the road to Mr Hingston's house at Woodbine. Faggots were provided by the aforementioned Mr Beauchamp. The national anthem brought proceedings to a close – 'God Save the King'. The band must have been very tired that day after the following three parades:

10.30a.m – from Carharrack chapel yard to Gwennap Parish Church
2p.m. – parading around the village
6p.m. – Carnival procession from the village to St Day and back to Trevarth

KING GEORGE V'S SILVER JUBILEE, 1935

Committee meetings, usually held at Cusgarne Council School, to organise and prepare for the events, began in March and continued into May. The Jubilee Day programme was as follows:

In the morning a large attendance was present for the radio broadcast of thanksgiving in the Mills' Hall. Later Mr S. Furze and Revd W. Cooper conducted the opening ceremony in the playing fields. Mrs H. Jory and Miss Downing judged the 52 children's fancy dress parade entrants. So pleased were the spectators that a collection took place to boost prize funds. Athletic sports and fun races were held in the field, supervised by Mr Charles Treweek and Mr Swithenbank. Three shillings was the top prize money for winning a children's race, with a massive 'ten shillings' allocated to the winning adult (men and women's) ten-a-side tug-of-war team. Mr Clemens presented mugs and buns to the children, and a public tea was held in the Billy Bray's schoolroom.

In the Mills' Hall, the 'Trail Blazer's Novelty Band' from Camborne, led by Mr S. Bryant, performed. During the concert there was a pause while the audience listened to the King's broadcast. A social and dance followed with Albert Pengilly as MC.

QUEEN ELIZABETH II'S CORONATION, 1953

A week of events celebrating Queen Elizabeth II's Coronation commenced on 1 June. This was organised by a committee with Stanley Chapman (chairman), Charles Treweek (honorary treasurer) and F.C. Crabbe (honorary secretary). The programme was as follows:

Monday – a United Devotional service in the evening *Tuesday (Coronation Day) – Afternoon: Children's parade led by the Carharrack and St Day Silver Band followed by sports in the playing field. Tea for all the children and presentation of souvenirs. Evening: Children's concert, including conjuring and magic by Peter Penwarden (member of the Magic Circle).* *Wednesday – Tea and children's social (free to all).* *Thursday – Afternoon: For the 'older folk' magic by Frank Vibert (member of the Magic Circle). Followed by tea and the presentation of souvenirs. Evening: Entertainment, including a sound film.* *Friday – A masked dance.* *Saturday – Afternoon: Gymkhana presented by Jack Polkinghorne. Children's carnival later on. Evening: Dance and social until midnight. Souvenirs for the children provided by the Camborne and Redruth Urban District Council.*

Jean Homer of Well Farm remembers entering the parade dressed as that 'Doggie in the Window', and her Mum used the old black-out curtains to make the outfit. Mavis, Jean's sister, entered as a 'Flower Girl' and won a prize of 2s.6d.

THE QUEEN'S SILVER JUBILEE, 1977

The weather was superb for the occasion. A grand carnival was held in the playing-fields as the centre attraction. Several bands paraded along with marching majorette troops, decorated individuals and numerous floats entered by groups and organisations making up the colourful procession as it encircled the village in the afternoon.

THE GOLDEN JUBILEE, 2002

The Golden Jubilee witnessed more patriotism than the Silver in the sense that private dwellings were adorned with union flags and attractive bunting draped frontages and gardens. There were a number of organised village events with several local streets, or housing areas – Menakarne for one – holding street parties on Coronation day. The recently renamed Carharrack Stars Inn had a spectacular fireworks display in the evening, with the skies above resounding to the sound of explosions and ablaze with flittering colour. Souvenir mugs were presented to local children later on in the year.

135

Above: *The three 'Maids of Honour' at the opening ceremony of the Mills' Hall and playing-field.* Left to right: *Sylvia Penberth, Roma Thomas and Dorcas Benbow.*

Above: *A photograph taken from the* West Briton *of the time. The inset shows Mrs Quinlan officially opening the hall, while the main view is of Miss Mills presenting the playthings.*

Left: *An interesting view of the pavilion which once stood in the playing-field. The man reading the speech is Colonel Barbary with Miss Enid Mills (right) and Lord St Leven (left).*

Right: *The hall nearly 70 years on. Recent renovations, both inside and out, have once again made this a building of which we should be proud.*

Left: *Miriam and Barbara Enstice standing at the end of the table on the day they helped to serve the refreshments at what is most likely the public tea.*

THE CONSTRUCTION OF THE MILLS' HALL & PLAYING-FIELD

On 3 August 1933 a meeting of the Carharrack and St Day Temperance Silver Band Committee passed the following resolution:

That the Carharrack and St Day Temperance Silver Band Trustees form themselves into a committee with power to co-opt and to make arrangements for the opening of the Carharrack Playing Field and Band Hall.

This committee were charged by Mr W.J. Mills to arrange the construction of the Mills' Hall, for which he was the benefactor. Upon the death of Mr Mills in December 1933, the committee took advice from Mr T.R. Mills.

Many meetings took place in early 1934 and eventually a site meeting was held on Saturday 21 April 1934 when the contractors, Mr Hensley, Letcher and Charles Treweek, were appointed. The actual position was agreed and the contract was signed for the hall's construction at a cost of £680. The site was purchased from Mr Fred Penrose at a cost of £50 on 17 April 1934. It was agreed by the contractors that the building would be ready for occupation on the first day of September 1934.

The Mills' Hall Trust, which oversees the running and maintenance of the hall, came into being in December 1935, with the following people making up the original trustees: Messrs J.T.E. Barbary, J. Odgers, C.H. Beauchamp, J.C. Treweek, E.J. Enstice, W.G. Pelmear, H.G. Teague and W. Cooper. In 1962 the trust became a registered charity.

Mills' Hall during construction. Standing, left to right: William Arthur Richards, Tommy Martin from Tolcarne and Bert Woodley. No other people known. (Photo courtesy of Nancy Woodley)

THE OPENING OF THE PLAYING-FIELD & VILLAGE HALL, 8 SEPTEMBER, 1934

For an hour or more prior to the 2p.m. commencement, activity in the village has increased. Flags and bunting bedeck the scene: the Mills' Hall entrance is decorated with an arch of greenery. Final preparations are made for forthcoming events. Local families and friends – their children excited by the growing hubbub surrounding them – edge their way towards better vantage points en route. Nearer the time Mr Blewett, aided by fellow marshals, Sydney Furze, Ernie Williams, Matt Moyle and Stevie Daniel, gently steer the gathering youngsters – numbering some 200 – into three sectional columns making up the procession. A friendly carnival atmosphere pervades in the early September sunshine, albeit a little watery.

Nervous excitement exudes from the 'Maids of Honour',

Roma Thomas, Dorcas Benbow and Sylvia Penberth, prettily dressed in their matching white silk frocks and attended by proud relatives who provide those last little words of comfort and encouragement to their offspring.

The pounding drum beat signals the 'off'. Strutting authoritatively, ensuring clear carriageways, are members of the local constabulary. The procession heads away from the Chapel Terrace assembly area, up past the rusting Railway Bridge, down to the Trevarth Road, back into Church Square before parading down to Brokenshire's Corner and hence to the Pound Crossroads, Railway Terrace and down to the events at the newly built hall.

Whilst the procession proceeds around the village, at the hall the reception committee of Messrs Joe Odgers, Charles Beauchamp, Charlie Treweek, Roy Gumma and T. Mills prepare to greet the dignitaries of the day; Brig. Gen. Lord St Leven, Major G.T. Williams, Mr and Mrs, Master and Miss W.J. Mills.

As the parade passes the hall on the first lap as it were, the 'Maids of Honour' are led away from the entourage, into the care of Barbara and Miriam Enstice, whose job is to prepare the youngsters in readiness for their task of presenting bouquets to the lady guests.

The 'opening groups' await the procession – the Mills family standing by the door facing the road, Mr Ryder lingers with the 'opening key' made by Mr Letcher on behalf of the contractors, the 'Maids' tightly clutch their sweet-smelling bouquets, Lord St Leven quietly discusses some details with Mrs Quinlan; the committee, plus Colonel J.E.T. Barbary, their chairman, complete this well planned scene. Lengths of rope, put in place by Clifton Allen, separate the crowd from the speakers.

The procession returns to the hall, settling themselves in readiness for the chairman's introduction to the proceedings. He calls upon Lord St Leven to invite Mrs Quinlan to accept the key from Mr Ryder, step forward onto the small platform (made for the purpose by Mr Treweek) positioned close to the door and declare the hall open. Mrs Quinlan dutifully steps forward:

I hope this will add greatly to the happiness of everyone and bring pleasure in the truest sense of the word into the life of this community, and thus fulfil my dear father's wish. I will now declare the Mills' Hall open.

A round of applause spontaneously breaks forth from the gathering. The 'Maids' present their bouquets to Mrs Quinlan, Mrs T.R. Mills and Miss Enid Mills, after which the committee chairman ushers the official party, plus guests and 'Maids of Honour' into the hall.

Those outside are now asked to move to the lower gate of the playing field, allowing room for the hall party to make their way over. Mr Treweek positions the platform in the centre of the field gateway where he has also fixed a cord across the gateway which will be ceremonially cut by Mr T.R. Mills. Mr Joe Odgers presents an inscribed knife to Mr T.R. Mills. As soon as the party from the hall arrive at the field gates, they pause while the band play a short item. Mr T.R. Mills steps forward onto the platform and cuts the cord, simultaneously Mr Conquest breaks the Union Jack as the gate opens. Again applause spreads through the crowd.

Mr Mills, along with Lord St Leven, is first through the gates followed by other members of the Mills family, guests, the 'Maids of Honour', the children, then the band and the general public. The band once again plays a stirring piece from their repertoire while the crowd are gathering ready for the presentation of the playthings, which is the task of Miss Mills, helped by the 'Maids' who between them will hold the ribbon to be cut and pull on the rope once the ribbon has been sliced. Loud cheers from the children engulf the field as Miss Mills cuts the ribbon connecting the mooring strings. Within minutes children gather around the equipment wanting to 'try them out'. At the roundabouts Messrs Pelmear, Swan, Moyle and Odgers have their hands full preventing overcrowding and queue jumpers, as do other stewards situated at the maypole, see-saw and swings.

With barely enough time for a few sessions on the new playthings there remains one more important function – namely the unveiling of his grandfather's memorial by Master W.J. Mills. A large group of children are marshalled just east of the memorial onto the path to witness the unveiling, the erection of the mechanism for which was undertaken by Mr Letcher. Once Master Mills had completed his task, a dedication service by the Revd Cooper preceeded the doxology led by the band. Speeches were forthcoming from Lord St Leven and Mr Mills, with the committee chairman giving a vote of thanks. A rendering of the national anthem concluded these events. There was little time to rest for the organisers. Within the next two and a half hours the following would be occurring:

4p.m. – children's tea to include tea treat buns and tea; the roll-call for which will be called by Messrs Blewett, Pelmear and Moyle. The bell and megaphone suggested by one committee member should prove invaluable!
4.30p.m. – the old folk's tea; invitations for which were checked by Messrs Pascoe and Pelmear.
5p.m. – public tea for those who wish to participate. Mr Moyle has organised all the tables, forms and boiler facilities needed for such a large number.

Children's sports will be the final event on this busy afternoon, arranged by the sports committee. Various running and fun activities should prove very popular with the younger element of course and their supporters. To round off a most successful day, which will surely prove to be exhausting for all concerned, prizes for the sports will be given by Mrs Mills. All those attending the events will wish to thank the committee and helpers for the efforts in presenting such an interesting and well-planned programme. Carharrack and those people present today will have witnessed a truly momentous event in their village's development.

The above article was based on the diligent notes made in the original minute-book of the Hall Building Committee by Mr E. Enstice, and a detailed annotated programme of the day's events.

THE MILLS MEMORIAL

The village committee, set up in 1933 to arrange the building of the hall and playing-field, decided at their October meeting to erect a bronze bust of their benefactor, Mr W.J. Mills, to be set in granite and to be situated in the field itself.

The plans of the memorial were drawn by Mr Ward Willis of London who also provided the specifications for the same. A total of nine companies were invited to tender and to submit samples of their granite along with their tenders. A sub-committee was appointed to inspect the samples of granite, and after consideration reduced the contractors to a shortlist of three. These tenders were forwarded to Mr T.R. Mills who, together with Ward Willis, decided to accept the tender of Cornwall De Lank Quarries of Bodmin. The total cost of the memorial including provision of the bronzes amounted to £158.6s.9d.; pennies collected from village children raised 7s.9d. towards the cost.

Mr W.J. Mills' grandson, Master William John Mills, as previously reported, unveiled the memorial. A book listing the subscribers was presented to Mr T.R. Mills and another containing the names of the children who had given their pennies for the purpose was presented to Master W.J. Mills.

Thanks go to Mr Alan Harris who researched the information for this article on the memorial.

Left: The Mills' Memorial in the mid-1990s.

FIFTEEN

❧✿☙

VILLAGE LIFE

ON LOCATION IN CARHARRACK

During the spring and early summer of 1994 film crews were a common sight at various places throughout the county. They were shooting scenes for an ITV detective series called Wycliffe, based on the books of Newquay author John Burley. Our village was used on at least two occasions: one in March when TV cameras and personnel descended upon No. 22 Trevince Park, the home of Mrs Harrison. Her property was chosen because it was basically unchanged since its erection in the 1960s. Whitsun Saturday in late May saw the return of the team and this time they commandeered the Wesley Sunday schoolroom, but it was such a pity that the weather outside was so lousy. The series began on network TV on Sunday 24 July 1994, with the Trevince scenes being featured in the first episode. Shots taken inside the schoolroom were used in the episode shown on 7 August.

Above: *The team move in on Trevince Park.*

Left: *Artificial sun brightens up the scene in Chapel Terrace.*

Left: *Miss Libbis' elocution class, pictured entertaining people at Trevince House in the 1920s. Miss Libbis' classes were held in her front room in Richmond House, Higher Albion Row. Her dramatic groups performed dances and plays at many venues in the district. Mrs Enstice usually played piano for them. Left to right, back row: ?, Gwenny Brokenshire, Lillian Cock; middle: Edna Teague, Barbara Enstice, Nellie Teague, Irene Loam; front: Sybil Roberts, Hilda Pelmear, Miriam Enstice, Nora Richards, Vera Richards, Audrey Thomas.*

Right: *Tea treats were annual events in Carharrack's chapels and churches, and were enjoyed by all. Here they all are, the Carharrack Wesleyan Choir, aboard the Stithians Red Bus, a Leyland charabanc, on a trip to Bodmin. Left to right, back row: Mrs Trebilcock, Albert Roberts the organist from 'over' Truro, Mrs Burrows, Irvan Trebilcock; fourth row: Willie Goldsworthy, Reggie Burrows, ?; third row: LeRoy Gumma senr, Edna Gumma, Lilian Goldsworthy held by Mum, LeRoy Gumma junr; second row:*

Bessie Penrose, Minnie Gay, Jane Jory, Eddy Jory (standing); front: Harold Knuckey (driver), Mrs Allen, Mr Willie Allen, Pearl Gumma. (Photo courtesy of Paddy Bradley)

Left: *This outing was in the early to mid-1920s. Left to right, back row: George Bray (in cap), Jack Combellack; third row: Dora Pelmear, Emily Eplet, Tom Benbow, Margaret Martin, Jack Pascoe; second row: Irene Pelmear, Lily Benbow, Lilian Moyle, Jack Odgers; front: Foster Pelmear, Phyllis Carbis, Grace Combellack, Chrissie Pascoe, Ada Pelmear.*

Right: *During the Second World War the area behind Alma Terrace was used as a nursery and market garden by Mr Couch. He was a tall man who wore a black outfit with a watch and chain and supplied the village with vegetables. Nishie Lawry had a wood store in the same area, and used to tour the district selling logs from his lorry. This group of men are gathered along Alma Terrace; only two could be named: (third from left) Willie Benbow; (sixth from left) Willie Collins.*

Left: *The 'Collegians' were a group formed during the early 1940s; four of them worked at Holmans. Left to right: Ronnie Exelby, Ronnie Roberts, Jack Brown (a Carharrack boy), Glenn Loze, Dolly Mitchell. Glenn Loze, from Camborne, also played the solo cornet in Camborne band and later went on to play with one of the famous works bands. During the war the Americans on United used to borrow the drum kit in exchange for packets of cigarettes or tins of soup.*

Right: *The 'workforce' who helped to clean up Carharrack Chapel after renovations in the 1940s. Left to right, back row; Miss Ethel Pelmear, Miss Eva, Mr J. Harris, Mrs Trevithick, ?, Mrs Warren, Mrs E. Jory, Mrs A. Cocking, Mrs Harris, Mrs V. Bray, Mrs Stephens, Mrs Trehar, Mrs Pellow, Mrs T.J. Allen; front: Mrs Smith, Mrs E. Cann, Mrs H. Pelmear, Mrs L. Moyle, Mrs Kinsman, Mrs Williams, Mrs Waters, Mrs Treloar; Judith Gay is the young girl, Mrs J. Allen.*

Left: *In all villages there is a willing band of people prepared to help organise, run and/or lend a helping hand when the occasion arises. These ladies formed such a group, and served refreshments at the Coronation celebrations in 1937. Left to right: Mrs Hitchens, Mrs Ash, Mrs Saundry, Mrs Tonkin, Mrs Williams, Mrs Thomas, Mrs Longman, Miss Jory, Mrs Pengelly, Mrs Paul, Miss Elsie Pascoe. The little girl is Naomi Joslin.*

Left: *Carnivals have been enjoyed in many villages throughout the years. They are a time for communities to unite as old and young alike find enjoyment in taking part or spectating. Since the Victorian era carnivals have been part of other celebrations in Carharrack and, following the Second World War, the village committee which was set up to organise the VJ and VE events decided that because the carnival was so popular they would have an annual one from then on. Since that time there have been many* carnival processions organised by village societies. They were regular happenings until the early 1990s, although there were breaks during certain years. The above image is the earliest carnival photo taken of a float, just after the war.

Right: *The 'Jazz Band' in the 1946 carnival. A few people in the photo have been named. Back row, second from left: Ronnie Bray. The man in the top hat and holding a drumstick is Tommy Allen. Playing the accordion is Stanley Chapman, who lived at Ting Tang. At the front on the left are Anne Young on the squeezebox with Lynne Stephens beside her.* (Photo courtesy of the Stephens family)

Left: *A flora dance held in the early 1960s. Leading off are Catherine Madge and Sheena Woodley. Thelma Treloar used to train the flora dancers.*

Left: *The crowning of our village carnival queen, Jill Chapman, in August 1946. Left to right:* Diane Woolston, Jill Chapman, Mrs Morrish, Patricia Jeffrey.

Right: *Roma Thomas being crowned, with Mona Matthews* (to her left) *and Ruth Daniels as her attendants.*

Left: *This photograph was probably taken in the 1950s; take a close look at the shop frontages, especially No. 1 Church Street – it has not changed since the early 1900s. The Austin pick-up carrying the carnival queen is probably driven by Percy Odgers, the local coalman from the 1950s until the 1980s.*

Right: *Carnival 'Diddymen' in 1975. Photo supplied by the Downing family. Left to right: Claire Uren, Julie Matthews, Debbie Hill, Gayle Holland, Tommy Calloway. The girl on the right was a solo entry, not part of the Diddymen group.*

Left: *Over the years many dances have taken place at the Mills' Hall. This photograph is of the first one in December 1934. It was organised by Eddy Enstice, aided by Charles Treweek, Albert Pengilly, Ernie Teague and W.G. Pelmear. Some 130 people attended. Music was supplied by the 'Mordaunt Orchestra' and Mr Conquest was the master of ceremonies. The five people in dark attire at the front presumably made up the musicians with the lady being its leader, Mrs Mordaunt, who lived down Sparry Lane in Orchard Cottage.*

Right: *This picture dates from the 1930s and was taken at the junction of Chapel Terrace and Church Street, looking towards Charlie Penrose's lane, so called because the lane led to fields owned by Charlie and used for various events. The site is now occupied by 7 and 8 Church Row. On the cart is Eddie Cann who worked for Robert Stephens, the coal merchant at the end of Alma Terrace. This pictured venue possessed a low wall, just the right height for resting on, and was a favourite place for men and boys to meet, chat and watch the world go by. The man in the 'easy' chair is possibly Mr Mills who lived down Sparry Lane.*

Left: *Pushball competitions were a feature of village celebrations for many years. The ball was supplied by a national newspaper for the event. They first came on the county scene in the late 1920s; this close-up, courtesy of the Osborne family, dates from about 1950. Albert Osborne is supporting daughter Jill with Minnie Pengilly and Mr Penrose watching.*

Right: *This 1920s party photo was taken in the back room of Bessie Jane Penrose's shop in Church Street. Kathy Penrose, Bessie's daughter, used to give music lessons in the same room.* Left to right, back row: *Hilda Penrose, Wilfred Penrose, Ruby Dower, Reggie Darlington;* middle: *Granny Line, Lilian Moyle, Foster Pelmear, Kathy Penrose;* front: *Willie Gay, Enid Penrose, Bessie Jane Penrose, Willie Darlington, Tom Penrose.*

WHO'S A PRETTY BABY?

On behalf of the St Day and District Nursing Association which looked after the health of the community for many years prior to the introduction of the National Health, a cake making, baby show and whist drive was held at the Mills' Hall in October 1935. Luckily there is a photograph of the participators and visitors of that day. A total of 34 bonnie babies, placed into five categories ranging from six months to four years old, were presided over by Mrs J. Williams of Scorrier House and Dr Enid Smith of Falmouth, who commented: 'One of the greatest dangers is rickets; also do not give children too many sweets.'

Above: *Village baby winners were: 6 to 12 months age group, Daphne Andrew; 1 to 2 years of age, Gregory Collins.*

Right: *Baby Show Committee, October 1935. Left to right, back row: Ida Penrose, Violet Bray, Pearl Lewis, Mrs Hugh Jory, Elsie Daniel, Lilian Moyle, Mrs Charles Treweek, Alethea Daniel; front: Mrs J. Allen, Mrs Stevens, Minnie Pengelly, Nurse Richards with June Lewis on her lap, Jane Rowe, Mrs Longman, Mrs Opie.*

Left: *Beautiful August weather for the Fun Day stall holders and their customers in the playing-field.*

Below: *The band, as always, supplying the music on one of many such occasions.*

FUN DAYS

In August 1995 Barrie May and Elaine Leigh organised a Village Fund Day to raise money towards the cost of refurbishing the Mills' Hall, the Mills' Trust being set the task of raising £1,200 as their contribution. Other funding came from various sources, i.e. through grants from social services, the Parish Council, the Rural Community Council and Kerrier District Council. The grand reopening, which took place on 29 March 1996, included speeches, light refreshments and entertainments, and in the evening the band performed a short programme for the onlookers. The completed work included a new heating system and toilet block, a ramp for wheelchairs and upgraded kitchen facilities.

Right: *In 1989 the Methodist Church inaugurated a community service and parade. The procession, which no longer takes place, used to commence at the Mills' Hall and, accompanied by the band, march 'loosely' to the church where several society members gave readings and the Sunday school, choir and band provided musical items. In this photograph the procession, headed by Parish Councillors and their families, makes its way to the Methodist Church in the mid-1990s. Kevin and Julia Bennetts and son lead with (left to right) Raymonde Reeve, Sue and Alan Harris and Revd Colin Allen, obscuring Colin King. The band are led by Reuben Long.*

Left: *In January 1942 the Wesley Chapel put on a Biblical play called Queen Esther. Left to right, back row: Mrs Treloar, Jack Harris, Lilian Daniel, Lilian Moyle, T.J. Mollard, Phyllis Odgers, ?; middle: Joe Allen, Thomas J. Allen, Mrs Williams, Ronnie Allen, Pat and Travis Treweek, Frank Mollard, Emily Pelmear, George Cann, Denzil Trevithick; seated: John Mollard, Thelma Treloar, Matt Moyle, Millicent Odgers, Steve Daniel, Elsie Pascoe; kneeling: Kenneth Pelmear, Jean Stephens, Margaret Teague, Douglas Downing, Joyce Tucker, Nancy Williams, Peter Pelmear.*

Above left: *This is an interesting picture in several ways. Jack Polkinghorne is giving a riding lesson to the children of Ian and Crystal Kellow in a field at the rear of the old Institute. The main structure is to the left, the small building behind the riders is the reading room, erected in the 1920s and used as a quiet place to relax, play cards and other games and browse the papers. Jack was a good horseman and he had a riding stables at Perranporth. During the summer months his pony rides along the sands of Perran and Gyllyngvase, Falmouth, were a great attraction to the visitors and locals. He over-wintered his ponies in the village.*

Above right: *Taken in 1935 this photo shows Jack Williams, his wife and sons, Alwin and Keith, in the lane at Croft Row/Laurel Terrace.*

Left: *The village pub has always been a place to meet, chat and relax. Both this and the photo below were taken in and around the Seven Stars in the late 1940s or early 1950s. Left to right: Albert Swan, Matt Swan, Hettie Jory and Bill Jory (landlady and landlord), Mr Pellow, ?, Donald Matthews (?), Albert Wills, ?, ?, ?.* (Photo courtesy of Albert Swan)

Right: *In the pub garden. Left to right, back row: Ronnie Ryder's father, Jack Annear, Bill Long (St Day), Henry Bland (who lived in a caravan on United then moved to the pound area), Bill Jory (landlord), Jimmy Mitchell, Fred Mitchell, Mr Pellow, Mr Watson, Willie Collins (watchmaker); middle: Matt Swan, Jimmy Burrell; front: Trevor Pellow, Ronnie Ryder.* (Photo courtesy of Trevor Pellow)

Left: *The WI used to put on summer variety shows. This picture dates from the early 1980s. Thigh performers, from left to right: Bertha Keats, Pat Hill, Pam Thomas, Ina Woodley, Beryl Kane, Sue Harris, Irene Leah, Sue Pickett, Margaret Osborne, Margaret Dawes.*

Right: *Children performing at the opening of a bazaar in 1966 in the Wesley Sunday schoolroom. Left to right: ?, Brenda and Karen Cavanagh, Catherine Madge, Sheena Woodley, ?, ?, Linda Thorncroft. On the far left seated in the pew is Miss Dunn, a teacher at St Day School.*

Left: *In 1991 the Old Cornwall Society embarked on a project to reinstate the village pump as close as possible to the original site along Chapel Terrace. Several local people lent their time, effort and skills, namely Roy Annear (master builder), Ronnie Wearne (master welder), Alan Harris (master sinker), Eric Rabjohns (labourer) and Ladds (rubble removers). Unfortunately it does not draw water. The project was jointly funded by the society and the Parish Council.*

WATER SOURCES

During the years prior to a piped supply reaching the village – about the late 1940s or early 1950s – there were two main sources of water: Carnmarth Shute (Shoot), and the hand-worked pump which originally stood along Chapel Terrace, just adjacent to the Wesleyan Chapel green. The pump in situ today was erected as close to the original site as possible by the Old Cornwall Society in the early 1990s. The following information was provided by local lass, Rita Wright (née Odgers):

Most women and children would congregate there early Monday mornings with baths, buckets and other receptacles, getting ready for washing. After struggling down through the village with their burdens, the tin bath had to be hauled on top of the Cornish range, filled with water and heated. If lucky, the washing would be completed in time to clean up and cook tea. Friday was another procession day, as Friday night was bath night; so the range was set to work again. This night Mr Williams would come around with his hand barrow and barrel selling water at 2d. per pail.

Right: *Mr Conquest filling his barrel, c.1933. Ankers and barrows were a common sight around the village. Dennis Woodley is the donkey minder. One of the biggest users of shute water, before a piped supply reached the village around 1950, was the Pop Works manufacturers, such as Carbis' and Jolly's. They were frequent visitors to this place, taking a while to fill their large barrel-type wagons before trundling off down to their premises. Several residents have supplied the water needs of the villagers, LeRoy Gumma being one of those. There is one change that has taken place since this photo was taken. The outflow used to meander across the rough road surface from where it would make its way to a leat, which carried it across the fields of Carndene to join up with Trevarth Shute. It became the habit of new car owners in the 1920s and 1930s to use the shute for their vehicles' weekly 'bath'. In due course engine oils polluted the water which was used by Carndene's livestock. To alleviate this problem a pipe was constructed that took the supply under the road to the leat.*

Left: *In May 1990 the South West Water Authority claimed that the hot weather had caused an abundance of algae to form in the reservoirs, and the resulting treatment of chlorine tainted the water. Bowsers appeared in the village from 9 to 12 May. Despite this several people reverted to their roots by seeking out the 'shute' for supplies, and are still around to tell the tale.*

Right: *The 'Village Pump' as painted by local artist S.J. Beer, c.1940. The pump with its lion-tailed handle survived into the 1950s. The foundations and walled area remained until road widening in the mid-1980s.*

Church Street

Left: *Mr Prater is seen wearing his bowler hat and standing in front of his shop which specialised in shoe repairs. A young lady is in the doorway of George and Mary Brown's grocery shop. Miss Johns' schoolchildren must have been let off lessons to attend the 'photo shoot'. Mr Prater seemed to like the limelight because he appears in half a dozen village views in and around Church Street.*

Village Fires

Royal Cornwall Gazette, 4 March, 1864
Serious Fire and Loss of Life at Carharrack
On Tuesday morning, a fire mysteriously broke out at Carharrack and three – one correspondent says five – cottages were destroyed, and one life was sacrificed. It appears that a woman named Mrs Stone, renting appartments off Mr Jeffrey, went out about twelve o'clock to take her husband's dinner; two little children were left in the house. On returning shortly afterwards, she discovered the place in flames, and at once raised the alarm. PC Hitchens from St Day arrived at the spot and succeeded, at risk to his own life, in rescuing one of the children and also a police constable who was ill in bed in an adjoining house.

On the arrival of Inspector Coombe endeavours were made to rescue the missing child but without avail, and she was not found until about three hours afterwards, when the body was burnt beyond recognition; the child's name was Maragaret Stone. The neighbours, under the direction of Inspector Coombe, rendered every assistance to their power to extinguish the fire and save the property.

Cornish Post & Mining News, June 1891
Two Fires in a Week
On Friday 5 June, a fire occurred at Carharrack Commercial School premises. A servant of Mr W.C. Edwards, who runs the school, had accidently set fire to the trimmings of the dressing table and within a few minutes the bedroom was ablaze. Luckily Mr Edwards plus other household members managed to extinguish the blaze without any injury to anyone. Damage caused amounted to £10. The previous Sunday night at 11p.m. Mr Kellow discovered that the stabling belonging to the Steam Engine Inn, run by Mr T. Johns, was on fire. Despite attempts to douse the fire, it had too strong a hold and the building was completely gutted.

Précis of a *West Briton* report, 24 November, 1927
Village Shop Destroyed by Fire: Businessman's Lucky Escape
The fire destroyed Poulter's, formerly Rooke's, Drapery Store in the Square. George Poulter was in the house alone when the fire took hold and had a miraculous escape. Mrs Poulter was away in London, having gone to purchase Christmas stock. On Friday evening Mr T. Deane, a village friend, had visited and about 10.30p.m. sparks were witnessed flying from the hearth onto the rug. Having tackled the situation Mr Deane left and Mr Poulter retired to bed at about 11.30p.m. Soon after 1.30a.m. George was awakened by a falling ornament downstairs. Under the impression that one of the cats was responsible for the noise, he let them out and again retired. Half an hour later he awoke to find the room smoke-filled. He hastily procured what clothes he could and attempted to leave. Downstairs he found that the fire, which had started in the sitting room, was spreading rapidly into the shop area. In attempting to open a door, which was jammed by debris, he sustained burns to his face and after great difficulty

reached the street. Almost immediately the place of laths and plaster burst into flames. Although exhausted, George roused neighbour, John Mitchell, to help and Henry Treloar hastened to Redruth on his motorcycle to summon the Fire Brigade. By the time Chief Officer H.E. Dallimore and his crew arrived the possibility of saving the building was out of the question. The work of the brigade was greatly hampered by the inadequate supply of water, which amounted to using the tanks of nearby homes. They directed their efforts to saving the adjoining property of I. and A. Penrose; fortunately they succeeded. Assistance was rendered by local PCs from St Day, Comford and Penryn, and villagers. A factor in preventing a quicker attendance by the fire service was the lack of a public phone in the village, one of the largest of its size not to possess one.

West Briton, 28 February, 1929
House Gutted by Fire at Ting Tang:
No Telephone and a Mile Long Hose
A serious fire broke out at the residence of Edward R. Simmons, a smallholder and general dealer, at Ting Tang, in the early hours of Thursday. When Mr and Mrs Simmons and two children retired to rest on Wednesday night, everything seemed in order. About 2a.m. one of the children awoke and the child's cries aroused other members of the family, who discovered that the premises were on fire. Mr and Mrs Simmons dressed hastily, and took their children to places of safety. By this time the fire had spread considerably.

The nearest telephone was Gwennap Churchtown, over a mile distant, and Mr Simmons hastened there on his bicycle and rang up Redruth Police Station, whence the alarm was passed to the Redruth Fire Brigade, which responded promptly under Chief Officer H.E. Dallimore. By the time the brigade had reached the scene, the fire had taken a strong hold of the building and the roof had fallen in. Difficulty was experienced in securing an adequate water supply, and eventually one was procured at Carnmarth Shute, necessitating the use of nearly a mile of hose. The house and its contents were destroyed and Mr and Mrs Simmons and family were fortunate to escape injury. They were accommodated at the residences of friends. The outbreak has again served to emphasise the urgent necessity for better water and telephone facilities in the Gwennap Parish.

Photograph of the fire at Poulter's, source unknown.

SIXTEEN

❧⊙❧

CARHARRACK IN THE NEWS

A photograph, source unknown, of the aftermath of a major village fire, Saturday 19 November, 1927.

West Briton, 15 April 1869
Singular Accident at the Wesleyan Chapel – On Sunday last, whilst the Revd Mr. Tweddle of London was preaching in the large Wesleyan Chapel of Carharrack, the weight of the clock fell from its position – the cord having broken. The chapel was full to overflowing and the people in the gallery thought the props of the gallery were giving way, which produced great consternation. A rush was made for the stairs, whilst the screams of the women were deafening. Many persons were more or less injured by fright and pressure, but none killed... the door leading to the gallery opened inwards, thus rendering escape almost impossible and in case of fire or accident, would be a trap to imprison an excited congregation.

West Briton, 1870
'The Chemistry of Light' was the title of a lecture given by G.H. Collins – F.G.S. of the Miners' Association of Devon and Cornwall – at the Mechanics Institute. It was illustrated by a number of 'beautiful experiments' showing the changes of colour and transparency produced by mechanical means, percussion and friction. The use of magnesium flares on a chloride of silver paper producing superb laced patterns.

West Briton, 1877
Trevince Arsenic Works has ten kilns which process 70 tons of pyrite a week for neighbouring mines. The works situated on a portion of the Beauchamp Estate is an auxiliary to Falmouth Chemical Works.

Royal Cornwall Gazette, 3 March 1879
Seizing the Bull by the Horns – On Tuesday last a crowd of men who had met near Carharrack were talking bitterly about the rise and fall of minerals. They had not discussed the subject long ere Mr W. Whitford junr, appeared and hearing their bitter talk, turned around and detained them for about 20 minutes on 'Sourness of looks has a great effect on bad times'. He wound up the latter part of his discourse with rhetoric and eloquence, and each returned to his home a wiser if a sadder man.

West Briton, 1880s
Alleged Ill-treatment of an Old Man. – 'Our Carharrack correspondent' sends us the following almost incredible story: Great excitement was caused in the village of Carharrack on Monday through the ill-treatment of a poor half-witted old man, named William Perry, by the relieving officer and two policemen. The old man, who is of weak intellect, is remarkable for his harmlessness and honesty – wheeling water and going on errands for the people, who are very kind to him. It appears there are parties around that are not satisfied with the old man getting his living in this way, for he has been more than once pounced upon by the parish authorities and dragged away – much against his will – to the Union, the very name of which excites him almost to madness. Last week a fresh order was made for his removal to the workhouse, which was carried into effect by the relieving officer, Sergeant Trenerry and PC Pearce. It appears that Trenerry saw the old man in the village, and decoyed him to Pearce's house by telling him that Pearce wanted him to wheel some water, which he was always ready to do. When there they informed him what they were going to do, although very inoffensive, it so horrified him that he almost went mad. They, evidently being of a nervous disposition, proceeded at once to put on the handcuffs which were too small for his

Left: *A damaged Govier view looking along the Poldory Valley with Carn Marth in the background. The buildings and stack* (left) *are part of the recovery plant run by Alfred Burrows. To the far right, barely visible, are the remains of the Trevince Arsenic works. On the skyline, to the right, are the engine-houses of West Wheal Damsel.* (Courtesy of RIC Library Archives)

wrists, and which he refused to have done, saying he would go quietly away without them, but they persisted in putting on the handcuffs. After a severe struggle, in which the old man was much maltreated – blood freely issuing from his hands and his arms – they succeeded in compressing the wrist, so as to put on one handcuff, evidently causing great pain. Not being content with this, wanted to make a spectacle of the old man by dragging him up the village – one by the collar and wrist, and the other pushing from behind until the poor old man lost his footing and fell to the ground. His cries for release were most heartrending; but the officers again tried hard to put on the other handcuff, and continued to worry the old man until he was almost exhausted with the same result. Finally they were compelled to... bring a trap and take him away quietly. Such inhuman treatment as the poor man was subjected to by those placed in authority over us need no comment.

West Briton, 28 October 1880
Carriage Accident at Carharrack – A carriage accident occurred at Carharrack on the 11th instant. Mr and Mrs Jose, of Mellingey, attended the home missionary meeting at Carharrack Wesleyan Chapel, and after the meeting they were taking home with them the Revd J.A. Macdonald, a member of the deputation, in their brougham with a pair of horses. Just after starting one of the horses became restive, and had not gone far before he threw his hind leg over the pole, which very much excited the other horse, and in the effort to pull them up the carriage got in contact with a low granite landmark beside the watertable, which lifted the frame and bottom of the carriage and jammed the doors so tight that the occupants could not open them.

There being no-one passing at the time, Mr Jose threw himself through the carriage window, being fortunately unhurt, and soon caught the horse by the head, the animal by this time plunging and rearing most fearfully, and had almost severed the front wheels and pole from the body of the carriage. The other horse was thrown over on its side in the watertable. The noise of the horses and voice of the driver soon brought assistance from the houses close by, and Capt. P.C. Martin came, and with the help of Mrs Blamey's strong arms, the door of the carriage was soon

wrenched open and Mrs Jose and Mr Macdonald liberated from their temporary but rather dangerous prison. The driver, the occupants of the carriage, and horses all fortunately escaped injury, except a little shaken with fright, which was soon got over by the nursing of Capt. and Mrs P.C. Martin, whose house was luckily close by. The springs and under gear work of the carriage were completely smashed, and a conveyance was procured to take Mr and Mrs Jose and Mr Macdonald to Mellingey.

Royal Cornwall Gazette, 25 May 1881
Special Notice to Builders – Just landed. A prime cargo of Delabole Scantle and Ladies Slate; Slate flooring; sills; headstones etc. To be sold cheap: several lots of square Delabole and Welsh Slate; 5 Delabole tanks from 90 to 700 gallons; one slab planed both sides; two large slate chimney pieces; granite trough 50 gallons; Portland trough; 3 grinding stones; variety of plain and ornamental roof ridges and roofing tiles; 60 dozen garden edge tiles; 12 dozen slug traps; 50 dozen flower pots; 60 chimney tops in terracotta red and cement. John Williams builder, Carharrack, Scorrier.

Royal Cornwall Gazette, 11 September 1885
Croft Row Death. A poor man died in a house in Croft Row, Carharrack on Saturday. He was dreadfully destitute, unmarried and had previously been in the workhouse.

West Briton, 14 December 1890
A Rapid Stenographer – One of the most rapid and expert technical stenographers in America is Mr William Whitford of Chicago, formerly of Carharrack. His chief task is reporting speeches on medical and scientific subjects at the American Physicians and Surgeons Congress. In 1888 he acted as the official reporter. Ten or twelve years ago, Mr Whitford was a raw uneducated miner in Carharrack and the progress he has made is due entirely to his own efforts.

Cornish Post & Mining News, June 1893
Sewing Group Gift – A new serpentine font supported by three pillars of another colour serpentine has been placed in the Wesleyan Church. A solid silver plate, handsomely engraved and bearing an inscription, has been given by Mrs Winter's sewing group class, May 1893. The silver

plate was made and fixed by W.D. Chandler, jeweller and craftsman, Redruth.

Cornish Post & Mining News, August 1894
Twopenny fine – At Truro Court Joel Blamey and William Davey, his employer, were summoned for working a horse in an unfit state. The creature was lame in both legs and suffering from a suppurating corn in one foot. Mr Blamey was fined 2d.; his boss £5.

Cornish Post & Mining News, 1890
Death of Young Cornishman Abroad – Mr T Tredre and family upon receiving a cablegram on Saturday 8 March, heard news concerning the death of their son, William, aged about 20 in Africa. Only 12 months previously Mr Tredre plus two sons had travelled to that continent. Mr Tredre had only just arrived back. He had intended to send out his third son, but this sad intelligence may probably alter the course previously intended.

In the 1881 census, William was listed as living with his mother, brothers and sisters in Albion Row; presumably his father was even then elsewhere searching for employment.

Cornish Post & Mining News, September 1893
Chemical Works Outing – On Saturday 9th, the Chemical Works Outing run by Mr W.J. Trythall, manager of both the Carnon Valley and Trevince Chemical Works, took place. The employees, 80 in number, met at Cusgarne and were taken by Jersey vehicles and the like to Falmouth where at 11a.m. on the Strand Pier they boarded the steamer New Resolute *for a trip around the River Fal and the harbour. One added bonus was the fact that the training ship* Ganges *was berthed nearby and its chief officer, Captain Prickett, gave a guided tour of the vessel. On returning to Falmouth they visited the castle, the polytechnic and some other shops before departing at 9p.m. for home, arriving back at 11p.m.*

Royal Cornwall Gazette, 25 January 1894.
Shaft Opens Up at Trevince – Whilst a colt was lying down in the field at Little Trevince, the ground suddenly gave under it. The animal fell with the earth down a disused shaft and was killed. The shaft was unknown until this incident.

Royal Cornwall Gazette, 30 March 1905
Collision at Carharrack Crossing – Near the Steam Engine Inn on Friday last there was a collision between the motor of Messrs Hoskin, Trevithick and Polkinghorne & Co. and a horse and trap belonging to Mr Hingston of Woodbine Farm. The horse and trap driven by the workman, Mr Fred Carbis, was returning from Falmouth and at the railway crossing at Carharrack, the driver saw the motor coming down the hill and the mineral train was on the line. The crossing is a very awkward one and the driver of the trap was caught at the corner against the wall by the motor. The axle of the trap was bent double and the wheel

crushed to matchwood. The horse was badly injured in the fetlocks by the wheel of the motor passing over its hoofs and the iron shoe both together. The driver was thrown out of the trap, being badly bruised and shaken. Dr Birchell was sent for to attend the man and Mr Smythe, vetinery of Falmouth, attended the horse. The man was taken home and is progressing favourably. The horse is alive but unable to stand.

Cornish Post & Mining News, July 1910
A Successful Carharrack Man – Our USA correspondent mentions a Mr Burden, who prior to his emigrating to the United States, had spent the previous two years as a lay preacher on the Gwennap Circuit. He left in the autumn of 1902 for the States settling in Sarles, North Dakota. In 1903 he enrolled at the State University obtaining a Bachelor of Arts and remained in a post at the faculty. Since 1905 he has been in charge of the Methodist Church in Sarles.

Cornubian, 29 October 1914
A serious accident took place on Friday morning 23 October necessitating the removal of Wesley Andrew to the Miners' Hospital, Redruth with serious injuries. Mr Andrew and his son, Wesley, were in the slaughterhouse when a noise was heard overhead and then the roof collapsed. Mr Andrew escaped with slight injuries but his son was not so fortunate, for the roof fell on him almost covering him with debris. A few neighbours came to his rescue and after some time managed to free him. Injuries sustained included several broken ribs. Mr Andrew has used the 'Billy Bray's Old Chapel' as a slaughterhouse for some time.

Cornubian, 23 February 1922
Family Strife – A Carharrack housewife accused her husband of assault. He had visited the Steam Engine Inn wearing his best coat and then sold it for beer money. When questioned he did not know if he had a coat or not, he was so drunk.

This rock is situated on private ground just behind Carndene and prior to the 1930s it was used as the venue for pilgrimages at Easter and Whitsun. Several villagers remember, as children, taking their dolls and suchlike to be blessed at the site.

Above: *Enjoying their Sunday school tea buns, 1938.*
Left to right, back row: *Sylvia Hold, Margaret*
Simmons, Joyce Pelmear, Rona Ryder, Margaret Teague;
front: *Pat Treweek, Sadie Penrose, Travis Treweek.*
The photographer was Thelma Treloar.

Cornubian, May 1923
They Don't Wash Either – T.R. Tripp enquired as to whether Dr Rivers – medical officer – had visited and was aware of a certain home in Carharrack where nine in one family were living in two rooms in filthy conditions; nothing except dirt – straw, nothing to eat. Dr Rivers in reply said, 'The complaint against the man is that he has a large family. If you are going to attack these people because they don't wash then you must attack a lot in St Day.' Laughter in the house. Mr Tripp: 'I beg to differ; I think it necessary that action be taken by the Medical Officer, Sanitary Inspector and Revd L.P. Porri.'

Cornubian, June 1924
Carharrack Lawn Tennis Club had matches against Chacewater, Gusgarne, Treleigh and Ponsonooth. Our team members were: Mr Pelmear, W. Darlington and V. Ellis.

Cornubian, 21 August 1924
Death occurred of Mary Phillippa Treweek (her husband, J.W. Treweek, died in 1917); she collapsed and died while attending Wesley Chapel.

Cornubian, 9 October 1924
A Man's Home is His Shed – At East Kerrier Court last week, a man living with his wife and eight children in a small shed (formerly used as a slaughterhouse) at Sparry Bottom was excused payment of 15s.10d. The assistant overseer mentioned that the family had been ejected from their home in the village.

West Briton, 22 January 1925
Re annual renewal of pub licences at East Kerrier. It was recommended that 'only one public house should suffice in the village', so said Supt T. Nicholls. PC Babbage, St Day, said, 'The needs of the neighbourhood are best served by the Seven Stars.' Mr J. Couch (of Messrs Stephens, Graham Wright and Co. St Austell) appeared for Treluswell Brewery Company, owners of the Steam Engine Inn.

The bench renewed the Seven Stars licence on condition that the dilapidated condition of the premises

must be improved if future renewals are hoped for.

West Briton, 15 April 1926
Death at Pound Cross Road – Matthew Nettle, widower, was killed by a motor cyclist at Pound Cross Roads as he was walking home. He was a mason by trade.

West Briton, 16 August 1928
Mrs Triniman, postwoman in the village, had an accident on Friday. After delivering to Mrs Penrose's shop she fell and broke an ankle. She had been doing the job for ten years, she had had only three days holiday.

West Briton, 20 September 1928
An extremely sad though happily rare form of incident occurred at Carharrack on Saturday morning and was attended with fatal consequences. A man named William James Douglas Smith, aged 19, son of Mrs Smith of Chapel Terrace, had along with his brother, Edward George Smith, aged 17, of the same address, agreed to undertake the work of deepening a well on the property of Mr W.R. Simmons, butcher of Church Street. On Thursday the elder Smith, who held a blasting certificate, descended the well, which was about 38 feet deep, and blasted some rock, which the brothers intended removing on the Saturday. About 8a.m. on Saturday, William James Smith left his home to proceed with the work, his brother intimating that he would follow him shortly afterwards. He had only descended the well a short time when he complained of the presence of fumes and gases which still remained from the blasting on Thursday, and he speedily returned to the surface by means of a rope ladder provided. Subsequently he went down again, remarking to a lad named Lloyd Pascoe, aged 11 years, who is employed by Mr Simmons out of school hours, that he was going to try to 'beat out' the gases.

Shortly afterwards Pascoe, who was standing on the surface, saw Smith attempt to climb up the ladder and then fall backwards as if overcome by the fumes and gases. Pascoe went and informed his employer, who was in the vicinity, and Mr Simmons raised an alarm. As soon as Edward Smith was made aware that his brother was in difficulty he immediately hurried to the spot, and descended the well and very narrowly shared a similar fate to his brother. Mr John Webber, a miner of Railway Terrace, very pluckily descended the well on three occasions. The first he was forced to made a quick return owing to the severity of the escaping gases and fumes, but on the second occasion he succeeded with assistance from the surface, in bringing Edward George Smith to surface. The lad, who was in an unconscious state, was removed to his home. Descending the third time, Webber managed to fasten a rope around what was apparently the lifeless body of the elder Smith and was drawn to the surface. Dr G.P. O'Donnell of Redruth, was quickly in attendance, but he could only pronounce life extinct.

Others who rendered assistance included Messrs W. Pellowe, A. Martin, J. Odgers, W. Curtis and J. Burrows. In addition to a widowed mother, Smith leaves a widow and two children, aged three-and-a-half years and eight months respectively. He, who was a native of St Agnes, was until recently employed at Falmouth docks.

West Briton, 20 December 1928
On Monday at the Wesley Chapel there was a service at which Mr Webber was presented with his bronze medal from the Royal Humane Society for his bravery in rescuing people from the well in Pop Lane.

West Briton, 31 January 1929
Carharrack Speedster – A local resident was fined £1 for speeding around a corner at Comford on his motor cycle.

West Briton, 18 April 1929
Washing water in the village costs 9d. a barrel.

West Briton, December 1929
At a meeting of the St Day and District Nursing Association it was stated that there had been 900 calls in Carharrack village by the nurse for sick persons. 60 people in the village subscribed to the funds. Annual income for the village, apart from charity funds, amounted to £13 – working out at 3¹⁄₂d. per visit.

West Briton, 28 May 1931
Prior to the band's performance at Penzance Contest, they practised their programme in the village Square for two hours... Mr C. Baker of St Dennis band conducted.

West Briton, 4 June 1931
Scorrier Crash – Joe Odgers' Singer touring car was in collision with a Talbot vehicle. Passenger Katie Chinn had minor injuries; Mrs Miriam Jenkin of Sparry Bottom was seriously injured and died from these days later.

West Briton, May 1932
The lowest milk price recorded since 1914–18 War; 3d. a quart.

West Briton, 22 June 1933
Billy Bray's Chapel Jubilee Celebrations take place.

West Briton, 13 July 1933
Carharrack's Great Days – Presentation to a well-known resident. Rosy memories of the 'good old days' when Carharrack was a teeming hive of activity; when the hillsides resounded to the roar of the mine stamps, and when everyone was industrious, prosperous and exceedingly regular at chapel, are recalled by Miss Helen Curnow Johns, who is leaving the village this week.
Having lived at Carharrack all her life, and educated in

Margaret and Betty Downing at Miss Kathleen Gay's school. Margaret vividly recalls her 'red satin dress with patent leather shoes.'

her private school hundreds of children, Miss Johns has become something like an institution there. Miss Johns' earliest memories go back to the time when as a small and very scared child, coming home from school, she used to meet the 200 bluff and noisy women employed at the United Mines. Those meetings were the terrors of her life. Miss Johns remembers rather affectionately the one horse van which used to ply between Carharrack and Redruth once a day, and went to Truro twice a week. In those days religion was the central interest of the villagers' lives and Miss Johns deplores the pleasure seeking trend of today.
A fitted leather writing case was presented to Miss Johns on Tuesday by Mr C.H. Beauchamp of Trevince, on behalf of her well-wishers as a token of their esteem. The ceremony was organised by Mrs Mordaunt and the Revd J.E. Darch of Gwennap presided. Miss Johns is spending her retirement at Lee-on Solent.

West Briton, 3 August 1933
A collision took place at St Day crossroads between a mail van of W. Goldsworthy, of Albion Row, and a butcher's van of R.T. Vivian of Trevethan – no injuries were sustained by those involved.

West Briton, January 1934
Deaths occurred of Mr Joseph Mills and his brother W.J. Mills during this month. Mr W.J. Mills, born in 1853, died in Torquay, and had given about £15,000 to the settlements of St Day and Carharrack via the W.J. Mills Benevolent Fund.

West Briton, 29 November 1934
Electric light was installed at Billy Bray's Chapel. Several concerts had taken place to raise funds for this 'enlightening event'.

West Briton, June 1935
A meeting was held at the Mills' Hall to form a village Community Council. Present were Messrs Swithenbank, Moyle, Cock, Pellow, Pengilly and Wakem; Mesdames Swithenbank, Pengilly, Hitchens, Woodley, and Misses H. Goldsworthy and E. Pascoe.

West Briton, July 1935
Notice given by Post Office of siting of post collection box at Higher Trevethan, plus a daily mail delivery.

West Briton, September 1935
Death of Thomas Williams, Tolgarrack House, Tuckingmill. He was recently employed at South Crofty and prior to that Dolcoath as an engine driver. He was

active in the Redruth Old Cornwall Society and solely responsible for finding the 'White Cross' from which White Cross Hill, Carn Brea derived its name. Born in Carharrack he emigrated to South Africa and spent some time there, working in the Transvaal Mine where he and other miners were captured by the Boers, but later released.

He is renowned for one brave deed during his service in the Boer War. A British Commissionaire's escort on returning to Lydenburg were attacked by 15 Boer troops. Mr Taylor of the Civil Police was badly wounded. Thomas went to his assistance, through enemy fire and brought him back to safety.

West Briton, December 1935
Christmas gifts of coal and groceries to the value of 6 shillings were discussed at a meeting of the Mills trustees; it is to be administered by the Carharrack Village Committee.

West Briton, 11 June 1936
Present from Africa – Mr R.T.B. Richards, hon. sec. of the Horticultural and Fanciers' Society, has received a Silver Cup plus miniature replica from Obuasi Sports Club, West Africa. Ex-villager W. Hedley Martin is a member of that club and has kindly donated the trophy. He has a mining appointment with the Gold Coast company.

West Briton, July 1936
Water Scheme Proposed – At present the water in Vogue Shute issues at 86,000 gallons in December and 5,000 in summer. The proposal is to take 45,000 gallons from Vogue and lift it by centrifugal pump, run by electricity, to a service reservoir of 45,000 gallons capacity from where it can gravitationally feed to the villages.

West Briton, December 1936
Emily Hitchens, widow of Elijah (Sparry Bottom), fell and hit her head in her kitchen; sadly she died from the fall. The Coroner's Court was held in the Men's Institute.

West Briton, June 1939
Village Hooligan aged 60 – A native of Carharrack aged 60

now of no fixed abode was in court for vandalism at St Agnes, also Helston and various venues. To quote the judge at the court, 'Everybody in St Agnes absolutely detests him.'

West Briton, 29 July 1942
The death occurred of gifted local musician Mabel Mordaunt, aged 55, of Orchard Cottage, New Road.

West Briton, 2 May 1945
A presentation was made of a children's bed to the Redruth Miner's Hospital. It is to be called 'the Carharrack (Mills' Hall) 1944 bed'. The WVS were a great help in the fund-raising.

Over 45 years on, when part of the Miners' Hospital was being demolished, the plaque relating to this 'Carharrack Gift' was discovered in the rubble and returned to the village, courtesy of Alan Harris.

West Briton, 24 October 1945
Gruesome Fun Fair – At a fun fair to raise money for the St Piran's organ fund the entertainment was entitled 'The severed but living head of Egyptian Princess Arite'.

West Briton, August 1947
The village carnival was held on 10 August, Roma Thomas was our carnival queen. There was horse jumping at Springfield – Mr Jack Polkinghorne was the ring steward. The tea for the under 14s was in Mr J. Odgers' field and the adult tea was served inside the Mills' Hall. There were 70 class entries, the same as last year. A parade, led by Miss Paula Mills on horseback as a marshal, went through the village and along Trevarth. Behind Miss Mills came the band followed by the carnival queen lorry.

West Briton, 31 July 1948
The rugby club organises a gymkhana in Ernie Teague's field. A display of horses/ponies, plus tricks by motor cycling skills by G. Andrew, V. Coward and P. Toy. Mr Dick Williams, the Cornish Sampson of Penryn performed feats of strength.

'Froggie' Skewes was a well-known purveyor of frogs and the like. Several older residents will have had dealings with him.

West Briton, January 1949
Mr John Henry 'Froggie' Skewes, Piece Carnkie, is claiming he is owed frogs by fellow 'frogger' Mr Shortman, also of Carnkie. In a reputed agreement Mr Skewes

Left: *In the late 1940s Mr and Mrs Webb from Lanner started up a 'Gay Nineties' dance club at the Mills' Hall. This photo taken in 1948 certainly proves that dancing was very popular.*

Right: Gerald Brown's pony 'escaped' down a mine shaft in the Little Carharrack area and several local men were on hand to help. The man part-way down the shaft on the left is Charlie Hocking (the slaughterman over Poldory). Left to right, the others are: Ernie Teague, Eddie Whitburn, Sam Brown at the back, the two side by side are unknown, Bill Lewis is far right in the cap.

was to sell Mr Shortman a motorbike and sidecar for 1,700 frogs in respect of these items. Mr Skewes reckons he was only given 1000 frogs by Mr Shortman. It seems the going price for 100 frogs is £1. It appears to be 'croak' and dagger stuff. No doubt the parties are hopping mad.

West Briton, June 1949
The Power of Song – A choir of 200 performed at Wesley Church; the largest number for over 20 years.

West Briton, May 1950
Chapel House Fire – There was a fire at the Chapel House which adjoins Billy Bray's Methodist Church. The occupants, Mr and Mrs Whitburn and their three children under five, were unhurt. Mrs S.J. Daniel, who lives opposite, saw from her upstairs window fire and smoke issuing from the door of Chapel House. She raised the alarm and within ten minutes the fire brigade arrived. The interior and furniture in several rooms were badly damaged.

West Briton, December 1950
The Singing Conductress – The Carharrack Sports and Carnival Committee held a concert at the Mills' Hall organised by Mrs 'Winnie' Pearson, the singing conductress.

For those who have never witnessed 'Winnie' in action, your first encounter with the 'singing conductress' may have caught you unawares. After trading your threepenny fare for a punched ticket and settling down to a pleasant journey courtesy of Western National Omnibus Company, you travels were suddenly 'enriched' by the dulcet serenading power of Mrs Pearson's lungs, bursting forth with popular tunes of the day. In house (bus) entertainment at its best.

West Briton, March 1960
Brands Hatch comes to Carharrack – Mention of a proposed 'Brands Hatch' style motor racing course for United Downs: the proposer was Douglas Watson of Mill Garage, Scorrier. Initial idea to include; 1¹/₃ mile circuit (longer than Brands Hatch); cinder track; restaurant; full pit facilities; and car park. Gwennap Parish Council back the idea.

During the year Camborne and Redruth UDC began a sewerage system for the Lanner/St Day Area; compulsory purchasing land for the proposed scheme.

West Briton, June 1960
Sunday Playtime – Camborne and Redruth Urban District Council to allow playing fields to be opened on Sundays – for a three month trial period.

The following extracts are from Caharrack Society's diary, which was begun in 1987:

5 November, 1988
The first Carharrack Club firework display took place. They decided to have such an event because the band-run displays, which began in the late 1960s, stopped in 1986. One much-loved feature of the band's event used to be the torch-lit processions through the village.

July 1990
The house price boom of the 1980s is over! A house in Manor Road valued at £89,000 in 1989, is now on the market for £65,000.

The following items trace the selling price of a two bedroomed terraced house in Chapel Terrace over the last 100 years:

1900 sold for £175 plus adjoining property.
1922 sold as one property for £95.
1935 sold for £200.
1965 sold for £1,500.
1984 sold for £9,000.
2002 valued at £90,000.

January 1991
A parcel of 'goodies' was collected within the village and sent to the nine local lads stationed in the Gulf War zone.

June 1991
The demolition took place of the old Carharrack Club building opposite the chapel.

SUBSCRIBERS

Bob and Stephanie Acton, Penpol, Devoran, Cornwall

Donna M. Andrew, Wheal Damsel Road, Carharrack

Anne Andrews, Aldridge, West Midlands

Henry C. Angove, Trevethan House

Dudley Bawden, Fox's Row, Carharrack

W. Bawden, Redruth

W.P. Benbow, Redruth, Cornwall

Nicola M. Bicknell, Rosudgeon, Cornwall

Edward G. Boram, Carharrack, Cornwall

Ina Branchett, Carharrack, Cornwall

David and Christine Branton, Carharrack, Cornwall

Ronald Bray

A.M. Bray, Camborne, Cornwall

Jocelyn Brew (née Stephens), St Day

Kevin Brown, Denmark

Graham Brown, Romsey, Hampshire

Mrs Gloria E. Burley, United, St Day, Cornwall

K.J. Burrow, Bucks Cross, Devon

Micky Burrows, Carharrack, Redruth

Terry Butler, Porthpean, St Austell, Cornwall

Courtney Butler, St Austell, Cornwall

Jack Buzza (Truro), Family History Researcher

Bernard Camm, Trevince Parc, Cornwall

In-Pensioner John C. Carbis, Royal Hospital Chelsea, London

William H. Chown, Carharrack, Cornwall

The Constable Family, Carharrack, Cornwall

Philip Curnoe, St Day, Cornwall

Roy Davey, Redruth, Cornwall

Michael Dawes, Carharrack, Cornwall

Margaret A. Dawes

C.D. Downing, Falmouth

Michael L. Downing, Carharrack, Cornwall

Elizabeth Dunn, Carharrack, Cornwall

Mr Denis Dunstan, Lanner, Cornwall

Valerie L. Dunstan (née Martin)

J.R. and A.W. Edwards, Carharrack, Cornwall

Mr Arthur Enstice, Burton Bradstock, Dorset

Nancy M. Evans, Camborne, Cornwall

Mrs Stella Evans (née Mably), Redruth, Cornwall

Mr and Mrs R. and K.A. Forrest, Carharrack, Cornwall

C.J. and A.J. Fox, Wheal Rose, Scorrier, Cornwall

Ntsebo and Geoff Garbett

Travis Gill, Falmouth, Cornwall

Pip and Liz Greenaway, Carharrack

Eric and Audrey Grey

Gumma Family, Crofthandy

Bryan Hammill, Forth Scol, Illogan

Vaughan Hammill, Paul's Row, Redruth

Kevin Hammill, Albany Road, Redruth

Alan and Sue Harris

Mrs Tamsin Hart (Johns), Carharrack

G. and M.E. Harvey, Carharrack, Cornwall

Drs D.G. and P.M. Hayes, Carharrack

Mrs Elizabeth M. Henderson, Redruth, Cornwall

Mrs Margaret Hill, Carharrack, Cornwall

Richard Cyril Hitchens, Camborne

Sapphire Mason Hodges, Anvoaze, Carharrack

Mrs Angela M. Holland, Redruth, Cornwall

Dr Hugh C. Hollingworth, Redruth

Mick and Sheila Holmes, Olde Alma Stores, Carharrack

Steven John Hopper (Landlord), The Carharrack Stars

Stanley M. Jewell, Carharrack, Cornwall

Mr Nigel J. Jolly

Mrs Sylvia Naomi Joslin, Carharrack

G.C. King, Carharrack, Cornwall

Alison M. Kirton

Philip G. Ladd, Perranwell Station, Cornwall

Antony R. Ladd, Chacewater, Cornwall

P. Pearl Lewis (née Gumma), Carharrack, Cornwall

Mr and Mrs J. Luker, Tresaddern Farm, St Day

Joan I. Macnamara, Carharrack, Cornwall

Mrs Judith Mankee, Redruth, Cornwall

K. and S. Manley, St Day, Cornwall

Pauline Manley (née Martin)

Marion Martin, Vogue, St Day
Marion E. Martin, St Day, Cornwall
Mr Barry F. Matthews
William G. Matthews, Camborne, Cornwall
Regan, Sally, Ryan, Liam and Samantha
    Matthews, Carharrack, Cornwall
Mr and Mrs Barrie S. May
Pat and David Maynard, Manor Road,
    Carharrack
Malcolm McCarthy, Padstow
Miss Jody and Master Ryan Mills, Carharrack,
    Cornwall
Ms Hilary and Mr Robert Mills, Carharrack,
    Cornwall
Joe Mills, St Day, Cornwall
Alan Edwin Mitchell, Creegbrawse, St Day,
    Cornwall
Peter and Rosemary Moor
Brenda Moore, Carharrack, Cornwall
Mike and Judi Morris, Carharrack
Mr and Mrs D.B. Morris
Norman D. Nicol, Shavertown, USA
Mrs Catherine B. Nurhonen, Carharrack,
    Cornwall
Mr Jonathan Nurhonen, St Erth-Praze, Cornwall
Mr Jeffery Nurhonen, Torpoint, Cornwall
Mr Terence Nurhonen, Johannesburg, South
    Africa
Arnold and Betty Oates, Carharrack, Cornwall
Mrs Jean Odgers, Carnon Downs, Cornwall
Alejandro Odgers, Mexico City
Joanna K. Orchard, Carharrack, Cornwall
Margaret Rose Osborne, Carharrack, Cornwall
Cathy Page, Carharrack
Mrs Clare Page (née Beauchamp), Stithians,
    Cornwall
Margaret Palmer, Carharrack, Cornwall
Mrs K. Parminter, South Downs, Redruth
Michael T. Pedley, Carharrack
Gerald and Joan Pellow, Carharrack
Alastair Pellow, Carnon Downs, Cornwall
Chris Pellow and Charo Caraballo, Getxo, Spain
Mr William Trevor Pellowe, Camborne,
    Cornwall
Philip Alan Pepper, Carharrack
Roy C. Peters, Carharrack, Cornwall
Kay Pettifer, Carharrack, Cornwall
The Phillips Family, Poldice, St Day
Hilary Phoenix, The Elms, Carharrack
Mrs Miriam Polglase, Redruth, Cornwall
Janet Polkinghorne, Carharrack, Cornwall
Alison I. Pooley, Carharrack
Ron Prescott, Redruth, Cornwall, grandson of
    George and Betrice Francis

John C.C. Probert, Redruth
Isolde Pullum, Carndene, Carharrack
E.W. Rabjohns, Carharrack, Cornwall
Raymonde A. Reeve, Higher Trevethan, Redruth
E. and L. Richards, Carharrack, Cornwall
Carol Robb, Surrey
A.J. Rogers, Carharrack, Cornwall
Kevin Rundle, Carharrack, Cornwall
John Frederick Ryder
Brian Saundry, Redruth, Cornwall
Terry Simmons, formerly Carharrack/now
    Illogan, Redruth
Valerie Stephens, Mably, Carharrack, Cornwall
Mrs Vanessa Stone (née Beauchamp)
Mark Stuart Sweet, Carharrack, Cornwall
Ken and Elizabeth Tarry, Carharrack, Cornwall
Auriol Taylor, Carharrack, Cornwall
Ernest A. Thomas, born Carharrack 1929/now
    Budleigh Salterton
Pamela Thomas, Carharrack, Cornwall
Mrs Frances Thomas, Roseworthy, Cornwall
Graham Thorne, Maldon, Essex
Ann Trebell, Carharrack, Cornwall
Andrew Trebell, Bude, Cornwall
Maria Trebell, Carharrack, Cornwall
Harry Tredre
Roy and Linda Trelease, St Day, Cornwall
Raymond and Grace Tremayne, Newquay,
    Cornwall
Dr Leonard Trengove, Ting Tang
Hiram R.L. Tresidder, Carharrack, Cornwall
Gill, Teo, Mark and Caroline Turner
John Uren, Carharrack, Cornwall
John F.W. Walling, Newton Abbot, Devon
E. Wearne, Carharrack, Cornwall
Lynne Webb
Debbie and Paul Webster, Carharrack, Cornwall
Mrs Mary Webster, Carharrack, Cornwall
Derek and Sandra White, Carharrack, Cornwall
C.N. Wiblin, Shrewton, Wiltshire
Sandra Wilkinson (née Nicholls), Surrey
Alwyn Williams, Carharrack, Cornwall
Patricia Williams, Redruth, Cornwall
Audrey Williams, Carbis Bay, Cornwall
Mr L. Williams, Bovey Tracey, Devon
D.J. and W.M. Williams, Carharrack
Derek Williams, Carharrack, Cornwall
Ronnie Wilson, Redruth, Cornwall
Mr and Mrs A. Wilson
Nancy Woodley, Carharrack, Cornwall
Ted Woodley, Church Street, Carharrack
Alec Young, Newquay
Laura and Poppy Young, Farms Common,
    Helston, Cornwall

Community Histories

The Book of Addiscombe • Canning & Clyde Road
Association & Friends
The Book of Addiscombe, Vol. II • Canning & Clyde Road
Residents Association & Friends
The Book of Axminster with Kilmington • Les Berry
and Gerald Gosling
The Book of Bampton • Caroline Seward
The Book of Barnstaple • Avril Stone
The Book of Barnstaple, Vol. II • Avril Stone
The Book of The Bedwyns • The Bedwyn History Society
The Book of Bickington • Stuart Hands
Blandford Forum: A Millennium Portrait • Blandford Town Council
The Book of Bramford • Bramford Local History Group
The Book of Breage & Germoe • Stephen Polglase
The Book of Bridestowe • R. Cann
The Book of Bridport • Rodney Legg
The Book of Brixham • Frank Pearce
The Book of Buckfastleigh • Sandra Coleman
The Book of Buckland Monachorum & Yelverton • Hemery
The Book of Carharrack • Carharrack Old Cornwall Society
The Book of Carshalton • Stella Wilks and Gordon Rookledge
The Parish Book of Cerne Abbas • Vale and Vale
The Book of Chagford • Ian Rice
The Book of Chapel-en-le-Frith • Mike Smith
*The Book of Chittlehamholt with
Warkleigh & Satterleigh* • Richard Lethbridge
The Book of Chittlehampton • Various
The Book of Colney Heath • Bryan Lilley
The Book of Constantine • Moore and Trethowan
The Book of Cornwood & Lutton • Compiled by the People of
the Parish
The Book of Creech St Michael • June Small
The Book of Cullompton • Compiled by the People of the Parish
The Book of Dawlish • Frank Pearce
*The Book of Dulverton, Brushford,
Bury & Exebridge* • Dulverton & District Civic Society
The Book of Dunster • Hilary Binding
The Book of Edale • Gordon Miller
The Ellacombe Book • Sydney R. Langmead
The Book of Exmouth • W.H. Pascoe
The Book of Grampound with Creed • Bane and Oliver
The Book of Hayling Island & Langstone • Rogers
The Book of Helston • Jenkin with Carter
The Book of Hemyock • Clist and Dracott
The Book of Herne Hill • Patricia Jenkyns
The Book of Hethersett • Hethersett Society Research Group
The Book of High Bickington • Avril Stone
The Book of Ilsington • Dick Wills
The Book of Kingskerswell • Carsewella Local History Group
The Book of Lamerton • Ann Cole & Friends
Lanner, A Cornish Mining Parish • Sharron
Schwartz and Roger Parker
The Book of Leigh & Bransford • Malcolm Scott
The Book of Litcham with Lexham & Mileham • Litcham Historical
& Amenity Society
The Book of Loddiswell • Reg and Betty Sampson
The New Book of Lostwithiel • Barbara Fraser
The Book of Lulworth • Rodney Legg
The Book of Lustleigh • Joe Crowdy
The Book of Lyme Regis • Rodney Legg
The Book of Manaton • Compiled by the People of the Parish
The Book of Markyate • Markyate Local History Society

The Book of Mawnan • Mawnan Local History Group
The Book of Meavy • Pauline Hemery
The Book of Minehead with Alcombe • Binding and Stevens
The Book of Morchard Bishop • Jeff Kingaby
The Book of Newdigate • John Callcut
The Book of Nidderdale • Nidderdale Musuem Society
The Book of Northlew with Ashbury • Northlew History Group
The Book of North Newton • Robins and Robins
The Book of North Tawton • Baker, Hoare and Shields
The Book of Nynehead • Nynehead & District History Society
The Book of Okehampton • Radford and Radford
The Book of Paignton • Frank Pearce
The Book of Penge, Anerley & Crystal Palace • Peter Abbott
The Book of Peter Tavy with Cudlipptown • Peter Tavy
Heritage Group
The Book of Pimperne • Jean Coull
The Book of Plymtree • Tony Eames
The Book of Porlock • Denis Corner
Postbridge – The Heart of Dartmoor • Reg Bellamy
The Book of Priddy • Albert Thompson
The Book of Princetown • Dr Gardner-Thorpe
The Book of Rattery • By the People of the Parish
The Book of St Day • Joseph Mills and Paul Annear
*The Book of Sampford Courtenay
with Honeychurch* • Stephanie Pouya
The Book of Sculthorpe • Gary Windeler
The Book of Seaton • Ted Gosling
The Book of Sidmouth • Ted Gosling and Sheila Luxton
The Book of Silverton • Silverton Local History Society
The Book of South Molton • Jonathan Edmunds
The Book of South Stoke with Midford • Edited by Robert Parfitt
South Tawton & South Zeal with Sticklepath • Radfords
The Book of Sparkwell with Hemerdon & Lee Mill • Pam James
The Book of Staverton • Pete Lavis
The Book of Stithians • Stithians Parish History Group
*The Book of Stogumber, Monksilver, Nettlecombe
& Elworthy* • Maurice and Joyce Chidgey
The Book of Studland • Rodney Legg
The Book of Swanage • Rodney Legg
The Book of Tavistock • Gerry Woodcock
The Book of Thorley • Sylvia McDonald and Bill Hardy
The Book of Torbay • Frank Pearce
*Uncle Tom Cobley & All:
Widecombe-in-the-Moor* • Stephen Woods
The Book of Watchet • Compiled by David Banks
The Book of West Huntspill • By the People of the Parish
Widecombe-in-the-Moor • Stephen Woods
The Book of Williton • Michael Williams
The Book of Witheridge • Peter and Freda Tout and John Usmar
The Book of Withycombe • Chris Boyles
Woodbury: The Twentieth Century Revisited • Roger Stokes
The Book of Woolmer Green • Compiled by the People of the Parish

For details of any of the above titles or if you are
interested in writing your own history, please contact:
Commissioning Editor Community Histories, Halsgrove
House, Lower Moor Way, Tiverton Business Park,
Tiverton, Devon EX16 6SS, England; tel: 01884 259636;
email: katyc@halsgrove.com